THROUGH THE SHATTERED GLASS

JEANIE CLARKE WITH BRADLEY CRAIG
AND NEIL CAMERON

ISBN-10: 1530387019
ISBN-13: 978-1530387014

DEDICATION

This book is dedicated to anyone who feels that they are suffering in silence, you are not alone and there is always a way out of misery.

And to my daughters, whose smiles provided a ray of sunshine during my darkest days.

CONTENTS

ACKNOWLEDGEMENTS

First of all, I would like to thank the efforts of Bradley Craig and Neil Cameron.

During the writing of my autobiography, Bradley challenged me to be brave and tell my story in its entirety. He made sense of my stories and forged it into a coherent narrative. His tireless research and effort connected the dots between my life and career, and his knowledge has helped me understand the context of issues that directly changed my own circumstances. As a result, he encouraged me to heal many old wounds which enabled me to grow as an individual. For that, I am truly grateful.

Neil was highly supportive and I am appreciative of his encouragement. He convinced me that my story could be a source of inspiration to others. I would like to express gratitude for his unwavering kindness.

I would also like to thank the following people for their generosity in providing thoughtful contributions to my story: Bill Apter, James Beard, Gary Michael Cappetta, Karen Burge Cole, Shane Douglas, Bobby Eaton, Bobby Fulton, Marti & Dory Funk, Jr., Linda Hanley, Jon Horton, Sam Houston, Missy Hyatt, Jerry Jarrett, Les Hudspith, Marty Jones, Marc Mero, Jacqueline Moore, Paul Neu, Rod Price, Mark Rocco, Laurie Rogers, Terri Runnels, Mal Sanders, Terry Simms, Tracy Smothers, Adrian Street, Kevin Von Erich, and my two wonderful daughters Stephanie and Cassidy Williams.

I wish to recognise my good friend Jean Huseyin for her ongoing support during the writing of this book.

Finally, I am grateful to Pastor Tom Kaplan, for helping me build a good foundation for my Christianity, and Pastor Billy Crone of Sunrise Baptist Church who was a source of strength during some trying times in my personal life.

Jeanie Clarke.

I would like to thank my parents, Jan and Graham, for their enduring encouragement and support. I wish to acknowledge my sister Lauren, who has been a great source of joy and enthusiasm over the years. I am grateful to the Pirie family, Andrew Sr., Jane, Andrew and Jill, and her fiancé Graeme Smith, for their kindness. I also want to thank my friends back home in the Bridge of Don, my fellow alumni from The Scott Sutherland School and my many friends within the professional wrestling industry.

Bradley Craig.

There are a few people I'd just like to thank. My parents, Margaret and Tom, who have always supported me in whatever choices I've made in life, my good friend Mark James in Memphis whose books have been an inspiration, all the Elvis 'Family', David Wade who has been a great boss and a good friend, to all of my family and friends. And finally I'd like to make a dedication to John - a true lover of books.

Neil Cameron.

FOREWORD

People often ask how I came to be involved in the wrestling industry. The answer is quite simple; wrestling was in my blood. It's the craft my father taught my brothers and I, and, in turn, it's the craft which I have taught my own sons.

But to begin with it was very different, because at first I never really had any interest in wrestling as such. What was more important to me was wanting, as many young boys do, to be just like my father. I grew up with my father as my first hero, my role model, the person I looked up to, and that admiration crossed over into wanting to be just like him.

It just so happened that my father was one of the biggest wrestlers of his era. So I was kind of pre-destined in life. It initially started as a summer job really. Wrestling back then was a little different though, it was very much the slow paced, rest-hold in the middle of the ring kind of matches, and the wrestlers were of a much older generation. My brothers and I were all athletes and had all excelled in different sports; basketball, football and the like; and the kind of wrestling we were seeing really wasn't fun for us to watch, let alone participate in. So we put our own spin on it, we were all young and athletic and so we just did what came naturally to us, something which was completely new and different and that turned everything on its head.

What we were doing just seemed to click and having this new, young breed with a new style in matches led to some major changes at the shows we were on. Our audience figures steadily doubled, and then tripled, with people wanting to see these completely fresh kinds of matches, and, as the crowds grew, our demographic changed too.

Before, the audience had been mostly made up of males in the 18-49 age brackets, but now there were more females coming along too and you could notice a change just in the sound of the shows as there was a huge presence of squealing from the young female contingent. It was even evident just through the concession stands at the venues too; beer sales were down and cotton candy sales were up! Dealing with this different side of the spectrum and the crossover appeal we now had really helped improve our shows and pushed us further into giving audiences something that was new and original.

And from there things just exploded. We had to get bigger venues, we were picking up more and more TV markets across the country and as a result of this expansion we seemed to attract the most loyal and diehard fans and not just in Texas, they were all over the USA. Our show even managed to beat *Saturday Night Live*, it shocked a lot of people at the time but we went head to head and we managed to beat them in the ratings. It was an exciting time and before long we were starting to make an impact overseas as well.

My father had already made a name for the family in Japan many years before. He was held in high regard out there and when it was time for us to make that journey too, the doors were open for us and we were lucky to be a big hit there as well. Talking about Japan reminds me of a funny story.

I remember watching a Godzilla movie once; these films were a huge part of popular culture in Japan and were made at the time when my father was wrestling. I just recall watching this one movie, *King Kong vs. Godzilla*, and these two monsters are fighting each other and in the middle of it all one of them puts a claw-hold, my father's signature move, on the other! That just felt like a milestone to me, that my father was being referenced in something that was so big in Japan.

One of the other international markets we became big in, and perhaps the one which means the most to me, and is certainly closest to my heart, was Israel. I have the utmost affection for both the country and its people and I'm so proud that our shows were able to resonate so deeply within society there. I once had the honour of talking to Shimon Peres, Israel's former President, who told me that wrestling was more than just entertainment in his country, it bought people together and the only real time there was a cease-fire during the war there was when wrestling was being shown. Our conversation is quite heavily documented and it is still one of the pivotal moments in my life.

Something else I get asked frequently is why do I think that what we did became so popular. It's a question which I have two answers for. Firstly, I think it's because what we did was relatable to those watching. We were a close family; we had to be, constantly travelling from town to town with a father who was the biggest villain in the industry.

At a time when people really believed what they were seeing, we only had each other and we soon realised from an early age just how important family was. This gave us closeness, a bond that was stronger than many other families, and this really became apparent to the fans. Seeing this close knit family of brothers, who they followed growing up really held their attention as it was natural; it was something they could invest and believe in because they could see the similarities to their own families. And that similarity translates to everyone, no matter where in the world they are. If people can see that you enjoy doing something, no matter what that is, then they buy into and they enjoy it as well.

The other reason is that I believe that we were blessed by God. I don't say that to have an ego or to come over as being brash, but I honestly think we were given this talent by the Lord and that's something I give thanks for every day. But when you have that blessing you have to use it to enrich others' lives as well. That's why we would put everything we had into our matches; so we could entertain.

We never forgot who was putting us in that fortunate position we were in; our fans. That's why none of us developed egos or acted like big shot celebrities and I like to think that's also why we were so over, because we thought of ourselves just like everyone who was out there watching our shows.

During our time in the ring we wrestled all the big names of that era; Bruiser Brody, King Kong Bundy, Big John Studd, One Man Gang and so many others. All the big names came through and worked with us, and this was way before The Fabulous Freebirds came in. Two others who came into the promotion and who did great business for us were Chris Adams and Gino Hernandez; they were just two of the greatest guys. I had known Gino for many years but Chris was new to us. He and I just clicked straight away.

At the time, we were looking for another big name to wrestle. That's how the business works; you either bring in a big name or you make a big name. For example, someone like The Great Kabuki, he was someone who we created. But with Chris Adams though, we just brought him in as he was a really good, versatile athlete. He didn't actually come here with a name, but because he was so good at what he did, we could use him straight away without having to change much about him.

Almost immediately, we just started selling out, building after building. Again, I think it was because it was something new to the fans when they watched our matches. We would just go at it in the ring. He would use judo on me and I would wrestle him back and we would just fight, and we would fight hard! It was so stiff that the other guys would wince.

Chris and I got on so good and I admired him so much. Other wrestlers would complain that I hit them too hard but Chris never complained. Chris would just give as good back. He understood that people want to see that, that it was our job to give people a good show. They wanted to see some intensity: they want to see guys going at it and see believability. It's just the same as them buying into the closeness of my family; the brutality that Chris and I put into our matches meant that people believed.

In a short amount of time, our matches caught on and we had such intensity in them that they're maybe better than the Freebird matches.

I do recall though that Chris had a hard time with interviews at first, because of his accent. That British accent just made you want to like him and so he had to work really hard to get the fans to hate him, but he did figure it out and found a way. He started saying that he was fed up with kissing fat girls, insulting the American people and things like that and soon he became a natural on the mic at pissing people off.

Despite playing the heel away from the ring, Chris was, in every aspect of the word, a gentleman. He kept his word, he was on time and was just a pleasure to do business with but sadly alcohol changed that. It hits some people harder. Chris actually knew this and would try to avoid it and would only order water when we would go out. I know this because I was there and it's sad that there are so many stories about Chris which aren't true, told by people who weren't there.

I can remember we went to Mexico, Chris and I introduced our hard-hitting style down there, and we went for a beer afterwards but he only had two beers and he wouldn't drink anymore. People often overlook that these things really only affected him in the last couple of years of his life. It was so unfortunate that these took control of Chris and that it happened so quickly. At the time, I was busy with my own life and didn't really see too much change in Chris before it was too late.

I do remember one night that the Police called after they had arrested Chris. They found his address book and he needed someone to watch his daughter Julia or she would be taken in by the child support services so we ended up looking after her a couple of weeks. I hadn't seen him for a long time before that and it was actually one of the last times I saw Chris. The path his life took was a tragedy that never should have happened.

I was one of Chris' pallbearers and, after he died, I went to see his family in England and went to a little service for Chris. I just wanted his family to know that Chris was a good guy; his word was his bond and he was a proud man.

He had honour and integrity and that it's sad that people only remember the negative things.

When Chris passed away it was said that he was just another victim of drug taking within the wrestling industry, but the reality is far bigger than that. People talk about the substance culture in this industry in the '80s, but to be frank it wasn't just the wrestlers, you have to look at the '80s at a whole. Everyone was doing it. All the celebrities, all the athletes, it wasn't just our business, it was the time we lived in and we looked at the world so differently back then. It was just the way of the world. But it's true to say that for wrestlers it was more of a hazard because of everything else that went with it.

For those who didn't experience first-hand that lifestyle it's sometimes hard to explain, but a good analogy I found was something I remember doing when I was in college. I had to do a paper on occupational hazards and which jobs had the shortest life-spans.

As I did the research I found it was rickshaw drivers who, on average, lived to just 29 years of age. It wasn't the job itself that caused them to live such short lives, but the peripheral aspects of that job; eating cheap food, living in squalid conditions and then actually doing the job without the proper nutrition or health.

It's exactly like wrestlers who away from the job are putting their well-being through huge amounts of abuse away from the ring – hours upon hours of travelling without rest, eating fast food on the road and then time after the matches spent in bars. And all of this night after night without an 'off season' like other sports and that's all compounded to a career that can run to 30 to 40 years, compared to say a football player who, if lucky, will only play for 15 years.

It's easy to say that 'pain pills killed him' when talking about so many who were taken before their time in this industry, but the real answer isn't that simple. Drugs may have contributed, but they weren't the sole contributor. If you don't eat right, sleep right or look after yourself then you'll age like crazy. It's an exhausting lifestyle and one that takes its toll.

I'm just glad I didn't follow the lifestyle of being in bars every night. Luckily, I was a married man and I wanted to come home to a clean and wholesome home life. That's why I treat my wife like a queen; I never messed around on her. I'm not trying to make out that I'm a great man, but with her being at home it gave me direction and kept me on a straight path. So that's what I did and that's why I'm still here and haven't aged as much as my other friends who are lucky enough to still be here.

But you can see why the life expectancy was so low. Like the rickshaw driver, it's the surroundings and the lifestyle as a whole, not just the drugs. There was a huge amount of wear and tear along with the substances in the wrestling industry and my generation had a mindset of 'it feels good so just do it'.

My generation just wanted to do it our way, and we never realised it was harmful and, for many, it was too late in the day before the realisation set in.

It's sad that so many of our peers are no longer here with us, but I give thanks for those who are.

Jeanie is someone who survived the horrors of excess, and her book aims to shine a spotlight on a lifestyle that claimed too many casualties.

I hope that her story can help set an example that it is never too late for anyone to turn their life around, even when the world seems truly bleak.

Things will always get better.

Kevin Von Erich

INTRODUCTION

I first met Jeanie Clarke at the famous WCCW Cotton Bowl show in October 1985. Jeanie and her oldest daughter Jade were there for Chris Adams, who headlined his biggest match in his career with Gino Hernandez against Kerry and Kevin Von Erich in a Double Hair match. I was only in my first two months in the wrestling biz. When I saw Jeanie with her movie star looks, British accent, and the way she carried herself, I instantly thought, 'this girl is money'. I was so lucky that Jeanie had no aspirations in wanting to be in the biz at the time, since I would probably be out of a job. Yes, I considered Jeanie as a potential threat. I'm not blind and oblivious in recognizing talent.

I was always impressed on how Jeanie and Chris Adams maintained a cohesive family environment for Jade, despite being divorced. They both lived in the same condo complex, which made it very accessible for Jade to see both parents.

Every person brags that they drew money. Jeanie was part of the package with Steve Austin against Chris and Toni Adams that helped rejuvenate a dead territory in USWA at the Sportatorium to respectable attendance, long after the territory was scorched to the ground. They had a ground-breaking storyline of the jilted lover hooking up with her ex's star pupil against him and his new wife. It had cat-fights, violence, and a soap opera which could have gotten over in this current PG-era of sports entertainment.

The fan in me was captivated when watching their feud in comparison to the drivel that the big promotions were producing at the time.

When Steve Austin debuted in WCW in 1991, he was originally managed by 'Vivacious' Veronica. I guess Veronica didn't realize about my initial opinion of Jeanie. This girl is a threat based on looks and talent. Plus, she had genuine chemistry with Steve Austin which, as corny as it sounds, was evident on how they held hands when they came to the ring. WCW realized they picked the wrong valet for Steve Austin and rectified it.

Jeanie knew when to interact at ringside, interfere behind the referee's back, cut a promo, and made 'Stunning' Steve Austin look like a million dollars and the next Ric Flair at the time, before he paved his own path and identity

Outside the ring, Jeanie was always fun to be around. There was never a dull moment.

When Jeanie came off the road from WCW in order to concentrate on raising a family, she was one of the coolest wrestling wives that I ever met. Many wrestling wives develop an ego based on their husband's successes and star power as if it was their own success and stardom. At the height of 'Stone Cold' Steve Austin in 1998, I was still able to hang out with Jeanie for the day in NYC. Jeanie was still cool and down-to-earth.

Over the years, I would correspond with Jeanie. I love her for never changing, always talking about her daughters, and just being a genuine friend. The last time I saw Jeanie, she was on a documentary. I had to call her immediately to tell her that she must own a 'hot tub time machine', since she never aged. Chalk that as another reason why I am jealous of Jeanie.

When Jeanie's editor asked me to write about her, I instantly said, "Hell Yeah!"

I have always been a fan of Jeanie in and out of the ring and she has, and always will be, a friend.

Missy Hyatt, the First Lady of Wrestling

PROLOGUE

Between 1983 and 2013 over a hundred people under the age of 50, who had all been involved in professional wrestling, had died.

For years, I seemed destined to become the next figure in this tragic statistic.

The majority of these names passed away due to substance abuse, a sad result of the excesses of their life on the road. A relentless touring and work schedule was based on a naïve belief that the show must always go on, no matter what. This, coupled with a party culture, bolstered the temptation for many performers to turn to drugs in order to cope with the daily grind.

There were drugs to put wrestlers to sleep and drugs to wake them up. There were drugs to numb their aches and pains, drugs to help them exercise and drugs which allowed them to perform their work, far away from their families for months at a time with barely any rest to their bodies and minds.

Recreational abuses of alcohol, cocaine and amphetamines were just as prevalent to survive the lifestyle which came with the job.

But many of the problems stemmed from the abuse of legal prescription drugs.

Fame ensured that large quantities could be easily attainable from crooked doctors and through the exploitation of failures in the medical system.

The sad fact about those who lost their lives so young is that many of their names are now barely remembered.

These men and women were husbands and wives. They were brothers and sisters. They were fathers and mothers. Many were my friends, leaving behind torn families. Just as sad were those who suffered without the love of a family.

These are people who have now just become a number, a digit on the shocking mortality rate linked to a life in professional wrestling.

I had spent close to two decades living amongst the wrestling industry. But despite finding fame and fortune travelling across the world, I had also found a crippling drug addiction as well.

Drugs don't care who you are. They can grip hold of anyone and turn your life into a living hell.

It is chilling to realise that in my darkest hour, I was at home, surrounded by my two young daughters.

My life had plummeted to the point where I was regularly consuming a cocktail of Xanax, Vicodin and Ambien in order to function. These drugs were my desperate solution to numb a life now devoid of emotional support, joy and love.

Drifting asleep in my living room, my daughter's nanny had been unable to wake me.

She called for an ambulance, but three firemen were the first to respond and immediately started CPR.

"Get her on the floor! Get her on the floor!" they screamed.

Those were the last words I heard as I slipped further and further away into unconsciousness.

Powerless, I couldn't fight to save myself and I just remember hearing my younger soul screaming.

I wondered what had become of the hopes and dreams of the little girl from Southend-on-Sea as my mind and body gave in to the blackness…

1 SANDY BEGINNINGS

I was born on 4th April 1959 in Brentwood, a small town in Essex, which is the county just next to London in England. My dad, Thomas, was an auto trader and my mum, Audrey, worked in a plastic factory. My mum was so beautiful; she had been a theatre performer and club singer before giving up her dreams of fame to raise a family.

I was the youngest of three children. My sister, Valerie, was just eleven months older than me and I had a half-brother, Phil, from my mum's first marriage nine years before I came along.

It's strange the things that stand out when you think back to your childhood and my strongest first memory as a child was my fifth birthday. My parents had split up some two years beforehand, and I was at my dad's house. I was timid of him and ran out of sight, secretly opening a present whilst being concealed under a piano. I can't remember anything else of that day but know that I was afraid of this stranger, a man I rarely saw.

Due to the divorce, I didn't really see much of my whole family other than on special occasions. My sister and I had been taken to live with my mum whilst my brother, being older, lived with his paternal grandmother.

We were taken to Southend-on-Sea, the stereotypical British seaside resort where we moved to when I was just three years old. Located about forty miles east of London, but still in the county of Essex, the town was a favoured weekend destination for the families who would visit from the city after a hard week working at the Ford plant in nearby Dagenham or labouring in the London Docks. It was a picture postcard dream of relaxation and bracing sea air.

But for those of us who actually lived there it was very different. It was a town where work and money were sparse and life could be tough.

I didn't see much more of my dad after we moved.

When I was seven years old, my mum took us on a rare visit to his house and for some reason I became very shy, perhaps it was just because I hardly ever saw him. When he came close to give me a cuddle I ran and hid behind my mum. It pains me to say that it was the last time I ever saw him. Not long after, I found out he had died.

Thinking back to that day, I don't know what it was that that made me frightened to go near my dad. Unfortunately, I just had an instinctive mistrust and fear of men ingrained in me.

Ever since leaving my dad, my mum had struggled with an alcohol problem and had attracted a string of abusive boyfriends. Most other children our age were taken to the park by their parents in the evenings, but my sister and I were left outside a circuit of bars and clubs. We would hang about as my mum and her latest boyfriend would drink all night until closing time. Our only joy would be hearing our mum's voice if she decided to go on stage to sing.

When not stranded outside the pubs, we always seemed to be living on the move. We lived in a constant cycle of at least eleven cheap bedsits, where my mum would be at home drinking and entertaining her latest boyfriend. We were shut in our bedroom and were expected to keep quiet. Through the long miserable hours came something more distressing than the silence. The drinking sessions would sometimes turn nasty and we would hear our mum being knocked about by a few of the men she brought home.

When yet another of my mum's relationships turned abusive, I ran to seek refuge at the nearest available place. The local churches were left open all the time and, as we had one at the bottom of our road, it became a place of escape. I was around seven years old when I first started hiding there.

I would roller-skate in the aisle and spend hours just sitting on the pews, enjoying the peace and quiet away from the unhappy and violent atmosphere at home. Because I was so young, I soon thought that God was an actual member of the community, as I heard people say that the church was his house. It always struck me as strange that God was never at home nor did I ever see his son, Jesus.

During one of my first visits to 'God's House', I stole some milk and a banana, as I was so hungry. I was ashamed and remember thinking that God made the moon follow me around afterwards as a way to shine a spotlight on me for committing a crime against the church.

As I started to spend more and more time there, clambering through the grounds, I noticed a playground and some swings.

I patiently waited for God and Jesus to return home so I could ask their permission to play on them, but my determination to play on those swings didn't waiver. I left a note for Jesus along with my skates and a copy of my favourite comic book *The Beano* and asked if he would like these in return for a go on the swings. When I didn't receive a reply to my offer, I presumed he was angry at my theft of the milk and banana. I tried to make amends by leaving an apple out for him.

With my sister, Valerie (right) praying for a deceased bird.

In my early visits to the church, I had no idea what the Bible was. When I first came across a copy, I just referred to it as the 'funeral book' under the presumption that it was only read if someone had died. After coming across a dead bird on the street, I borrowed one from the church. Wanting to uphold the traditions of God, I tied a string around its clawed feet and dragged it all the way home. I held a funeral service for the deceased, and made my sister pick flowers to place at the grave after we buried its tiny feathered body.

Our little service proved how my childhood imagination could bring fun into the bleakest of circumstances, and I never lost my sense of wonder at the world.

A big part of my exposure to the wider world was through the advent of television. We had a small black-and-white telly in the house, and I used to love watching it whenever my mum was out of the house. I was a fan of the old sixties series of *Batman*, but my absolute favourite was *Lost in Space*. Every week, I would rush home to watch that show. I dreamt of joining Will Robinson and Robot in the safety of a faraway planet, and in a future where poverty was non-existent.

Another place where life seemed happier was at my maternal grandmother's house, or as I called her, Nan.

Sometimes my sister and I would get to stay with her for a week, if our mum was struggling to cope. I remember that it was the small things which used to amaze me when we would stay with her. She would actually set the table for us, and we would sit down together and eat at fixed mealtimes. We never did this at home; we only ate whatever we could scavenge around the house. Valerie and I soon realised that our Nan's house was the warm, loving home that we never had. Once we were back with mum, we would often fantasise about running away to live with Nan permanently.

Once, we did try to run away from home, and escaped to Priory Park. We took a dolls' pram and a carrier bag filled with a toothbrush and clean underwear. We spent the whole night in the park before we got too cold and hungry. Defeated, we returned home.

As grim as our home life was, we were forced to accept that it was better than sleeping rough.

With the unsettlement of running away or dreaming of a life beyond the stars, my education at school was being affected. I would do what I could to avoid homework. Whenever I tried it and got stuck, my mum would snap at me if I asked for help.

My relationship with my mum really hampered my development. Emotionally, I felt stunted. I would often feel unwanted as she never encouraged me to aspire for anything. I had no direction, or discipline, and sometimes I would rather play truant than face the embarrassment of having to explain that there was nobody at home who could assist me with my homework.

Nevertheless, I had lots of friends at school. I was a popular kid, and I excelled at sports and drama.

I remember my first part in a school play. I played a frog, and had to wear this ugly mask and jump out of a cardboard well. It wasn't the part I really wanted, which was to play the princess, but it was enough to install a love of acting in me. Escaping reality for a brief moment, I enjoyed the pretence of living the fantasy of being someone else.

Beyond performing in plays, there were some other aspects of school for which I was grateful. Pupils from single-parent families were entitled to different benefits. I was eligible for free school meals, which ensured I got something decent to eat during the week. I was also given a free school uniform each year. It was the only time I got to wear new clothes. Everything else was either a hand-me-down from my sister or bought from the second-hand shop.

As I grew older, I spent more and more time away from home. I was rarely ever indoors, instead spending my time roaming the streets of Southend. During the longer nights of the summer months, I would stay at the seafront as long as I could.

I was doing what I could to live a normal childhood.

Like so many other children in the neighbourhood, I was at an age where I badly wanted a pet. As the other kids had to be indoors for a certain time, I would get very lonely when they all went home after we played at the beach. For company, I would often play with any stray dogs that I found prowling the streets. I knew that it would not be possible to take them home, so I had to think of another way of getting a pet.

I came up with a cunning plan. I would find a plastic cup, and wait until the tide was out on the beach. I would then gather as many little crabs as I could. I panicked at the returning waves, and I scurried away. I was so worried that I would get sand on my clothes that I dropped my little collection on the beach, and the crabs shuffled away from me.

Undeterred, I was adamant that I needed a pet, and I decided that an assortment of smaller creatures would be easier to manage.

I went out to the garden and collected as many snails as I could find, and put them in a box along with some turf I had lifted from the lawn. I hid them in the living room and went to bed, content in the knowledge that I was at long last an owner of some pets.

The next morning, my short lived happiness came to an abrupt end. I was woken by the sound of my mum screaming and shouting in anger.

Overnight, the snails had escaped their box and left a trail of sticky, slivery trails in their wake all over the floors, furniture and even the walls! She soon discovered that they'd been given a helping hand getting into our house and I was 'rewarded' with a firm smack across the back of the head.

As I got older, I learnt every trick and scam that there was to clasp at some semblance of a happy childhood. I was quite mature for my age and I soon developed a street sense which allowed me to survive, and even thrive, in bleak poverty.

It wasn't unusual for me to nab some milk from the house doorsteps and I would often steal fruit from the neighbour's trees. Sometimes, I would even sneak into gardens and play with any toys I could find. I think the neighbourhood understood my circumstances and they seemed to feel sorry for me. They would occasionally give me slices of cake or sweets.

I could never afford anything as a child, and it seemed that everything I owned was second-hand. In the sixties, jumble sales were hugely popular in Britain. People would donate all of their unwanted belongings and household items, and the goods would be sold to help raise funds for a local charity. These sales were usually in aid of the church and, since I was always spending time there, I was the first to know when these events would take place.

On the morning of each sale, I woke up eager, and I was always the first to queue in line. Once inside, there were books, clothes, and toys; all costing mere pennies! I would load up with armfuls of goodies and stagger out with as much as I could carry.

By the time that the next jumble sale came around, I had developed a little system to guarantee that I could return with a pocket full of loose change.

Like so many other coastal resorts around the U.K., Southend seafront boasted rows of amusement arcades. These arcades were full of gaming machines, aiming to tempt punters to try their luck at winning a small fortune with challenges of skill and chance. With nobody looking, I'd give the machines a nudge, and the pennies would spill from them. I would then run as fast my little legs would carry me before anyone could see.

It wasn't long before I got noticed and was banned from all the amusement arcades in the area, but I was a persistent and stubborn child. I would merely wait, hiding across the street, until the staff that knew me had finished work for the day. As quick as a flash, I would dart across to the nearest machine, give it a quick push, and then I'd be gone with a handful of pennies.

On one occasion the owner gave chase, but my speed left him trailing. My years of roaming the streets gave me the advantage; I knew all the routes to find a quick escape. I quickly gave him the slip after hiding up a fire escape, and I remember watching him hunting for me as I sat just yards away from him. I patiently waited for him to give up his frustrated manhunt, and then I scarpered to the nearby chippy and bought a bag of chips with my riches.

As my little arcade heists became less frequent, I had to find other ways to make money. Despite being such a young age, I quickly became quite the entrepreneur.

I would go 'bottling', by going out and collecting all the discarded milk and soft drink bottles I could find and then return them to the nearest shop for the deposit. I would go out in the morning with an empty crisp bag and, by the end of the day, it would end up full of loose change.

But one evening, while I was out collecting some empty bottles, I experienced my most terrifying and unsettling moment as a child.

I was probably around eight years old at the time, and was approached by a man on the beach asking if I wanted to be 'twizzled'. Twizzling is when an adult lifts up and playfully swings around a child. He seemed friendly and I was just happy to break the loneliness I was feeling walking the beach on my own.

Playing outside in the garden, at age 8.

The man picked me up and started swinging me around and around. It started off as great fun and I was giggling, however after a few minutes I felt dizzy and asked to be let go. He completely ignored me and continued to swing me about. I asked again. I was feeling nauseous and so I started yelling at the top of my lungs. His grip just got tighter. I was starting to panic. I couldn't see any other grown-ups on the beach.

In fact, I couldn't see anyone.

Luckily, the man lost his balance and we both tumbled to the ground. I ran as fast as I could, escaping to one of my hiding places.

A short time after this incident, I saw the man's face again, but this time on the news. He was wanted by the Police for molesting several children. I considered myself extremely lucky that day.

Despite the incident on the beach I still needed to find a way to earn money for myself. I used to hide the loose change that I had raised to stop it from being discovered by my mum and wasted on her drink habit. The safest place was under the carpet, and I found other hidey holes for my purchases of chocolate, sherbet and hard candy.

With my little riches, I also treated myself to small toys and comic books, but my absolute favourite thing that I ever bought was a dress from one of the jumble sales. It had a print of ducks all over it and I would wear it all the time. Even when it was freezing outside, I refused to put a coat over it. I wanted everyone to see my beautiful proud garment.

By age nine, we found ourselves on the move again. We occupied two upstairs rooms in a cramped block of flats. One of the rooms was a living area which doubled as my mum's bedroom. The other room was the kitchen, with a couple of bunk beds set up about a foot away from the gas cooker. We had one bathroom which we had to share with the other residents, who all seemed strange and scary to me.

With nowhere to move in the house, our lives became impossible as my mum's drunken boyfriend came to stay after a night getting wasted with her in the pub.

As our situation seemed to get worse, social services were called and they arrived to check up on our living conditions. After making an assessment, the authorities had to intervene. My sister and I were told we were going to boarding school.

We were immediately taken into care and sent to a former orphanage in Sawbridgeworth, a town about forty miles north of Southend. It was an unnerving experience, as we didn't know what to expect. I was just glad to have Valerie along to give me strength.

It was a difficult adjustment as we were faced with the challenge of fitting into the regime of life in the home. In spite of everything that had happened, we missed our mum.

One night after my tenth birthday, I was cuddling up to a toy Koala bear I had been given. I would speak to him, and told him I wanted to go back to Southend.

Homesick, I decided that my Koala and I would be better off if we made a break for it, and run away.

I managed to get out of the dormitory and took off into the nearby woods. Undetected, I carried my Koala up into a tree and sat there. I also had a bottle of perfume I'd taken from a girl in the same dorm. My plan was that if I was captured, I would drink the perfume.

I had given up, and was ready for the worst. It was not the kind of idea a child should have, but I was just so sad to be in the home.

After moments of reflection towards my deprived upbringing, I had a change of heart and headed back to the dormitory.

My impoverished childhood had made me a survivor. I was determined that my situation would change now that I had been given a fresh start, as I had spent enough of my time running away or hiding.

I was still a child, and ready to live life to the full.

2 GO AWAY LITTLE GIRL

Within a few months of being taken away from my mum, I eventually started to accept my new surroundings, and I even began to enjoy being at Sawbridgeworth.

A lot of the children there had come from similar backgrounds, and I still had the comfort and protection of my sister Valerie.

We got proper meals, and a regular bedtime. At the school, I got to resurrect my interest in drama and I even became the sports captain. I learned to play tennis, how to swim, and I even tried horse riding.

For the holidays, we would get to visit our mum, but her situation hadn't really improved. It was actually a blessing when our trips home would end, as we realised how desperate our old life was.

Unfortunately, the joy of my new life wouldn't last.

At age eleven, I had been given notice that I was to be returned to Southend, while my sister would stay at the school. The council had given my mum a flat, and she needed a child at home to claim social security money.

I was devastated.

When I got back, I felt deserted. I was missing my sister, and my mum's alcoholism had gotten even worse. She would be out all night with her latest boyfriend, and I hardly saw her.

In the meantime, I enrolled in Shoeburyness High School, which was a two-minute walk from the flat. I tried to maintain a positive outlook, and endeavoured to make new friends in this unfamiliar area.

The strongest memory I have from my time in High School involved an awakening to the purest of form of love.

One Easter, the class were set to view a film called *King of Kings*. It was a film which depicted the life and times of Jesus Christ. After I watched that film, I burst into floods of tears.

In the portrayal of Jesus, I saw a compassion and kindness that I had never experienced, and it moved me. I sobbed uncontrollably, and couldn't stop. With no alternative, the teacher sent me home for the day.

The movie was unlike anything I had ever witnessed in my upbringing, and I had never known that such warmth could exist from a person. It made me realise what I had missed in my life, a nurturing figure to provide me with love and kindness.

Not only had I been raised to feel unloved, but most of my experiences with adults had been unsavoury.

To me, grown-ups were the people who chased away a hungry child, tried to snatch and molest a youngster, used authority to break up siblings, or neglected their own kin.

A large part of this distrust stemmed from the place that a child should never feel scared; the home.

The most frightening experience I had there occurred when my mum's boyfriend came in past the house.

His name was Jim Baker. I had seen his face a few times when I had sneaked into my mum's favourite singing venue, The Eagle Club, to watch her perform.

Cleaning my clothes in the kitchen, I was in the house alone and wearing only a pair of shorts and a T-shirt.

I heard the back gate and, clutching an opened bottle of Johnnie Walker Red Label Scotch whisky in his hand, he trudged into the house. I knew he was going out with my mum, so I was not alarmed to see him.

"My mum's out just now," I informed him.

I noticed his eyes glancing at me, and he smiled.

"I know your mum's not here. I came to see you," he leered.

I was confused, I couldn't quite understand what he suggesting, but I was starting to feel uncomfortable around him.

I had an idea by his body language that there was a fondness for me, but at thirteen, I was still very much a child.

He advanced towards me.

"Just lay back. Let me give it to you, I won't make you pregnant," he whispered.

Shaking with fear, I sprinted out the house, with tears streaming from my eyes.

I found my mum, and I told her what had happened with Jim. She had an angry look at me, I am not sure if it was jealousy, but it was certainly disgust. I knew she really loved Baker, and she refused to accept what I was telling her.

Upset, I went to see my friend Janice, who lived in a nearby flat above our one. She could feel my pain, and she was a great support to me.

Posing in my favourite dress, at age 12.

Her family could sense how destitute I was. They would frequently have me round for dinner and even offered me a job. I would clean their house for some pocket money. Enjoying the escape, I soon offered to do similar odd jobs for other families in the neighbourhood, including outdoor gardening work.

I already knew that happiness would not be handed to me, but if I worked hard enough, I could possibly earn freedom from misery.

Increasingly independent with each day, my life seemed much happier as I entered my teenage years. I was a regular girl of my age, and would spend most of my time with my school friends. I was interested in fashion and music, and also started swimming at the local pool.

As puberty dawned, I started to gain an interest in boys. After noticing that some of the lads at school were quite cute, I developed a huge crush on the television star Donny Osmond.

He was the lead singer from the famous brother group, The Osmonds. My infatuation developed as soon as I heard the song *Puppy Love*, and I would listen to it over and over on the gramophone.

Stricken by the love bug, I completely covered the bedroom walls with pictures of this American teenage heartthrob, and my fantasy was to travel to the United States and meet him.

At thirteen years old, I found out The Osmonds would be playing a tour of the United Kingdom.

Brimming with excitement, I caught the earliest train and made my way to the box office. I wanted to be the first in line to get tickets for their show the famous Rainbow Theatre in Finsbury Park, London.

On the night of the gig, my little frame was put to good use. I managed to worm my way right to the front, screaming so loud I couldn't speak for days. It was such a thrill to see my idol in the flesh, and was the happiest memory of my life.

The rush of live music was infectious, and I revelled in the crowd atmosphere of a concert.

Exhilarated, I wanted to share the experience with my friend Marion, and we started attending all the gigs that we could. I got a couple of part-time jobs, securing work at a greengrocer and at a local hairdresser, to fund my interest.

Over the next few years, we saw performances from David Bowie, Slade, Queen and countless others.

We would often hitchhike to the events, and after a while we made friends with some of the road agents who would sneak us in for free.

Our faces became well known, and it was not long before we were invited backstage to the VIP after-parties.

The most amazing of these was held at the London Hilton, where I met David Essex. To top it off, he even autographed my arm and complimented my frock.

I was star struck. Afterwards, I travelled to Wales with his roadies, and hung out with his supporting act, the 1970s soul group The Real Thing.

However, all the travelling about and chasing of bands had caught up with my school life and my absences were starting to be noted. Nevertheless, my imagination was captured by the thriving music scene, particularly with the explosion of punk rock in 1970s Britain.

I saved all the cash I could to afford tickets to the shows, and Marion and I would spend hours talking about forthcoming tours. When we weren't on the road, we became the best of friends, and I would love spending time at her place.

Marion's house almost felt like a second home, and she had a really nice family. Her mum worked in the same factory as mine, and her dad was a bricklayer.

At the weekend, we would hang out in the kitchen and would sometimes hear these fantastic noises from the living room television. I was intrigued.

It was the sound of crowds roaring and bodies being slammed to the mat.

We went through to watch what was being broadcast, and it was professional wrestling.

It turned out that Marion's dad was an avid fan of the sport, and I discovered that he tuned in every Saturday afternoon to watch the matches.

Marion's dad seemed to know everything about the wrestling. He had watched it for years, and the weekly coverage was a genuine highlight for him.

Every week, professional wrestling was featured as part of a programme called *World of Sport*, a regular fixture on the British channel ITV which showcased a range of athletic events.

Knowing all the top stars, he spouted off the names like Mick McManus, Jackie Pallo, Kendo Nagasaki and the nefarious Les Kellett. He told us that all the moves had wild and impactful labels too.

There were punishing holds such as the Surfboard, the Half-Nelson and the dreaded Power Lock, spine-crushing throws like Body Slams and Backbreakers, to exotic attacks like the Kamikaze Crash and the vaunted Japanese Stranglehold.

And just like our passion for the music gigs, Marion's dad would go to all the wrestling events that he could.

But one afternoon, Marion came over with excitement in her face.

Her dad was feeling a bit ill, and couldn't attend an upcoming event at the nearby Cliffs Pavilion in Southend.

He offered her the pair of wrestling event tickets that he had already bought and she was dying to go.

At first I was hesitant, but Marion had gone to all those music gigs at my urging. It was only fair that I accompanied her to an event that she wanted to see.

Reluctantly, I agreed.

I was on my way to my first wrestling event.

3 SECONDS AWAY, ROUND ONE!

At first I couldn't see what all the fuss was about, nor why Marion's dad was so obsessed with the wrestling. But once the crowd warmed up, I started to be drawn towards the drama in the ring. The British crowds were notoriously rowdy and would really get into what they were seeing. The touring villains would play to the audience as they would sneakily cheat, argue with the referee, and hurl insults at the baying crowds who were so desperate to see them get their comeuppance.

I soon learned that it wasn't uncommon for members of the audience to actually get physically involved in the matches to help their hero.

Any self-respecting bad-guy wrestler, or heel, would only think they had a good night if they were thrown a couple of punches from the local punters or if they were battered by the handbags of the many elderly ladies who seemed to populate the front rows of every show!

Some of the wrestling's finest villains have come from the UK. Mick McManus, Steve Logan, Adrian Street, Dave 'Fit' Finlay and many others were all able to get under the skin of their audiences and cause near riots just by their arrogant demeanour, which I later realised was the exact purpose of their job.

One of the very best this country produced was Mark 'Rollerball' Rocco. He was the first thing that made me sit up and take notice during the show. With his jet black hair and rugged good looks, I actually found him incredibly cute.

Mark 'Rollerball' Rocco, former wrestler: "British wrestling had the highest viewing audience during the 70s and 80s. The TV coverage inspired not only the fans but also the main advertising agencies that appeared on Saturday 4pm during World of Sport became household names. Every wrestler had an image and the public followed no matter what. Some of the conflicts carried on for many weeks. I was fortunate enough to be among the wrestlers who attracted the public to the intense storyline. I never spoke to or made eye contact with the public as my job was to make them insane with anger - it must have worked as I found it difficult to leave the venue as the public thought they had permission to damage a wrestler was included in the entrance fee."

As the evening went on, I started to really enjoy myself. I could relate to the sheer exuberance from the crowd, as it was exactly the same kind of highly-charged atmosphere that I experienced at music concerts.

I also loved the showmanship of the matches too, having spent all those years enjoying taking part in school plays and shows. I could really empathise with the theatrics of it all and the way these guys in the ring adopted their characters to enhance the drama.

To me, the wrestling was like a stage production – it just involved a lot more physical attributes. But the storytelling, even down to the facial expressions and voice work, was exactly the same concept.

The British wrestlers were true masters of their craft. They could create a narrative and make people believe every second of it.

As the show finished, we thought we'd hang back and let the heaving surge of bodies leave the venue before we attempted to exit. So we ventured to the bar to have a drink. In the midst of the throng we were casually standing there, chatting and minding our own business.

A tall, dark haired guy then approached us, adorned with the cutest smile I had ever seen.

"Hi, I'm Chris Adams," he said.

At the time I first met Chris, he had only been wrestling for about a year. He had broken into the business almost by accident through a friend, as his first love was actually judo.

Growing up in Warwickshire, in the West Midlands of England, Chris had been practicing judo since the age of nine and he had followed his father Cyril into the sport, much like his younger brother Neil. He was a natural sportsman and also played football, cricket and rugby, but judo remained his passion.

When we met for the first time, Chris was training to be an architect whilst doing a variety of odd jobs including selling toys in a market and working for the Yellow Pages. Wrestling was really a hobby for him. He first got hooked on it when he was invited to a show by Tony 'Banger' Walsh who had trained in the same gym as Chris in Leamington Spa.

Chris was completely blown away by his first event, particularly by the athleticism of a young wrestler named 'The Dynamite Kid' Tom Billington. Back then, Tommy was performing all the high-flying and high-impact moves which would solidify him as one of the all-time greats. His flashy style made him a rarity on the British wrestling scene, which was mostly centred on mat-based grappling.

After seeing Dynamite in action, Chris wanted to enter the ring to emulate his new hero and asked if he could meet the local promoter.

The promoter was aware of Chris' athletic background and asked if he would like to try wrestling. He was excited to give it a go and was given the nickname 'Blackbelt' Chris Adams, in recognition of his judo ranking. Unusually, he wasn't really given any pro wrestling training before starting on shows and instead relied on his judo repertoire to back up his martial artist moniker.

At first, he was put into tag matches with Big Daddy, a huge behemoth of a man who was British wrestling's most popular hero. Unfortunately, Daddy was so overweight he found it difficult to work a full-length match. I would soon discover that promoters would hide this shortcoming by booking him in tag team contests to give his massive frame some respite.

Chris Adams (left) with Big Daddy (right).

By having a small and agile tag partner who was first into the ring allowed the match to be padded out. Usually the smaller man would fall prey to the villains' cheating as the crowd started chanting for Daddy to come into the fray and clean house. Moments of absorbing punishment would pass before the smaller athlete would finally make the hot tag to the huge man from Halifax, who would then deliver a short beating, and score the all-important pinfall.

On the outside, Daddy looked like the hero. He received all the cheers but would barely have to break a sweat. For most new wrestlers, this was their rite of passage before being allowed to go into individual matches. Stars such as The Dynamite Kid, Davey Boy Smith and Steve Regal all started like this before being established as legitimate headliners in their own right. Chris took to it like a duck to water.

Whenever he put his mind to a task he just became a natural at it. Nothing seemed to faze him.

Marty Jones, former wrestler: "The first time I met Chris Adams, we hit it off straight way with both of us having a sporting background, Chris with his judo and myself with amateur wrestling, both being champions in those respective sports and both breaking into professional wrestling at the same time. Other than his natural ability in the ring, the thing that always stands out about Chris is how smart he was in his appearance, especially his ring attire. I think often he felt in the shadow of his brother Neil's success in judo and this spurred him on to be the very best. He certainly made his mark very rapidly in wrestling, which is something not many judo practitioners have done."

Chris was also a very complex individual too, a complete enigma at times and one who had many different facets to his personality. He was charismatic, intelligent and highly talented, but most of all, I found him to be a caring and kind individual.

Mal Sanders, former wrestler: "I liked Chris Adams very much; he was a good friend of mine. Whenever we saw each other in the dressing room we would go up and give each other a big cuddle and would chat between our matches. I was a big fan of his too because of his style. He wanted to emulate his older brother Neil, who was an Olympic silver medallist, and be a big success, which really we all wanted to be, and Chris did become a success. He was just a nice lad and he was always the same, always happy. Whenever you saw him he had a smile on his face, and it's his smile I remember most about him and how he would always be laughing and mucking about. It was always lovely to see him."

I was really taken by this tall, dark-haired and handsome man. He had the cutest dimples when he smiled. We didn't talk for long as Marion and I were ready to leave, and he needed to get away and meet up with the guys with whom he was sharing a car.

Before he left, he asked for my phone number.

I must admit although I thought he was gorgeous when I first met him, resembling a young version Paul McCartney from The Beatles, I was slightly hesitant to fall for him. I figured that asking a local girl for her details would be a regular occurrence for these guys. Turn up at a town, wrestle, meet a few girls, flirt, hopefully get a date – and repeat. And the next time they were back in town they knew they would have some female company waiting for them; a sailor-with-a-girl-in-every-port type of deal. I'd seen it all before at the concerts. Whenever I went to a particular group's gigs there were always the same girls who were waiting around for the company of their idols.

But I was still more than happy to hand over my number. To be honest, I never thought he would actually call anyway.

Not long after our first grappling experience, Marion and I were keen to see some more events. In addition to the Cliff Pavilion show, we travelled to Catford in south London and Fairfield Halls in Croydon, just to witness the matches. With my busy life travelling to gigs and wrestling cards, my young mind became distracted from Mr Adams and his pledge to call me.

The relationship I had with my mum hadn't improved so I found that it was easier to avoid her. I was rarely at home; I would leave early to go to work and be back home late, when I knew she'd be in bed. Our flat was basically just somewhere that I got a few hours' sleep and a change of clothes.

One evening, I arrived home earlier than usual and was greeted by my mum, complaining about incessant phone calls from 'that damn Chris guy'. He'd been driving her insane with the amount of calls he had been making to try and reach me. I had no idea that he would have been so persistent and it was a real compliment.

To stop him being a nuisance to my mum, I promised I would ring him back, although deep down I was very flattered that he was making such an effort. Our meeting had been so fleeting that I was amazed that he had even remembered me.

I returned his call and, after a bit of small talk, Chris asked if he could take me to the Birmingham Motor Show. This was a huge event in the UK. As well as all the car manufacturers showing off their latest models, there were all sorts of entertainment going on too. I'd never been before and it sounded like fun, so I told him I'd love to go.

At the time, I couldn't drive so I had to catch a couple of trains to his home town of Leamington Spa in the Midlands.

As I sat there on the long journey watching the scenery change out of the window, I had the strangest of feelings. I was nervous and excited all at the same time. My stomach was doing somersaults as I had no idea what to expect and, after going all that way, I was just praying we would get along. The nearer I got to my destination, the more the apprehension started to build.

As soon as the train pulled into the station I noticed Chris. In all honesty, it would've been hard to miss him. Standing there, he flashed his gorgeous smile and was dressed to the nines in a three-piece suit, completed by a smart tie and a pair of dress shoes.

I walked towards him with my eyes wide open. Suddenly, I became very self-conscious of the casual t-shirt and jeans combination I was wearing. There I was thinking we were off to a rough and ready car show and he was dressed up like he was going for a day at the Ascot races!

The first thing we did was go to his local pub and we chatted over a drink. I can remember almost everything about that date even now; the weather, the layout of the pub, what we were wearing and what we had to drink. It was a pint for him and a Babycham for me. This champagne-type drink was quite cosmopolitan back in the seventies and I wanted to appear more worldly-wise to Chris than I actually was.

In truth, I've never enjoyed drinking. The first few times I tried, it made me feel incredibly sick and I think seeing the effect that it had on my mum was enough to put me off it. As we sat talking, with me politely sipping my drink and pretending to enjoy it, I could see that he was looking more and more stressed and it appeared that he wasn't enjoying himself. I was worried I had said something to offend him.

"Do you mind if I go home quickly and get changed? This suit is really uncomfortable!" he suddenly blurted.

I just burst out laughing and so did Chris. He returned about twenty minutes later dressed in a more casual T-shirt and jeans. He may have made himself uncomfortable dressing in the suit but he was just so incredibly sweet taking the time and effort to make me feel special. And I must say – he looked just as handsome dressed down as he did in his suit.

The time just flew by as Chris and I sat in the pub, we just talked and laughed like we'd known each other for years, he was so easy to get on with and we just clicked straight away. We had scampi and chips at the pub for lunch (everything from that day is etched in my memory) and then he said he'd love to introduce me to some of his friends.

So we went off to meet a chap by the name of Steve Palmer and his girlfriend Isobelle. We listened to some music and just generally hung out, chatting and joking. In the evening, Chris took me to his favourite Chinese restaurant for a meal.

It was just a perfect day. Before I knew it, we were back at the station in time for me to get the train home to Southend.

Just before my train left, Chris asked me to come back the following weekend. He had a show, and he wanted me to come and see his match. There was no hesitation; I was thrilled.

As the train pulled away from the station, I looked out of the window waving as long as I could until Chris faded from view.

Sitting back in my seat, I suddenly realised that we never actually made it to the Birmingham Motor Show after all! I didn't care though, inside I was starting to fall for this handsome wrestler, and I knew he liked me too.

I was on cloud nine. The next weekend couldn't come soon enough.

4 WHEN SATURDAY COMES

After the week had dragged on for what seemed like an eternity, Saturday finally arrived and I was off once more to meet up with Chris. We travelled to the venue and I sat in the front to eagerly watch his match. I can't even remember who his opponent was that night, as quite frankly it didn't matter. I couldn't keep my eyes off Chris.

Bearing in mind that we'd only met a couple of times it came as a bit of a surprise that on the next date he wanted to show me the flat that he owned in Warwick. He was so proud of the flat that he managed to buy he was almost excitable, like a little boy showing off his favourite toy.

It was a spacious second storey, two-bedroom flat that Chris shared with a friend who rented the second room; a friendly and cheerful guy called Robbo. The first thing that struck me about the flat, considering that two males lived there, was how tidy it was.

This was Chris all over, he was always fastidious. Everything always had to be in order and in its place. He was incessantly organised, almost to the point of being annoying, his office was perfectly filed and his shirts were always colour co-ordinated.

Chris had a match that night and after we got back it was far too late to make the train back to Southend, so he asked me to stay for the rest of the weekend. Looking back now I think it was then I first fell in love with Chris Adams.

We had the most perfect weekend. He took me to Warwick Castle and showed me where he played as a child, we walked hand-in-hand for miles, talking and laughing, our hands almost glued together neither of us wanting to let go of the other.

Before I caught my train home, he took me to Stratford-upon-Avon. There, we browsed the shops and wandered aimlessly, just content in each other's company.

21

When I arrived home my Mum didn't even ask where I'd been for the last few days. I sat in my room in our tiny council house replaying over and over in my mind our perfect weekend. Although I was physically in Southend, my heart was in the Midlands.

Marion soon called wanting to hear all the gossip from my sojourn, and also to invite me to some more wrestling shows. I didn't have the heart to tell her the news; Chris had just asked me to move in with him before he left. I was flabbergasted.

After just two dates, it seemed to be too soon, but there wasn't a minute of the day I wasn't thinking of him and also how happy I was when I was there, compared to being in Essex. Chris would ask me whenever we spoke on the phone if I had made a decision, but I just couldn't help thinking we were rushing in too quickly. I decided to compromise and said I would come and stay for a week and see how well we got on living together.

A few days later, I was back on the train, this time with a suitcase packed for the week. As soon as I arrived, he sprang a surprise on me; we were going to meet his parents. Living together and meeting his parents, Chris didn't do things by half. But this was another thing about him that I soon learnt, Chris didn't have time to sit about, he was all about actions, not just words. When he set his mind to something, he went for it and didn't back down at all. It was this attitude that he knew would take him far in the wrestling industry whilst many of his peers floundered.

I was nervous as hell that day, but as soon as we walked into his parent's house, I started to relax. His mum, Jean, immediately made me feel at ease. She was always so kind and loving towards me and even from that first meeting she gave me a feeling that I belonged. His dad Cyril was very laid back and extremely funny, he had us all laughing in no time and any apprehension I had about the meeting soon disappeared. We were joined by Chris' brother Neil and we hit it off straight away as we were the same age. For a guy who was seriously tough, Neil was also incredibly sweet. Despite their competitive natures when it came to sporting achievement, the brothers were very close and I could see how much Chris loved his younger sibling. In fact I could feel the affection that they all had towards each other – at long last I felt I had finally found the family for which I had so longed. Years later, Jean would kid me about that first meeting as when I was asked where I came from I pronounced my hometown in the broadest Essex accent and it came out "Sarfend" – and they were unsure of exactly where I meant!

The week came and went and I decided to stay around, we were so happy together that we didn't want to be miles apart for any length of time. I started to accompany Chris at all of his wrestling matches around the country and I quickly became good friends with the rest of the wrestling crew.

Chris worked for Joint Promotions, which was the UK's premier wrestling operation. Joint Promotions was a syndicate of local promoters, who had an agreement to share talent and resources as necessary, effectively creating a monopoly in the industry. Joint also had national television on ITV as part of its *World of Sport* weekly programming each Saturday afternoon, and so every British worker wanted to be on their books to get that much sought after exposure.

By the late seventies, Joint Promotions was headed up by promoter Max Crabtree, whose brother Shirley wrestled as Big Daddy. I soon realised that this was the reason Daddy was so protected in his matches, as it was rumoured that Max felt he could only trust a family member to lead the bills of his shows, and an injury would be devastating to a card built around the name of his top drawing star. But slowly, it started to seem that the burly champion of the people was now becoming weary and tired. He was being booked to compete almost every night, as Max tried to capitalise on the demands of Daddy's adoring fans. Nevertheless, wrestling was so popular that, as well as the TV tapings, there were dozens of shows all over the UK every month, and so many of the boys used it as their primary source of income. It was a glorious time for the wrestling industry in the United Kingdom.

Chris had already packed-in his other work commitments to make a full-time job of wrestling. He was being heavily featured on cards all across the country, and was starting to regularly appear on TV since his *World of Sport* debut in July 1978. This increased workload meant a lot more travelling and so, to stop us from being apart for any great periods of time, I offered to do the circuit with him. To keep the travelling more cost effective, we would car-share with a bunch of boys also from the West Midlands. Usually, we were accompanied by Tony 'Banger' Walsh, Jackie Turpin and Les Hudspith (who wrestled under the name Ringo Rigby).

I have fond memories of these days with the banter and camaraderie that went on between us all. We travelled all over the UK. Chris worked frequent circuits in Southampton, Porthcawl, Skegness, Yarmouth and all points in between, driving a good couple of hundred miles between each show.

One thing that made Chris stand out from the others was his handsome appearance. That's not a knock on the other wrestlers, but at that time the business wasn't about being body-beautiful. The real focus of the sport was centred on competence in the ring. Many of the British wrestlers came from the shoot style of catch-as-catch-can amateur wrestling and were visibly rough and tough guys with lumps and bumps all over them. They each had an aura of hard-man credibility and were taught a deep respect for the business in order to enter it. It was deeply ingrained into their professional code that they must protect the image of the sport at all costs, especially from any member of the public who might decide to try and challenge one of the TV wrestlers to a fight.

Before long, Chris was beginning to attract a large female following and, to capitalise; we set up the 'Chris Adams Fan Club' which I ran from the flat. For £2.00 (about $3.50), members would receive a welcome letter from Chris, a personally signed 8"x10" promotional photograph, and other perks which I've long since forgotten.

Like many managers of attractive male music stars, I knew that the secret to getting Chris' adoring fans into the halls to watch the shows and join the Fan Club was to make their star look available.

Despite us living in domestic bliss, Chris and I never publicised our romantic relationship. It certainly worked as we couldn't believe how much mail was flooding into the flat, most of it propositioning Chris for a date. With his popularity seemingly skyrocketing further each passing day, he came up with a plan that would gain us huge amounts of publicity and really make him a standout star in the UK wrestling scene.

Welcome
to
Chris Adams Fan Club

Short Biography:
Born 10.2.55
Place: Warwick
Height 6'0 Weight 13st 7lbs.

Chris left school at 17 with 9 'O' levels and 2 'A' levels hoping to become an architect. After 4 years of studying he decided that Architecture wasn't for him and he went into selling advertising hoping it would be more exciting with a chance to travel and meet people.

By May 1978 Chris still hadn't found the right job for his outgoing way of life and he had to find something else. But what?

JUDO Since he was 11, Chris has practised judo, gaining many championship places. At 13, Chris won a gold medal at the Midland area championships, and went on to win them 10 more times, the National Championships 3 times, with 2 silver and 3 bronze medals. He has also been a member of the national squad 5 years running and has represented Great Britain several times. During 1977/78 to improve his judo Chris would have had to do it full time which is difficult as it is an amateur sport.
What should he do?

WRESTLING It was strange because, when Chris was undecided about his job he was also undecided about his judo. It was the luckiest day in his life when Chris had the opportunity to start wrestling. It was a tough decision because he would be doing something he knew little about, however, Chris hasn't looked back since and is looking forward to gaining a title in the near future.

FAN CLUB Chris wrestles six nights a week and he is asked many questions, one of which is "What sort of girls does he like?" Says Chris:- 'There is no particular type of girl, as long as she has a friendly personality, and a good sense of humour – this is more important than looks.'

I would like to thank you for joining the Fan Club. We will be holding all sorts of competitions and discount offers. If you have any questions, please send a s.a.e. to the Fan Club and I will be pleased to answer them.

Best wishes,

Chris Adams

The Welcome Letter to the Chris Adams Fan Club.

Mark 'Rollerball' Rocco, former wrestler: "The young Chris Adams was a shining light. I tried to help with advice as I was an established wrestler - he took my advice to heart and I watched him improve. He was on the right track and would have had many years of being a public hero. Chris fell in love with a top girl Jeanie Clarke. Chris brought Jeanie into the wrestling world and she became his valet or second. This worked great as Jeanie was the target for all the villains to attempt to do her damage always and to be saved by Chris. This got the crowds on their feet if not on the seating screaming at the villains, an amazing reaction."

Before I go any further I must explain for anyone who hasn't seen any British wrestling from this period that it was much different to the wrestling product that fans see in rings today. The matches were fought under 'Mountevans Rules' and were set out in a similar structure to boxing, with each fight being broken down into rounds lasting several minutes. Contests were determined when the first wrestler to win two pinfalls, two submissions, or a knock-out would be decided the winner.

In boxing, the role of a 'second' is for someone to be set at ringside and provide advice, give pep talks and clean up any injuries in-between rounds. Chris wanted to have someone at ringside who could compliment his persona of being a smooth ladies man. He didn't want a valet or manager who would get involved in his matches; instead the notion was for me to be his 'second'.

His idea was for me to come into the ring after each round to give him his water and rub him down with a towel, and provide the necessary inspiration by cheering him to victory. Having a pretty girl come into the ring with him worked a treat for Chris; it reinforced his image as a real heart throb and was the start of the 'Gentleman' character that he would later adopt.

Marty Jones, former wrestler: "When Jeanie first started with Chris, I was away working in Mexico and Japan, but I do remember the first time I laid my eyes on her. I think we were working at the Colston Hall in Bristol, and I just thought - nice arse! But seriously, I thought it was a masterstroke by Chris and they were so good together. I'm sure Max Crabtree would've loved them to have got married in the ring with the service done by the famous 'wrestling vicar' Michael Brooks. What an angle that would've been!"

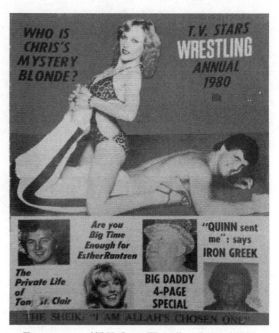

Front cover of T.V. Stars Wrestling Annual 1980.

It was a real head-rush being with Chris and around the wrestling industry. The wrestlers were revered as genuine celebrities and a maelstrom of mainstream publicity started coming my way too with magazines and newspapers all wanting to know about Chris Adams' and his sweet and bashful ringside second.

With Neil (left) and Chris (right) Adams.

Front cover of the Leamington and District Morning News, 20ᵗʰ September 1980 edition.

The largest British tabloid, *The Sun*, asked to do a feature article on us, and we were thrilled to learn that Chris' brother Neil was a silver medallist in judo at the 1980 Summer Olympics.

Having a family of successful sportsmen was of tremendous interest to the media, and we were asked to travel down to the photo studios for a pictorial article. Little did we realise that the story would be picked up by other local and national newspapers.

One newspaper article went on to describe the rare times that I got physically involved in matches. I had taken a swing at the manager of the Black Baron, after he suggested that women had no place in a wrestling ring. On another occasion, at the Belle Vue in Manchester, Chris battled Mark 'Rollerball' Rocco, which led to Adams being taken out of the match on a stretcher. As he was being carried away, Rocco kicked him off of it, so I felt compelled to retaliate with a hard smack across the head!

By the autumn of 1980, I was now a fully-fledged member of the crew for Joint Promotions, the UK's biggest national wrestling syndicate. At the youthful age of nineteen, I was appearing in cards held all over the country and Chris even suggested I would soon be on television.

Max and Brian Crabtree had told Chris that they were impressed by my glamorous model image, and girl-next-door charm, and were keen to showcase me on the 18th October edition of *World of Sport*.

I was thrilled to learn that my debut would be taped ten days prior in the hometown venue that started it all, the Cliffs Pavilion in Southend. After Chris and his opponent 'Bad Boy' Bobby Barnes were announced, I was so shy, and could barely look up to the crowd when I was introduced. All I can remember is timidly encouraging Chris to victory, as the men in the audience wolf-whistled for my attention.

By now, the cat was truly out of the bag about our relationship, but it didn't seem to affect Chris' popularity as the post was still flooding in for the Fan Club on a regular basis.

As I was now involved in the matches it also meant that I hung out in the dressing room during the shows instead of being in the audience.

At first I was quite scared and intimidated, being the lone girl in the private sanctuary of all the boys, but in fact the lads couldn't have been friendlier. They were like a great big family who immediately warmed to me and accepted me as part of it.

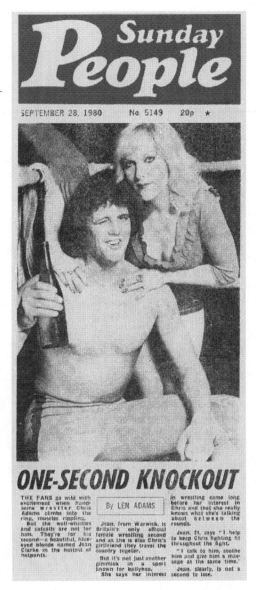

Sunday People, 28th September 1980 edition.

The dressing room was full of some of the biggest names ever to work on the UK wrestling scene: Big Daddy, Mark 'Rollerball' Rocco, Tony St. Clair, Mal Sanders, Marty Jones, Steve Grey, Johnny Saint, The Dynamite Kid, Pat Roach, Dave Bond, Wayne Bridges and the Midlands trio of Turpin, Walsh and Rigby.

I learned so much about the psychology of wrestling from these guys in the backstage area, and got a great education on the sport just by mixing with its best teachers. I was slowly starting to become smart to the business.

Chris had never sat me down to wise me up on the inner workings of wrestling; I just started to figure it out by being around the boys and listening to their discussions backstage, or if we were out in the pub following a show.

Most of the boys would enjoy a pint after the matches. For them it was a chance to let off some steam and relax. Our regular hangout was Tops nightclub in Leamington Spa. One evening there, we ran into Jeff Lynne from the band Electric Light Orchestra and ended up at a party with him. This was a huge thrill for me as ELO were one of my favourite acts and their 1975 hit *Strange Magic* still remains amongst my most cherished tracks.

Another time at Tops, we met the ace Snooker player Alex 'Hurricane' Higgins, who was ranked number one in the world at the time. He came to the flat for the evening, but he and Chris drank so much that he ended up crashing with us for several days.

Generally, Chris would only drink alcohol on a social level, and rarely let his intake get out of control. If he did get drunk, it sometimes ended up in violence.

I first witnessed it whilst we were having a Chinese meal. Somebody knocked into him on the way out of the restaurant. It angered Chris, who felt that the man should have apologised. Chris stood up, stormed outside and caught up with the guy in the car park. He casually tapped him on the shoulder and when the guy turned round Chris head-butted him, breaking the man's nose.

On a couple of other occasions, he returned from a night of boozing covered in blood. Naïve, I could not believe anyone would want to pick a fight with Chris, I saw him as such a nice, sweet guy. Luckily, these incidents were not common.

Despite this, Chris' career was still soaring. Business was booming all over the country and wrestling was continuing to sell out illustrious venues including The Royal Albert Hall and Wembley Arena.

It was such a prestigious industry as the British style of wrestling and its workers were so highly regarded.

Many international stars also passed through the UK system in the seventies and eighties, including such legendary names as the enormous French attraction Jean Ferre (better known as Andre the Giant), The Samoan Chief Peter Maivia (the grandfather of The Rock) and future Canadian greats Bret and Owen Hart.

Another was Yasu Fuji, a Japanese wrestler who had worked in the United States and Canada. He actually had his British debut match in 1980 against Chris. The pair instantly clicked as Fuji also had a background in competitive judo.

Fuji soon recommended Chris to Mike LeBell who, along with his brother Gene, ran a wrestling promotion in Los Angeles, California.

The promotion, named NWA Hollywood Wrestling, was one of several territories within America's version of Joint Promotions, the National Wrestling Alliance. Chris appealed to the LeBells, as Gene had competed in judo and had helped to popularise the sport in the States. After some written correspondence, Mike called and offered Chris a job.

Chris was over the moon. Performing internationally was an aspiration he had set himself ever since setting foot in the ring.

He felt that his career had gone as far as it could in the UK, and he knew that the only way to make big money and be a huge star was to wrestle in the States. When the opportunity came, he grabbed it with both hands.

When Chris told me we were both like children on Christmas Eve. The time seemed to drag as we waited for the date to come round for us to fly out to America.

We just couldn't believe how our fortunes had changed, and quickly arranged for someone to look after the flat as we packed up all of our essential belongings. Neither of us knew for how long we would be there as there had been no indication.

Our gut feeling was it would be a short tour to give Chris a trial run before we were bundled back to the United Kingdom.

All the boys were really pleased for Chris as they knew international success was his ambition. Nobody tried to dissuade him, and to be honest it wouldn't have made any difference if they had. When Chris put his mind to a goal there was no changing him, he was incredibly stubborn and wouldn't stop until he achieved it.

Mal Sanders, former wrestler: "When Chris went to America we were really pleased for him, as there weren't many going, so anyone who got on the American circuit we were pleased for and would wish them the best…. So whenever anyone like Chris or Dave Finlay or anyone else went to America we would always wish them the best."

We put together the little money that we had saved for our overseas adventure. With a couple of suitcases between us and all the best wishes from our friends and family, we arrived at the airport ready to take the leap into the great unknown.

Both of us were in a complete daze of excitement and nerves. This was the first trip out of the country that either of us had made, and although we'd already had quite a career in the UK, I was only 23 and Chris was just 26. As we waited to board the plane, we hugged each other and just smiled and laughed.

We were on a complete high; our life was like a dream.

Next stop: America.

5 CALIFORNIA DREAMING

As soon as Chris and I arrived in States, we immediately fell in love with the country.

The only experience we had of America was what we saw on television and in the movies, and the country had always embodied such a hopeful spirit in its cultural exports. It was a far cry from the United Kingdom, which had been rocked by a major recession during the turn of the decade.

Each view in Los Angeles looked like a picture postcard. The streets were lined by palm trees and illuminated by blazing sunshine. So many of the people had golden tans like movie stars or famous models, and there were dozens of convertibles driving around the coast. We gazed in wonder at the golden sands and the crystal blue ocean as we made our way to Santa Monica, a beachfront city in Western Los Angeles.

Our home in Santa Monica was within a downtrodden, three-storey hotel called The Flamingo West. Located at 1733 Ocean Avenue, it was a favoured accommodation for wrestlers working the area.

We had a tiny one-room apartment, with a small kitchen area in it. We had no car when we arrived but there were lots of buses on the boulevard, so it was fairly easy for us to get about. There was an enormous shopping mall at the end of the street, but most of the time we just hung out on the beach.

It was heavenly to lay in the glorious sunshine on the soft sand or to take a swim in the warm ocean.

Chris was originally scheduled to wrestle each Friday at the Olympic Auditorium, a large venue which was about fourteen miles away from where we stayed. At the time that he started working for the LeBells, he was incredibly optimistic. The territory had become one of the biggest drawing markets for wrestling in the States.

It was a great place for Chris to be introduced to the American style of wrestling, although being there on a trial basis was far from ideal. As a newcomer, the pay-outs weren't great and he was infrequently booked.

Our savings started to dwindle and soon, his bookings could not even cover our rent. Being young, we were excited by this enthralling new country and we weren't ready to leave it. I offered to get a job to help with our finances, but I didn't have a green card to allow me to work in the States.

All along the ocean front were these dispensers with free newspapers, so I would spend each day collecting them up and circling any adverts for jobs which I thought might be suitable. Worryingly, time was running out for us.

Chris and I couldn't afford to keep our apartment, so we slept on the beach. A huge bag of monkey nuts was the only sustenance that we could afford. Despite not having any money, these were some of the happiest days of my life.

We were young and our homelessness didn't seem to matter. Each night, we would curl up to each other, in the cool night air and listening to the ocean waves. It never once occurred to us to return home, even though in the morning we'd have bugs all over us and be forced to take freezing cold showers on the beach in our bathing suits.

One morning at the beach, I was reading a paper and stumbled upon an advert from an agency that was looking for models. I had done quite a few photo shoots with Chris back in England, and knew that this was something I could easily do.

After responding to the advert, I was asked to attend an interview at the agency, which was based in Hollywood.

The man at the agency was really nice and explained that it was 'glamour modelling' which was mainly for magazines, adverts and calendars. He offered me an immediate start, and I accepted.

Selected images from my glamour modelling career in Los Angeles, early 1981.

On top of my new modelling job, I had also found another job working as a hostess at a restaurant on Santa Monica pier called Moby's Dock.

At the same time that I was working the restaurant and doing modelling jobs, Chris was starting to get a few more wrestling bookings. Our money situation had only slightly improved, and we moved back into the Flamingo West. It was a tiny studio room with no air-conditioning, but we were so busy and we were spending most of our free time on the beach anyway.

It was when we were out strolling along beach one day that our lives were about to change once again. As we walked along, we passed a guy who kept staring at us.

"Hey Chris, how are you?" enquired the man.

I soon realised it was an old friend Chris had from his time in Leamington Spa.

It turned out this guy, also called Chris, was now working in L.A. and was living in nearby Venice in a two bed-roomed apartment. By sheer luck, he was looking to split the costs of his accommodation, and offered us his spare room. So, we left our sweltering studio flat and moved into the spare room in Venice.

The apartment share significantly improved our finances, and it was not long before were finally able to buy a cheap second-hand car which made our life so much easier. As Chris' wrestling commitments were usually restricted to evening shows, he would often drive me to work, before spending the day with our new flatmate.

While I was at work, the pair would hang out drinking at the famous Ye Olde King's Head, a British-style pub in Santa Monica. It was highly popular with tourists and the local ex-pat community.

The return of Chris' heavy boozing caused a little tension between us. He sometimes failed to collect me from work as promised. Let down and annoyed, I would be stranded, with no way of contacting him.

Having grown up around an alcoholic, I often worried about the frequency of his drinking and I was concerned that it would get out of control.

I was glad when Chris was able to pick up a few more bookings on spot shows in San Bernardino and Long Beach, as wrestling commitments always curtailed his meaningless binges.

Chris was perceived as a reliable worker by the LeBells. By the end of the year, his wrestling schedule had drastically increased. On 13th February 1981, he teamed with Tom Prichard to capture the vacant NWA Americas Tag Team Championship.

It was a title that the pair had been chasing for almost a year.

On a few occasions, I would accompany Chris to the ring and hand him a bouquet of flowers before his match, just as I did during our early appearances in Britain.

The sustained work and championship status was a huge boost to Chris' confidence. With both of us earning regular money, we eventually settled into the Venice apartment.

Just as we seemed to have regained control of our destiny, we received some unexpected news. We found out that I was pregnant, which was a huge shock to us both. The information came at a time when my work was still heavily supplementing our shared earnings, and we knew that I would soon have to stop modelling.

Chris and I had a serious talk regarding the pregnancy, but realised we both wanted to be parents. It was a gift that just happened to come sooner than we would have planned. We had struggled before and got by, and we would just do the same again.

The following week, Chris received a call from a promoter in Mexico. He was asked if he would consider travelling there for a tour, to face the legendary Perro Aguayo in a series of matches. Aguayo had engaged a hot feud with Marty Jones six years prior and wanted to replicate its monstrous success with another Brit. He had really learned to respect the skill and toughness of the English wrestlers, and was keen to face Adams.

Just before setting off to Mexico, Chris got a call from his old friend Hulk Hogan, a wrestler who he knew from working a tour of Japan. Hogan had won a role in a movie, and was going to be filming a key scene at the Olympic Auditorium for the third instalment of the popular *Rocky* franchise.

Hogan invited some of the boys to come along to the set to hang out, watch the filming and be a part of the audience during the scene. Chris took me along, and I was so excited to witness a film being made. The scene itself was unforgettable, as the valiant boxer Rocky Balboa took on an arrogant wrestler named Thunderlips, played by the enormous Hogan. I fell in love with the underdog character of Rocky Balboa in the first two films which were just so inspirational and uplifting. It was such a thrill to be a part of *Rocky III*.

Chris with Hulk Hogan, 1981.

We were both sitting fairly close to the ring for the scene, and during a break in filming I walked up behind Sly and tapped him on the shoulder. He turned his head, catching me with his smouldering Italian looks.

"Hi, can I have a picture with you please?" I asked.

Within seconds, a huge pair of arms came between us as one of his bodyguards tried to separate us.

Just when I thought the moment was lost forever, Sylvester looked at his minders and gestured for them to take it easy.

"It's okay, she's alright," he reassured.

I was bursting with excitement. He said he'd come over in a minute and asked where I was sitting. True to his word, he walked across and we had our picture taken together. He also posed for a picture with Chris.

To this day, the photo I have with Sylvester Stallone is one of my most treasured possessions. Unfortunately, when Chris and I swapped places, I was so overcome at having a photo taken with Sly that when we got our photos back, Chris' photo was missing the heads off both of them. I must have been shaking with excitement. Nevertheless, it was such a great memory for us to share before Chris had to leave for Mexico.

With Sylvester Stallone on the set of Rocky III.

As he set off south of the border, I stayed in Venice. Being pregnant, I had doctor's appointments to keep and couldn't make the trip. Through a bit of English charm, I had managed to wangle these for free despite having no medical insurance. I had also met a girl called Norma, who was a friend to many of the wrestlers and owned a house in Redondo Beach. She kindly offered me the chance to live with her.

I absolutely loved the area and Norma and I got on really well. I was missing Chris so much, as his tour of Mexico had been the longest time we had ever spent apart.

Wanting to see him, I flew down to Mexico City for a few weeks. It was not the visit I had intended. Being six months' pregnant, the food and water made me very sick and I noticed that Chris had started drinking heavily again.

When I returned to Redondo, I was worried about going into labour in the States. Although I'd managed to get medical appointments for free, I wasn't convinced I would be able to deliver the baby without being financially penalised. With my work and childcare options limited, raising a baby with Chris out of the country would be almost impossible.

With Chris during my first pregnancy, 1981.

After a couple of telephone calls to Jean and Cyril, they kindly offered to help. I decided that I would return to England for the birth of our first child.

On 16th October 1981, Jade Fiona Adams was welcomed into the world. Born in Leamington Spa, she was a healthy and happy baby and brought so much joy to my heart. Although Chris missed the birth of Jade, he flew back to see her as soon as he could.

In the hospital with my first child, Jade Fiona Adams.

We moved into our old flat in Warwick for a few months, and he managed to find work on a few shows for Joint Promotions while I stayed at home with our new-born child.

It was a temporary situation and we both coped well, but we had dreams of returning to the sunshine of the United States.

By the beginning of 1982, Chris was asked to return to Los Angeles. He was being promised a larger role for the LeBell brothers' promotion, with a greater financial incentive.

As luck would have it, one of the old West Midlands crew, Les Hudspith, had just started wrestling for the Los Angeles territory. We decided that our young family would return to America, and we were able to share an apartment with Les and his girlfriend Debbie.

Les Hudspith, former wrestler Ringo Rigby: "Debbie and I arrived in L.A. first and rented a place in Pasadena but not long after Chris, Jeanie and Jade came back and so we all ended renting a place in Ventura together. Chris and I made many trips to Las Vegas to wrestle, working at the old Show Boat Casino and Hotel in Las Vegas, just off Fremont Street.

It's strange but all of four us ended up doing modelling in different ways. I remember a British national newspaper renting a villa in Palm Springs for us and we did a photo shoot in the swimming pool. It was great fun in a great place, a blonde, a brunette plus Chris and Ringo. Fantastic days!"

This seemed like the perfect arrangement, as we all got on really well. When the boys were away wrestling, Debbie and I had each other for company. Chris was thriving in the territory, and his good looks and boyish English charms were starting to secure him a solid spot in the promotion. And like before, it also got him a lot of female attention.

Unfortunately, Chris had started to act on the temptation. I sensed he was straying when he began to stay out overnight after drinking. But I actually found out that he was cheating on me with some of the girls who attended the matches when one of them called the house.

At first, I was really hurt and bitter. I had come all the way out to the States to create a new life with Chris, and helped elevate his career by launching and managing his fan club. I supported him with my modelling gig when times were tough and I even became the mother to his daughter.

I felt so betrayed.

Conflicted, I confided in my two neighbours in the above apartment. The question on whether or not I could trust Chris again tore me apart.

Even though I was devastated by his cheating, I still deeply loved Chris. I also considered the best interests of our daughter Jade. I did not want her to be raised in a fractured family.

Crying at my knees, Chris begged for my forgiveness and swore he would do anything to regain my trust. I wanted to believe him. I was still young at 21, but the love of Chris had brought so much comfort to my life. He deserved a second chance.

Ultimately, I agreed to return to Chris.

I held on to the dream that we could try and repair our relationship.

6 THE GRASS ISN'T ALWAYS GREENER IN PORTLAND

Having spent months faced with relationship doubt, I was fully committed to making things work with Chris when I gave him a second chance. As the father of Jade, I was looking to bring some stability to our young family.

Unfortunately, further uncertainty came into our lives when the security of Chris' burgeoning career in America came to a grinding halt. Due to diminishing box office returns, NWA Hollywood Wrestling had ceased operations on 26th December 1982. With Les and Debbie splitting up and moving from the apartment, we had to accept that our time in California was coming to an end.

Having impressed many within the industry during his run with the LeBells, the word spread that Chris was a dynamic and daring young performer, and a star of the future. A free agent, he was soon called by Don Owen, who ran a promotion in Portland, Oregon.

Owen's company, Pacific Northwest Wrestling, was also a member of the NWA, and had established links with a number of promoters across the country. Pulling resources, they would trade talent and work together to keep their respective rosters fresh for their home fan base.

As a result, the Portland territory remained strong during a time when various other promotions were struggling to survive.

Chris was very lucky to be given an opportunity for alternative work as quickly as he did, but he was hesitant to leave Los Angeles. But he had to accept the inevitable, and we got ready to relocate northwards.

I will never forget the coastal drive on the route to our new destination, passing through San Francisco.

The scenery was breathtakingly gorgeous, with each mile framed by a series of picturesque vistas.

But as we left the state of California, there was a noticeable change of weather.

A wild storm had brewed. Under a dark grey sky, we drove for hours into lashes of rain. Fatigued by the journey, we needed to stop for some food and provisions. We pulled over at a Wendy's burger restaurant, where there was a noticeable blankness in Chris' eyes.

Noticeably bothered, he was struggling to eat his food.

"I'm not going to like it here," he sighed.

There was nothing I could say. Our options were limited.

Getting back in the car, we continued to Portland.

Once we arrived, we found our way to the apartment, a grim little unit filled with worn-out furniture. On the upside, our next-door neighbour had offered to show us around town. His name was Tommy Rogers, and he was another wrestler who was working for the Pacific Northwest outfit.

With business thriving, Chris was booked intensely to keep up with the demands of the promotion. The territory's main strongholds were Portland, Salem and Eugene, and spot shows in neighbouring towns were added to fulfil the needs of the local audiences. However, despite solid business, life at home with Jade was tough, as we did not have the privilege of the two incomes that we needed to raise a child.

In the Portland apartment with Chris, 1983.

As beautiful as Oregon was, it lacked connectivity for a young mother without her own mode of travel. There was not the public transport network that I relied upon to pick up our weekly shopping or to take Jade out for the day. To exacerbate matters, we just happened to arrive during a very rainy season, which further restricted our activities.

When Chris was unemployed in California, I had worked extra shifts and split my income with him to ensure he never suffered. Unfortunately, when our roles were reversed, he never returned the sentiment.

Without the privilege of a green card or anyone to assist with childcare, I was unable to secure work. As a result, I had to rely on Chris to provide me with the money required for essential purchases, such as food and toiletries. He tightly rationed my expenditure, and I struggled to make ends meet as Jade and I were stranded at the apartment.

Frugal, he would often question the requirement of any outlays. I was uncomfortable in my dependence on my partner, but I had started to see a selfish side to Chris that had remained hidden in the years we had been together. He still managed to find money to go out and get drunk with the other wrestlers, and he had even started to smoke increasing amounts of cannabis too.

If we would spend time together with Tommy, it would usually end with the lads ending up stoned while I was left to pick up the pieces. I found myself coming to resent Chris and his irresponsibility, and I became increasingly irritated with his greed.

Chris could tell I was starting to be disillusioned, and offered me a break from my daily monotony. We arranged a babysitter and visited the local bar. After we had finished our drinks, we again headed over to see Tommy. It was not long until a bong was taken out so the lads could take a hit.

Tommy then passed it towards me, and insisted that I take a puff. Initially refusing, I eventually gave in to the pressure.

Following a deep inhalation, the effect was more bizarre than I could have imagined. It was the first time that I had ever touched dope, and I didn't expect the weed that the guys were smoking to be so potent.

Freaking out at the warping of my senses, I went to lie down in the bedroom, and I yearned for the strange feeling to pass.

In the midst of an anxiety attack, I was convinced I was going to die. Frantic, I called for an ambulance to rush me to the hospital.

With flashing lights beaming through the windows, Chris and Tommy burst into the room to attend to me. They sat me up on the edge of the bed, with Chris reassuring me that I would be okay.

The paramedics entered the room, and saw me hyperventilating. They acted with urgency, placing an oxygen mask over my face, and tried to calm me.

Chris was worried that the emergency call would affect his career, but the police were never notified. He still felt indebted to Owen for the chance to wrestle after the LeBell's office had closed.

Moreover, Chris had become increasingly interested in the fans perception of him as a clean-cut hero.

When I would go to the shows on which he was wrestling, I would see crowds of young girls clamouring for Chris' attention. Once they realised that I was his girlfriend, they would look at me with angry glares. During our time in Joint Promotions, it was common for him to get the admiration of the local girls, but it had reached an invasive level in Portland.

One of the fans did manage to find friendship with the wrestlers, a local drug dealer known as 'Dirty' Ralph. He was a seedy character, who always seemed to be surrounded by women. As Chris liked to dabble with grass, he would sometimes party with Ralph, even though it made me uncomfortable.

But it wasn't long before I noticed a pattern emerge as the parties became more frequent. Chris had stopped coming home at night.

With his previous issues of heavy drinking, I was worried for Chris.

However, before I could approach Chris with my concerns, I had to return to England. Due to the death of a close family friend, I needed to fly home and attend the funeral. Given how young Jade was, I asked if Chris would look after her. I gave him the contact details of my regular babysitter in case he needed any help.

When I returned to Portland, I started to get a number of calls to the house late at night. It was a girl called Amanda, who had been asking to speak to Chris.

Having already cheated on me in Los Angeles, I questioned why a female would call the house in the middle of the night.

Chris tried to brush it off, explaining that she was a friend of Ralph's who was asking if he needed any weed. But his face told a different story. There was guilt in his eyes, something that I had already seen in previous months.

As I continued to visit the arenas, the joy in Chris' face had drastically changed. He carried an awkwardness that I was not used to seeing in him, and his usual outgoing confidence seemed to be eroding each day that I was around the promotion. One Wednesday evening in Salem, a female fan approached me, and introduced herself.

Her name was Ruth, and she seemed to be overly interested in my family, especially Chris. Some of the other fans warned me about her, so I told Chris when he got back to the apartment. When I mentioned her name, his face dropped and he became defensive.

By that time, I knew that Chris had failed to keep his word to me. He had resumed his old ways of sleeping around with other women. He had taken advantage of my naivety and vulnerability.

I accepted that he was not going to change, and I needed to find an escape from a relationship which was doomed to fail. However, with no green card, no job, and a child, I was stuck.

I knew that I could not return home to England. I could not live with my mum, or have Jade being raised in the environment of an alcoholic. And crossing the Atlantic wasn't even an option, as I had no money to afford the flight.

Knowing that I could not move, it was a real strain as I struggled to co-exist with Chris in the apartment. If he tried to embrace me in bed, I could not stop but think that his need was tainted. There was a grief that my desire for him was forever lost.

The damage had been done and I no longer looked at him in the same way. I was saddened, as I realised that the love would never return.

During my troubles with Chris, I got a call from the wrestler 'Playboy' Buddy Rose. He was going to be working with the World Wrestling Federation, and asked if I would leave Portland to join him in New York as his valet. It was a nice offer, but I couldn't.

A few days later, a wrestler named Billy Jack Haynes came over for coffee. I knew Billy from the arena shows, and always thought he was a really soft-natured, humble gentleman. Knowing I had few friends in Portland, he offered to listen to my problems.

As I told Billy Jack about my issues with Chris, he looked down and shook his head. He confirmed by suspicions were true. To make matters worse, he told me that he had confronted Chris about his behaviour with the local girls.

"I couldn't believe it when I asked Adams why he cheated on you. He told me that if you have steak every night, you occasionally fancy a piece of chicken," explained Billy.

As soon as Billy confided in me, my feelings of sadness towards Chris were replaced by other emotions. After Chris' constant promises that he would never cheat on me again, I now had the confirmation that he had lied.

I was angry and repulsed by Chris. He was not the man I thought he was.

Billy also seemed to be disgusted by how I had been let down by Chris.

"You deserve better. I'd be more than happy to help you out. Come and stay with me, and I'll treat you with the respect you deserve," he offered.

It was so sweet of Billy to console me with a gesture of such kindness, but I explained the situation with my finances and my green card. I knew that there was no way that he could really help. But he said he was serious.

Before he left, I told Billy that I needed to sleep on it. It was too big a decision to make over an afternoon, even if I was eager to escape the apartment which I was sharing with Chris.

As I pondered what I should do, Chris stayed out all night after yet another party. It was clear that there was only one option for me.

The next day, Billy came round and we went for a drive around town, before parking his car. I told him that I had decided to accept his offer and started packing my belongings.

That night, Chris was again late in coming home. I decided to stay up until he returned to the apartment.

As he opened the door, I was shaking with nervousness.

"I'm leaving you," I firmly sighed.

Chris dropped to his knees and fell to pieces. He started to sob, and it moved me. However, I had seen it all before, and nothing was going to alter my decision.

As he pleaded with me to change my mind, I knew I couldn't allow myself to be hurt by him again. It was not a decision I had taken lightly, as I had tried to make a stable home for my daughter. However, it soon became obvious to Jade that her mother was deeply unhappy.

I left the apartment, and Billy was waiting for me in his car with Jade. I remained silent as we drove to his apartment.

My relationship with Chris, which had lasted almost five years and taken us across the world together, had come to an end.

Once I settled into Billy's apartment, he did everything he could to make me welcome, and really took me under his wing. Realising that I couldn't drive, he immediately set about teaching me, and arranged some lessons with an instructor. He also knew that I craved financial independence. As a foreign citizen with no green card of permanent residency in the States, my work options had been restricted.

Without hesitation, Billy offered yet another solution to help me, suggesting that I marry him.

It was another selfless act from him. He knew that if I married an American citizen, it would allow me to remain in the States, and enable Jade to stay in the same country as her father.

Thinking of my daughter, I accepted his proposal. We visited the local Registry Office to arrange a date for our marriage in the summer of 1983. Passing my driving test, he also surprised me with an unexpected gift; a brand new Chevrolet Camaro. I was touched and it moved me to tears. I was so happy.

Billy Jack provided a generosity that I was not used to, and I felt humbled to be valued so dearly by him.

But a caring spirit was in his nature. After meeting his father, a blind man who lived alone, it was obvious that Billy would do anything to provide comfort to the people in his life.

Gradually, I realised that Billy viewed me as much more than a friend, and I became drawn to his sensitivity. I felt safe around him.

Our friendship had progressed into a very special bond, and we became lovers.

Although mutual attraction and companionship had led to our intimacy, Billy and I started to realise that we each wanted different things in our lives. We remained on good terms but we both knew that there was not the love required to sustain a lasting relationship.

Slowly, we drifted apart. By Christmas, I returned to England.

Billy and I continued to talk, and he was now looking to move to Tampa, to wrestle for Championship Wrestling from Florida. He asked if I wanted to return to the States, and offered to fly me to Florida.

We knew that our relationship was over, and he sourced an attorney for our uncontested divorce.

With our short romance running its course, I will always feel indebted to Billy. We remained amicable and I would forever hold his friendship and selflessness dear to my heart.

At a time when I had lost so much faith in myself, he really built my confidence and gave me the greatest love of all; the gift of freedom.

As a parting gift, Billy arranged for me to stay at an apartment in Tampa Bay, and secured a six-month lease for me while I searched for work in Florida.

The beaches and climate of the state reminded me of California.

I secured a job as a make-up artist at a department store and settled into the Florida way of life right away. Through my work, I made lots of new friends and would regularly go out for dinner with them.

After a while, all the unhappiness from my time in Portland faded away.

Gradually, I felt happy and free, enjoying the relaxed lifestyle of the Sunshine State.

After the lease on the apartment was up, Chris offered to look after Jade for a while so I could find a new residence. At the same time that I had left Billy to return to England, Chris had started to wrestle for a promotion in Dallas.

As a temporary measure, I moved into The Hall of Fame Inn, a hotel that was a famous haunt for many wrestlers. It was right next door to the Tampa Bay Buccaneers football grounds and some of the players stayed at the hotel.

I started dating one of their star players, Danny Spradlin, and I became good friends with Steve Courson. We would often hang out by the hotel pool or go clubbing.

One night, we went out to the local nightclub called Confetti, and by chance we bumped into the NWA World Heavyweight Champion Ric Flair who was in there partying. I had met Ric a couple of times when he'd been wrestling in Portland and he recognised me. Within seconds, he had a drink sent over to me. He then sent another. And he sent a few more after that.

I rarely touched alcohol but that was one of the few times I did, and I got extremely drunk. Somehow, I staggered back to the hotel and felt extremely sick. I do remember Ric phoned my room afterwards. He must have been calling to make sure I was okay, as he was keen to check up on me.

After living out of a suitcase for weeks, I was finally able to move into an apartment which was at the other side of the Buccaneers stadium. As soon as I settled in, I got a visit from my mum, who I had flown over from England.

I asked Chris if he would not mind giving me Jade now that I had secured a fixed address. He obliged, and his new girlfriend Toni Collins arrived at the airport to hand her back to me.

With my mum in Florida, 1984.

Toni had been working as an assistant in the front office of WCCW and that's where Chris encountered her. I only briefly met her but she seemed really nice.

Although we had gone our separate ways, Chris and I were starting to talk quite regularly. He wanted to keep up to speed with how Jade was doing, and his steady work in Dallas meant that he could afford to see her more frequently. The distance had worked out well for us, as the animosity I had for him started to subside. Slowly, we became amicable again.

By the summer of 1984, Chris rang me and started talking about a notion he had in mind for WCCW.

He wanted me to perform as the female valet for a wrestler called Gino Hernandez. I politely declined the role; I was too busy having a great time in Florida with my job and new friends.

I wanted to start a business, and I had already discussed the idea with my friend Kathy. We had both been working in the make-up industry, and agreed that we would branch off on our own and offer cosmetic services for models and events.

We designed a logo and placed an advert in the local Tampa Bay paper for our new venture, which we decided to call The Face Place.

For the next few months it went really well. We had several clients a day and were making great money by selling our products too. Within a short period of time, I was able to buy a gorgeous white 1984 Corvette.

During the course of another telephone conversation with Chris, he said he was heavily missing Jade, and again asked if we would consider moving to Dallas. He said he could find me work in World Class and that he was really keen to run with an ex-wife angle.

An angle is a wrestling storyline, and his pitch was for me to be introduced as the wicked ex-wife to set up an on-screen feud between Chris and another wrestler.

The idea of involving females in feuds had been already been big hit down in WCCW a couple of years earlier when Jimmy Garvin brought his real-life wife Patti into the promotion to aid his valet, Sunshine, and named her Sunshine II.

Garvin would later ditch the original Sunshine after she cost him the WCCW Television Championship. Patti was renamed Precious and the three ended up feuding, and Chris bought in to the storyline to even the sides up for Sunshine.

This feud, which led to a number of mixed tag team matches, led to phenomenal business in the promotion and Chris was really keen to replicate its success.

I told Chris that I was not really sure about returning to wrestling, but I agreed to move to Texas so that he could spend more time with Jade. There was nothing keeping me in Florida.

By the end of the summer of 1985, Danny had been released by the Buccaneers and was drafted by the St. Louis Cardinals for the National Football League's 1985 season. With his relocation to another state, our relationship faded.

Once again, it was time to move. I was excited by the pioneer spirit of the Lone Star State, and I was ready to take a trip.

7 THE DALLAS TRIP

Upon my arrival in Dallas, I went to visit Chris. He had since moved into an exclusive apartment on Lovers Lane, which was part of an expensive complex of condos that were built around a private swimming pool for the residents. I was looking forward to catching up with Chris, and properly getting to know his new wife, Toni. They had wed just nine months prior in Hawaii on 20th December 1984.

I had no problem with their marriage; even though Chris and I were friendly, any romantic feelings that once existed between us had long gone.

The first time I went over to visit them after moving to Dallas, Toni burst into tears and ran into the bedroom to cry. She was very insecure that Chris had just asked his ex-girlfriend and daughter to come and live in Dallas.

When she finally came out of the room, with tears and mascara running down her face, I felt so bad. I could tell she was a really sweet, fragile soul.

I reassured her that she had no need to think of me as a threat to her marriage with Chris. I was really happy for them.

In one of the adjacent apartments lived a girl called Vicky, and Chris had organised for Jade and I to stay in her spare room. Chris also had a spare bedroom where Jade could stay when she had time with her dad. It worked out really well that we could both share the responsibility of raising Jade.

With Chris and Vicky offering to provide childcare for Jade, I resumed my work as a makeup artist in a freelance capacity.

As for Toni, she quickly accepted that I wasn't in Dallas to rekindle a dead romance and we started to bond as good friends.

Terry 'Garvin' Simms, former WCCW wrestler: "I will never forget the day I met Jeanie, because it was both a shock and an eye-opening experience at the same time. I had moved to Dallas to wrestle for World Class in the 80's, and had been invited to the home of Chris Adams (who I had been wrestling every night for the previous two weeks). I'd been told that Chris' wife was easy on the eyes, so when the graceful lady with the beautiful face and knock-out body opened the door and greeted me with a British accent, I thought to myself "Easy on the eyes, my ass! She's stunning!" Imagine my surprise when I walked in and was introduced to someone who could have been a sister to this lady and was told this is Toni Adams; the woman I'd just met was Jeanie Clarke! Both Jeanie and Toni were sweet women and very close friends. I thought I'd entered the Twilight Zone (and didn't care if I had!) because Chris was not home and I had a chance to sit and talk with two beautiful women for hours."

It was not long before Chris and Toni asked if I would like to go to one of the World Class events.

Chris really hyped up the show, so that Friday night I headed to downtown Dallas to find the Sportatorium, the legendary home of World Class Championship Wrestling. The Sportatorium was the least glamorous place you could find, and not the place you would expect to find the most high-tech of wrestling television tapings.

It looked like a rustic and beat-up white asbestos-clad barn, and it had a very distinct smell which was reminiscent of an old gym. But when the fans started arriving, the venue became truly electric. They were so intense; a loyal group of followers who went each week to the matches and helped create such a special venue. The octagonal dome of the Sportatorium captured the acoustics and made it an incredible environment to be inside, amplifying the loud volume of the die-hard WCCW audience.

World Class was so different to anything I had ever experienced before. It had an energy to it that cannot be described, and its popularity was not limited to the weekly shows. The promotion had a major television deal to syndicate its programming across the country, and into international markets.

Bobby Fulton, former WCCW wrestler: "WCCW was an amazing company, it was a first class promotion and the Von Erichs were just so over with the fans and the rest of the talent was so strong, it was a great company to work for and was a highlight of my career. I'd say it was perhaps the hottest place that Tommy [Rogers] and I, as the team The Fantastics, got over in.

I also think it was one of the very first worldwide companies, we would be seen on TV in Japan and Israel and would do tours over there too. Because of how strong and how well thought of WCCW was it really gave a lot of guys the opportunity to tour overseas. But we also expanded right across the US too. I remember we went all the way up to Massachusetts and we sold that out, and then through to Chicago where we did the same. People would know about us before they knew about wrestlers in other promotions, because of how strong WCCW was."

The company's success was due to the efforts of a strong roster of stars. It boasted some truly great names, but the most revered of all were the famous Von Erich family.

Behind the scenes, the promotion was owned by Jack Adkisson, the ageing patriarch of the family who was known to fans as Fritz Von Erich. On-screen, the product was anchored by his sons, who had all excelled in athletic competition before turning to pro wrestling.

The Von Erichs seemed to live a royal existence in Texas. They appeared in television commercials, and featured on all sorts of popular merchandise; from posters and T-shirts to even their own board game. Their likenesses seemed to be everywhere and they were mobbed wherever they went.

As the beloved hometown heroes, the Von Erichs would face a rotation of dastardly heels to keep the WCCW faithful glued to the product. Chris had originally joined the company as a wildly popular hero, but had since betrayed the Von Erichs when there was a requirement to freshen up its main event scene.

When I arrived in Dallas, Chris was working in a tag team with our mutual neighbour Gino Hernandez.

Together they were known as the The Dynamic Duo, and were the most hated heels in the company. They would come out to the song Bad to the Bone by George Thorogood & The Destroyers, and flaunted their style and wealth to rile up the fans.

Gino was so naturally gifted. As well as having great wrestling skills, he was a master of the microphone and was able to churn out amazingly cocky promos. Oozing class and sophistication, Gino used these qualities to back up the arrogant character he portrayed. He had a great fashion sense and always dressed so well, even in his workout clothes. I'm not ashamed to admit that I had a little crush on Gino.

After defeating their opponents, the Dynamic Duo had started a unique post-match ritual, giving their defenceless foes humiliating new hairstyles with a huge pair of scissors. This routine was used to set up a match with Kevin and Kerry Von Erich at the second annual *Cotton Bowl Extravaganza* on 6th October, where the losers of the contest would have their hair removed.

That night, Chris and Gino were forced to taste their own medicine. After losing the bout, they had their heads shaved in front of a raucous crowd of 26,000 fans who all went wild as the pair's locks were shorn.

I remember sitting in Chris' apartment after the match. Gino came over with a strange expression and glassy eyes and sat right next to me.

"Feel my head, feel my head," he kept repeating. He seemed in disbelief of his new crew-cut.

Rambling incoherently, he would then just start crazily laughing for no reason. Soon, we all decided to head out and hit a nightclub that we used to frequent on Greenville Avenue. Gino asked if I would ride with him.

He owned a Porsche, and started driving with reckless abandon, weaving in and out of the traffic and careering all over the road. We must have been speeding at 100 miles per hour on the way to the club.

Within moments, he overtook yet another car without looking and went into his pocket to look for something.

"Here try this," he said, handing me a tiny piece of paper.

"What is it?" I wondered.

"It's good stuff. I got it from Hawaii - just chew on it," he countered.

I shoved the piece of paper in my mouth. Gino uncontrollably laughed again.

"Don't worry, I'll lookout for you," he giggled.

I had no idea what he was talking about, and I figure he didn't either, but I had only popped it in my mouth for a second or two.

After about ten minutes, I still didn't feel any different. I just figured it was Gino acting bizarrely in a drug-fuelled binge.

We arrived at the club and made our way to the bar.

Half an hour later, it happened.

I just started laughing and laughing for no reason. I couldn't stop and Gino started cracking up as well. So there we were, in absolute hysterics at absolutely nothing.

"I have to use the bathroom," I conceded.

I didn't get much of a response, as Gino was in a world of his own merriment. As soon as I put one foot in front of the other, it was like walking on a cloud. I was floating and couldn't feel a grip beneath my shoes. This made him laugh even harder.

Later Gino recalled that I shuffled over to the edge of the club with a look of sheer terror on my face and then walked to the bathroom, via a circuit of the whole club.

Timidly and awkwardly, I motioned with my back to the wall as if I was creeping along on the narrow edge of a skyscraper.

When I returned, Gino offered me a drink to make it better, but I quickly declined. I wasn't going to trust his judgement any more that night as I was already so far out of it.

He could tell I wanted to leave, so Gino drove me home. I was petrified, as the drive home was even more erratic than it had been on the way to the club.

When we finally made it back to the apartment complex, I just wanted to go to bed. Unfortunately, I was buzzing so much I couldn't get to sleep. I headed over to Chris and Toni's as they had just arrived back from the club.

They were so far out of it as well. Spaced out, Chris stripped naked and ran outside. He then hurled himself into the pool, splashing and shouting at the top of his lungs at 3.00am.

Gino had never told me what was on that piece of paper. I later learned that we had all taken an acid trip.

Despite the hard partying, Chris and Gino could turn off the excesses, and appear perfectly lucid once it was time to perform. The office had felt that the Dynamic Duo had peaked as a villainous duo, and wanted to create a storyline feud between the pair.

On 27th January 1986, the two were set to face each other in another hair match in Fort Worth. During the end of the contest, Gino threw some hair remover cream at Chris, seemingly blinding him.

When Chris returned on television, he was filmed with bandaged eyes. He stated that he was unable to wrestle and would be gone from World Class. The angle was the first step to set up a return grudge match. The eye injury was a device to explain Chris's extended absence, which he was using to visit his family back in Britain.

While Chris was away, I had the key to his apartment. I saw Gino from the balcony about to go for a tan. He waved and called out for me to join him, so I went over and we hung out together. Since Vicky was at home with Jade that evening, he asked if I would go out for a few drinks with him.

He took me to The Rio Room, a private and highly-exclusive club. It was renowned for its very strict guest list and was only open to the extremely wealthy. No matter where Gino went, the doors were opened and everyone wanted to party with him.

He was so outgoing, and came across as the coolest guy in the world.

Once we got in the club, we both sniffed a line of cocaine from Gino's never-ending stash. I tried it out of curiosity and figured I needed to try it if I was going to fit in at such a classy venue.

We were flying really high and we had an amazing night in the club. When we got back to the complex, Gino asked me to carry on partying at his apartment.

As soon as we got inside, he reached for a cereal bowl from the top of his kitchen cupboard. It was full to the brim with cocaine.

He started chopping out long, thick lines of the powder and sniffing them up at a rapid pace. He was talking extremely quickly, most of it garbled nonsense, and peppered his speech with crazed laughing. And then, just like if a switch had been flicked, he went very quiet.

A look of sheer panic and paranoia crossed his face.

He stood up and rushed into the kitchen. With worried urgency, he turned on the taps full blast. He put the plug in the sink and the water started overflowing, spilling onto the floor.

I went to turn the taps off, but Gino came up from behind and grabbed me in a vice-like grip around my shoulders and waist.

"Be very quiet… don't move," he whispered.

"Can you hear that?" he snapped, with wide-eyed panic.

Gino kept his grip on me and I couldn't move. There wasn't any noise other than the dripping of the water.

I grabbed the door of the fridge to try and escape his clutches but it was an impossible task, as he was extremely strong. I managed to wriggle and twist around slightly and saw that Gino had a loaded gun in his hand.

"Don't talk. Don't move," he breathed.

All the time, his eyes kept glancing between the door and the window as if someone was outside.

For fifteen minutes, I just froze in complete silence, praying for my life.

All of a sudden, Gino let me go and then walked back to the couch to snort another huge line of coke. I sat down next to him to reassure him that everything was okay.

Everything I said just fell on deaf ears. All of his paranoia was fixed on looking at the door, interspersed by the consumption of even more cocaine.

He rose up again, and stormed over to the window, craning his head to peer into the inky blackness of the night, and then came back to the couch to do another line. Five minutes later, he repeated this bizarre cycle. It continued on and on for about an hour.

I was extremely afraid and wanted to go home.

"Don't go. Do not go near the door!" he warned.

I sat with him for several hours trying to calm him down and get him to relax but it was hopeless. Suddenly, the day was breaking and, just as the first rays of sun came through the window, he snapped out of it. The fear of whatever was out there in the night had passed. He finally laid down, content and safe that nothing was going to get him.

I saw him later on that day and he came up to me with a sheepish look on his face.

"I'm so sorry Jeanie, you must think I'm a moron," he winced.

I could tell he'd tortured himself over the ordeal, so I wanted to give him reassurance.

"Of course not, but I'm really worried about you," I softly smiled.

Gino apologised again before reverting to his cool, cocky self and tried to laugh off the incident. It was clear that Gino's drug use had spiralled beyond a recreational pastime and was now a serious problem.

A week later, he was coming back to the apartments after picking up a peach pie. He loved sweet pies and used to buy them from an expensive deli. Whether it was clothes, cars, drugs or food, Gino always sought out the very best.

"Hey kiddo," he shouted across to me.

"The pie's looking great Gino, save me a slice," I replied, waving across to him.

"Sure thing, come across in the morning for one," he flirted.

Later that night, I was getting ready for bed after watching TV, and happened to glance out of the window. Gino had come back from another night partying at the Rio Room and I could see he had dumped his Porsche at a strange angle in the parking bay.

The next morning I went across to see him as arranged and knocked on the door. There was no answer. I knocked harder and there was still no reply. I looked through the window to see if he was crashed out on the couch.

The peach pie was on the table but there was no sign of Gino. I presumed he was sound asleep in bed. He must have crashed out after another hard night of partying, so I headed out into town.

When I returned, I saw that his car still hadn't been moved. I went up to his apartment to see if he had awakened. I banged on the door but there still wasn't any response.

I went back to my apartment and asked Vicky if Gino had been over but she hadn't seen him. I told her about the gun incident from the previous week and said that I was extremely worried about his mental state. I wanted to check up on him, but felt I couldn't call anyone for help. The last thing I wanted for my friend was to have him arrested if the police found the large amount of drugs that were in his apartment.

The day after, I heard a commotion outside and saw a group of people outside Gino's apartment, breaking down his door.

A body bag was carried out of the complex. It was then wheeled into an ambulance.

My heart sank, as my worst fears were confirmed. In the short time we had spent together, we had become much more than friends.

Shaken, I called Chris in England to let him know our friend was dead. Toni answered the phone, and her blood-curdling scream chilled me as I told her the devastating news.

We were all in absolute shock. It took me about six months to stop grieving over my friend's tragic death at just 28 years of age. Whenever I thought about him, I would burst into tears. He may have faltered to addiction, but Gino Hernandez was a kind and caring man.

Gino's death hit me hard. I couldn't bear to see his apartment anymore so I told Vicky that I needed to move out of the complex. I needed to make a fresh start in Dallas. Reeling from the pain of Gino's untimely demise, I moved into a new rented apartment on Greenville Avenue.

To help with the additional expense, I started to look for a source of some extra income. A friend of mine was working for Eastern Onion, a company which specialised in novelty telegrams. She would turn up at workplaces, bars, and even restaurants and then perform a dancing strip routine on anyone who had been set-up to receive this service. She told me it was a real laugh seeing these people get a show in the middle of a public place completely out of the blue. When she told me how much she was making I was amazed.

I looked up the company in the Yellow Pages, and after contacting them, I was offered the opportunity to work as one of the dancers.

As the appointments always took place in a public area, no nudity was allowed. Once the music hit, we simply stripped down to a bikini or lingerie. It was actually rather tame and quite a good laugh.

After a year of working for the agency, I decided that I could create a more comfortable life if I was self-employed. As my own boss, I would have more flexibility to schedule my appointments around valuable time with Jade. Having successfully launched a make-up venture in Florida, I had a new dream. I wanted to open my own telegram firm, and set about designing a business strategy for my fledgling company.

Genie's Novelty Tele-Grams

343-3406

Genie's Novelty Tele-Grams promotional card, 1987.

I called it Genies, and set about creating a number of 'characters' for my new venture, which was due to be launched in early 1987. I purchased outfits as a police officer, a nurse, a business lady and a few others. Each persona would turn up at the specified location acting perfectly normal, before the surprise of booming music hit and the dance routine started.

From the onset, I was swamped with so many gigs. Due to the demand, I couldn't cover it all and had to draft in some new girls to cover the workload. It was a roaring success and it quickly became the biggest telegram company in the whole of Dallas. Eventually, we grew to a close-knit team of ten dancers. I was blessed to employ so many lovely people, including my friend Laurie Rogers, and we all formed such a wonderful social circle.

Laurie Rogers, friend and former Genie's entertainer: "Jeanie and I met around 1989, a magical time in Dallas, when the 80's where in full form. Jeanie owned a unique company that set our industry on fire. She was beautiful and smart, and I was so excited to begin working with her. I was hired as a dancer, or an entertainer as I liked to be called, and I would wear different costumes for the performances – it was a blast! We soon became the best of friends, hanging out at the best clubs and meeting exciting people. We were enjoying life to the full!"

Even though I had moved from the complex in Lovers Lane, I remained a very close friend to both Toni and Chris. We spent Christmas together and I quickly offered Toni a position at my new business.

As Toni joined the roster of Genies, Chris also decided to set up a little private enterprise of his own. He wanted to open his own wrestling school, and filmed adverts which would appear throughout World Class programming.

I was excited for Chris as he aimed to open the training camp in 1988. Genies had been going strong and afforded me the financial security to buy my very first house in the Garland district of Dallas. I used one of the rooms as a little office, and would sit and write little skits for the routines based on the costume and occasion.

With some of the money that I had earned that year, I wanted to use it to reach out to my brother back in England. I had only seen Phil sporadically since we were children, and I yearned to spend some quality time with him.

I arranged to fly him out to Texas, and I was so excited that we would be reunited.

All those lost years didn't make any difference, and we clicked straight away. In the years since our childhood, Phil had become such a talented artist and musician. He had excelled academically, and he was studying towards a Master's Degree in Fine Art. I was so proud of my big brother.

During the visit, we went to the famous Southfork Ranch where they filmed the hit TV show *Dallas*, and even travelled to Elvis Presley's Graceland mansion in Memphis.

We had the best time together, and I was grateful to get the chance to reconnect with my brother. He loved getting the chance to meet his niece, who was now a cheerful little seven year old. It was great being a little family again. I was just saddened that he couldn't stay.

With Jade and Phil at the Southfork Ranch, 1989.

Not long after Phil went home to Canterbury, I got a call from Chris. Once again, he wanted to pursue the idea of me returning to the business. But this time, he was not going to take no for an answer.

Chris had been training some new recruits at the Sportatorium and wanted to pair me up with one of his students in a storyline.

Outside Elvis Presley's Graceland mansion, 1989.

He spoke with a conviction that I rarely heard from his voice.

Chris was certain that this rookie possessed some real potential.

8 A STUNNING DISCOVERY

For almost five years, I had resisted the urge to return as an on-screen performer within the wild and wacky world of professional wrestling. But Chris was determined that the time was right to run with a storyline involving two feuding couples, as he had fostered a promising talent at his fledgling wrestling academy.

Chris' classes at the Sportatorium were notorious for being brutal. He harboured an old-school mentality to protect the wrestling business from outsiders, as the secrets of the industry had been closely guarded for generations.

During his seminars, he would often punish young trainees to establish if they had the desire to come back for more. In his mind, only the elite who could persevere through his sadistic stretching and in-ring bullying would stand a chance of enduring a career in professional wrestling.

From the opening of his school, he had encountered lots of young wannabe wrestlers, many of whom did not have the desire, skills, or physical attributes to make it in the industry.

There was one exception, a former college football player from North Texas State University.

After dropping out of college, this rookie had been scraping a living by any means necessary. He had secured a job in the small city of Denton by loading boxes on a freight dock for Watkins Motor Lines, until enlisting in Chris' wrestling school at the Sportatorium.

In this newcomer, Chris had found someone who could help realise a storyline that he had developed for half a decade. He wanted to know if I would hear him out on his new idea, as he was convinced that my involvement would be critical to its success.

Having grown comfortable as a performer during my time with Genies, I decided to listen, and visited Toni and Chris' apartment. It was not long after I arrived that Chris started to describe his notion for the angle involving me.

His plan was to engage in a series of matches with his top trainee in a 'student versus teacher' rivalry, but wanted the story to escalate into a personal issue. To make it a truly bitter feud, he needed a foil. And that foil would be me.

Using our former real-life relationship as a precedent, Chris wanted me to portray his evil ex-wife, the scorned lover who was intent on doing anything she could to exact her revenge on 'The Gentleman'. To further antagonise him, I would align myself with his ungrateful student, as Chris would struggle against uneven odds.

When the time was right, Chris would introduce his current wife, Toni, into the fray. He was certain the story would connect to the Dallas wrestling faithful.

Meanwhile, Chris wanted to retain a sense of intrigue over the story, which he intended to play out over the course of a year, and he wanted my reasons for harbouring such a grudge to remain unknown. My motivations would be slowly revealed in a slow-burning, episodic tale. We were going to create a soap opera storyline, complete with twists and turns, and all set within the genre of pro wrestling.

I wanted to know more about my character, so I asked Chris for guidance.

Being from an English background, Chris' envisaged me as a pretentious (albeit elegantly-dressed) wicked lady. He referenced the character Alexis Colby from the hit television series *Dynasty*, a power-dressing vixen brilliantly played by Joan Collins. Chris wanted me to base my performances on her character, and even wanted me to claim that I had spawned from Royal descent.

Far removed from who I really was, it was the pantomime-villain aspect of the 'Jeanie Adams' character which really fascinated me. I would arrive in luxurious evening dresses, flaunting my wealth and insult the local fans as Chris, the people's champion, would defend their honour.

His idea sounded fun, and I knew I could easily arrange cover at Genies which would allow me to participate in the saga. I told Chris I would do it.

Excited that his storyline was coming to fruition, Chris wanted me to make an immediate impact. He asked if I could be in attendance at the next schedule of tapings held at the Sportatorium the following Friday night and Saturday morning. Before he could finalise the commitment, he needed to get approval from the new booker of the Dallas territory, Jerry Jarrett.

For so long, the territory had been the exclusive stronghold of the Von Erich family, as World Class Championship Wrestling became a staple of Dallas sports culture. Due to financial pressures within a decade in which the wrestling industry was changing, the majority of promotion was sold.

WCCW merged with the Continental Wrestling Association, a Memphis-based outfit owned by Jerry Jarrett and Jerry Lawler. In an attempt to create a national promotion, both were unified under the banner of the United States Wrestling Association.

Jerry Jarrett, former USWA promoter: "We had an exclusive contract with the Sportatorium, so we had access all week. Chris and I began a wrestling school. He did the actual training, and I handled the business end of the school."

For World Class, Chris had been one of the company's top stars, and he was keen to make a good impression to Jarrett. He carefully laid out his vision for the ex-wife angle, knowing it could really raise the profile of the new USWA.

Jerry Jarrett, former USWA promoter: "Jeanie Clarke was first introduced to me by Chris Adams. Looking back even now, the story seems surreal. I have been divorced, and based on my situation I had never seen a situation where the ex's were civil, let alone friends. Anyway Chris introduced us and also suggested we might do a little ex-wife angle.

To say Jeanie was an attractive woman would be an understatement. She was a real knock-out. She was attractive, had a great body and was well endowed. Chris's wife at the time was also attractive. I immediately saw box-office potential to the ex-wife soap opera so we began the program right away."

After his meeting with Jarrett, Chris called and said the idea had been approved, but Jerry had requested some publicity photographs of Toni and me. After seeing them, he was convinced that he could really put something together with what he had seen, and wanted us to go to the April television tapings.

Days later, I headed to my first show for the USWA.

At the Sportatorium, there was a separate access for performers to arrive, and after getting through the door, I saw Toni.

She ushered me to this tall, blonde-haired and blue-eyed young wrestler.

"I want to introduce you to Steve Williams," she said.

"Hi", I smiled.

"Yeah, hi," he grunted, before turning and walking upstairs to the crow's nest, a private area where the wrestlers could watch the show without being seen by the crowd.

Williams performed under the name 'Stunning' Steve Austin, and was the newcomer who Chris had praised. But in my first meeting with Steve, I found him to be a bit abrupt, and somewhat aloof. Nevertheless, we met again briefly in the downstairs office that was being used by Chris as he laid out the direction of the storyline.

Given how inexperienced Steve and I were in our roles, it was important that we followed Chris' instructions to the letter, as we launched the opening salvo of the Adams-Austin feud.

Jerry Jarrett, former USWA promoter: "Chris kind of took Steve under his wing and began pressuring me to book Steve on the Dallas cards. Chris was Steve's opponent so he could cover for the usual greenhorn mistakes."

It was now time for me to come out as the mysterious new valet of Steve. The intention was to build to the angle over a long period of time, so it was important that we revealed very little about our new alliance, or any history that I had with Chris.

With the cameras rolling, Steve was set to face the preliminary favourite Frogman LeBlanc in a singles match. But immediately before the contest, Austin was asked for some pre-match comments on his arrival to the USWA by commentator Mark Lowrance. He brushed off the questions on his career, instead focusing the interview as the introduction of a new ally.

"I wanna bring down the sexiest girl in America; the gorgeous, and lovely, Jeanie!" proclaimed Austin.

Within moments, I sauntered my way to the ringside as Mark tried to establish the link between 'Stunning' Steve and this mystery lady simply known as Jeanie.

"Mark, I just want to say how wonderful it is, tonight, to be here with a real man like Steve," I proclaimed, flirtatiously patting him on the chest.

Steve wrapped up the interview, and took away Lowrance's ringside chair. He asked me to take a seat, and watch him punish LeBlanc with ease.

As I was urging Steve, the crowd cheered as Chris made his way to ringside. Confused, he wanted to know why I had aligned myself with his turncoat pupil. I gave him my answer, not in words, but with a thunderous slap to the face.

Humiliated, Chris stormed off in a rage, as Mark and his co-host Ronnie P. Gossett were left to speculate on what had just happened in the middle of a match. Booked to look strong, Steve rapidly polished off the Frogman with a spinning Samoan Drop to gain the win.

We embraced and we were leaving ringside, as Lowrance rushed over to question the motive behind my strike at Chris.

"Why are you slapping Chris Adams?" asked Mark, in a bemused tone.

"I have no comment on that right now," I smirked.

Puzzled, Mark turned to Steve for an answer.

"Do you have any comment?" he asked.

"No comment, Mark. Blondes have more fun baby, and we're on our way to the top!" Austin yelled, before we both walked away from ringside.

Backstage, Jerry and Chris were elated at how my ambiguous debut had created a buzz in the arena, and they discussed ways to elevate Steve to a level where he would be accepted as a worthy competitor to Chris.

The plan was to feed Steve a long list of enhancement talent, who he could beat up without mercy, in an effort to make him look instantly strong. Meanwhile, I would slowly reveal myself as not only an old flame of Chris', but moreover, his ex-wife.

Jon Horton, former USWA announcer Craig Johnson: "I can remember the first night I saw Jeanie. First off, her British accent hit me. It completely entranced me. Then on top of that she was, well you know, amazingly beautiful. I knew the camera would love her. I was right. But the fans.... what would the fans think? She had the fire of a scorned women; the venom of the worst witch. She was a dominatrix without the leather, the devil without the horns. She made herself evil and the fans believed it."

I became much nastier, as I was fed lines to antagonise the crowd. In one interview, after insulting Chris and his loyal fans, I professed to have only dated the most eligible of bachelors. I even pulled out the picture with Stallone from the set of *Rocky III*, and claimed him as a former flame. It was a real thrill when Kevin Von Erich, who was visiting the arena, complimented my interviews. My sheer viciousness made him chuckle, and he knew that on live shows there was only one chance to get our delivery right.

With 'Stunning' Steve Austin. 1990.

Steve and I got a kick out of being so mean to the crowd during our interviews. As we plotted the derogatory phrases and arrogant mannerisms for use in our next segment, Steve and I would crack up backstage at each other's conceited antics.

I can recall a match where I caught the bottom of my dress under the high heels of my shoes on my way to the ring. As I stumbled and tried to regain my balance, I looked across to Steve. He could not hold a straight face and burst out laughing, which set me off too. For the rest of the match, we would try our best not to break character, but we could not compose ourselves.

Slowly, Steve warmed to me as we spent more time together. Within weeks, our relationship developed from awkward, small-talking colleagues, to friends.

"You know, when I met you, I wasn't sure of you. But after getting to know you, I can say you are a real sweetheart," Steve smiled.

We were developing a real chemistry and it seemed like the angle could elicit some real drama.

It was an audacious task for Chris to undertake, as all of the burden would be placed on his shoulders. With less than a year's experience as an in-ring performer, Steve needed to be carried to have an acceptable match for such high billing on the card, even though he was working hard to progress and seemed to have a natural aptitude for his craft. Similarly, although I had worked as Chris' second during by time in Joint Promotions, all of my experience in wrestling had been in a role that was heavily limited, and not as engrossing as the Jeanie Adams character. As for Toni, although she was enthusiastic to be involved, she had absolutely no experience in wrestling at all.

But even though he would have to plan out each match, interview and angle from the viewpoint of each person involved, Chris was up for the challenge. Thinking for the four people in the storyline, he was naturally gifted at understanding the psychology of the fans, and booked us in ways that could conceal our individual limitations. The execution and expert planning of the saga should be fully attributed to him, as he made sure we knew exactly what to do and when to do it.

Chris wanted our storyline to connect with the crowd, and would often tell Steve and me exactly what to say and do to generate the intended reaction from the crowd, or as the wrestlers refer to it, heat. It had been a while since he had been able to portray a dastardly villain, and he would get immersed in our characters. His inner heel was able to live vicariously through 'Stunning' Steve and Jeanie Adams in every show.

But Chris was able to get the best of both worlds, as he was still able to portray the lovable hero, the babyface in whom the fans could believe. He was inventive as he figured out ways for Steve and me to maximise heat in our conflict against him.

By May, Steve and I were doing all we could to depict ourselves as truly nasty villains, with Chris valiantly fighting against the odds.

In one match, I helped Steve cheat a victory, and then entered the ring to blind Chris by spraying his eyes with a can of hairspray. A few weeks later, in a barbed-wire match, I sneaked in a pair of brass knuckles to Steve which he used to knock out Chris. To further insult him, Steve battered the neck of Chris with a number of shots from a steel chair, as the outraged fans went crazy.

As the feud caught fire, Toni became increasingly impatient and could not wait to start.

When Chris returned to television from our assault on him with the chair, he was wearing a neck brace and was scheduled for an interview with the USWA's lead announcer Craig Johnson. As he gave an update on his fragile condition, I entered the ringside area to berate Chris, before Steve ran in and attacked him.

The fight ensued into the ring, as the crowd were infuriated by the focused attack on Chris' weakened neck. After gaining an advantage, Steve grabbed a hold of him as I entered the ring. I mocked Chris and started slapping his face.

Moments later, the crowd exploded, and I turned around. Toni had finally had enough and charged up the aisle, flooring me with a punch and even squaring off to Steve.

The boys continued their brawl, and as I was left with Toni in the centre of the ring. We furiously went at it until being forcefully separated.

Facing Toni Adams in a match at the Sportatorium, 1990.

Toni had finally been introduced, and what a reaction she received. She evened the sides to give my despicable ex-wife character Jeanie Adams a taste of her own medicine.

The angle continued to build to a series of special mixed-gender tag team matches, including one on a huge 4th July show.

Jon Horton, former USWA announcer Craig Johnson: "Her tag team with Steve and their matches with Chris and Toni were explosions of emotion and raw action. I knew the four of them were good friends, but in the ring, in their character, it was hard to imagine."

The audience seemed to really erupt with excitement whenever the two of us would catfight. As soon as we got to the back, we would even get a standing ovation from the crew.

Jacqueline Moore, former USWA wrestler Miss Texas: "It was great wrestling at the Sportatorium. The crowd were die-hard wrestling fans. All the top wrestlers appeared at the Sportatorium. Chris, Steve, Jeanie and Toni had the hottest storyline around. That place sold out every week."

Some of the wrestlers asked if there was a legitimate issue between Toni and me, as they thought that some parts of our catfights were real. Neither of us had any wrestling training, we just improvised and hoped for the best. Sometimes our lack of training would cause us to get hurt, as we were never trained how to protect our bodies during a match.

In one tag contest, I had fallen to a seated position within the ring when Steve then flew from the top rope onto me, crunching all of his weight down onto my spine. The impact was so crushing that I lost control of my bladder, wetting myself in the middle of the match, and I could hardly walk away to hide my embarrassment.

Of course, the local fans thought it was part of the show and had little sympathy, offering only laughs and catcalls as I got helped backstage.

Once the adrenaline wore off, I couldn't straighten my spine and had to call for my friend Laurie to take me to the hospital for an X-ray. If a move in the ring looked like it hurt me, it usually did.

My brief spots during the matches gave me a further respect for the men and women who chose to wrestle as a full-time vocation, and I could only imagine the physical punishment they had to endure.

Nevertheless, it was so cool to find out that the workers believed in what we were doing, and the reality of the angle had impressed the USWA booking office.

Jerry Jarrett, who had spent a lifetime in the wrestling business, came rushing over, pumped up and beaming with enthusiasm. He had been watching our work from a monitor in the back and complimented our chemistry. He saw value in the girls and even booked Toni and me to headline a show at the Dallas Sportatorium.

Jerry Jarrett, former USWA promoter: "Jeanie was a natural in the business and this program was in no small part responsible for our early success in bringing Dallas wrestling back to sell-out crowds. The old adage, 'sex sells' sure was true in this case.

During my promotional career, I always had success in reality based wrestling angles and this was as real as it gets."

I could not believe it when my grudge match against Toni managed to sell out the Sportatorium. Chris was so nervous about it being a singles contest, given that neither of us had actually been trained to wrestle, but knew it could draw money if it was correctly promoted. His main concern was the stipulation that he and Steve had been barred from ringside, and couldn't distract the crowd if our inexperience was exposed.

With Percival Pringle III and Steve Austin prior to an outdoor wrestling show in Dallas, 1990.

For days, Toni and I rehearsed in detail all of the spots within the match. To cover for us in case we got lost during the heat of the moment, I was paired with a new manager, Percival Pringle III. Warm and friendly, Percy had a great mind for the business, and I was thrilled to have his support.

On the night, we did everything possible to follow Chris' instructions to the letter. It was pretty cool that not only did two girls work in the main event, but we managed to steal the show. At the end of the match, Percy's repeated interference provoked a run-in from Toni's friend, Chris Von Erich.

As I was distracted by the brawl between Percy and Chris, my top was ripped off by Toni, leaving me with only a bra to cover my modesty. To try and salvage my dignity, Percy shuffled over and covered me with his star-spangled jacket. The pair of us fled the ring, vowing vengeance on Adam's and Von Erich the next time we saw them.

Even though the feud between Steve and Chris had been raging for months, it never seemed to get stale. So many unique and creative scenarios ensured that the matches felt fresh. In addition to using the girls, the lads fought in lots of 'gimmick matches' to heighten the rivalry.

For those who don't know, a 'gimmick match' is any wrestling match that does not follow the rules of a standard contest. In the matches between Steve and Chris, not only did they compete in a barbed-wire contest; they fought in a kendo-stick match, and even in a 'Come As You Are' street fight, where both turned up in any outfit they decided to wear that day.

As a martial artist, Chris came out wearing his trusty judogi, while Steve, a former college football player, arrived in full protective padding and headgear.

I remember getting a real blast out of that match. Steve riled up the audience who felt it was unfair that he was allowed to wear his football attire, given how padded it was. I wondered how the match could be topped, but Chris had yet another idea.

On the 31st August, the two warring couples, and their new allies, would face off in a match enclosed by a Steel Cage.

In the weeks leading up to the event, we did all we could to heighten the dramatic elements of the storyline.

The accusations Steve and I were making on television against Chris would get even more personal. First off, Steve had taken custody of his dog Blue, and then seized his beloved wrestling boots, before we started taking aim at his marriage.

As part of the storyline, I claimed that Chris' old cheating ways had continued into his new relationship with Toni, and teased the camera with nude photographs of him. We played on her insecurity by showing a series of pictures of Chris with other women, including one taken four years earlier with the valet Sunshine.

To add insult to injury, I presented Toni with photographs of Chris with another woman (actually my friend Laurie Rogers), which were captured at a local restaurant with a hidden camera. They showed him at angles which were incriminating, as Chris claimed that it was just a business lunch.

In front of the live audience, Toni burst into tears and slapped Chris, before walking away from him. We gloated that his second marriage was in tatters, as the live crowd jeered our foul accusations.

Backstage, Toni wanted to hug me, as she felt the content of my interviews were starting to touch upon the truth. Despite knowing that all of my direction was still coming from Chris, it was still hurtful hearing such venom.

But it was the sense of reality that made the feud work, and it started to capture the attention of the American press.

The National Examiner ran a story chronicling the dispute, and we took advantage of the press coverage by parading a copy of the tabloid on television.

We needed to up the ante, and came up with fresh ideas to make people want to watch the match.

After suffering a broken wrist during a match (a legitimate injury which was actually caused when I nailed Chris with a hammer for the timekeeper's bell), I vowed to give Toni a humiliating new look, by means of a brutal haircut.

Jon Horton, former USWA announcer Craig Johnson: "I remember the angle continuing with Jeanie and Steve attempting to cut the hair of Toni. The problem was that in the match leading up to it, Jeanie either broke or sprained her wrist. The result was her wrist in a cast. Saturday morning, Austin and Jeanie were joined by Percy Pringle for an interview to talk about the ongoing rivalry.

Jeanie was holding a very large pair of scissors and she was doing a snip-snip motion to the camera and then when Jeanie took the microphone, the hand with the scissors dropped to her side. The problem was the scissors were aimed right towards my groin. I jumped, happy not to have met a very painful injury, and had to leave the interview set. Percy picked up the interview as Jeanie realised what had happened.

Wanting to keep her mean look she, as we call in the theatre, broke. She was laughing so hard but trying to keep her mean exterior at the same time. It was a beautiful moment of realism. Afterwards I saw her backstage and she asked how I was. I laughed and said luckily she'd only grazed me. We both completely cracked up with laughter."

Making my way to the ring for the mixed-tag Cage Match at the Sportatorium, 1990.

The crowd were at a fever pitch before the match started. As we waited for Chris and Toni to make their way into the ring, Chris Von Erich appeared behind them. The three grabbed Percy, who had been providing commentary from ringside, and forced him into the Penalty Box. The box was a black steel-barred cell that looked like a shark cage, and the crowd cheered as they knew that Percy would not be able to help us cheat the Adams' out of victory.

Clutching the only key that could allow Percy to get out, Chris Von Erich remained at ringside as Toni and Chris Adams entered the ring to face Steve and me within the confines of the Steel Cage. The fight was on, and there was no escape. The action went back and forth, with both couples trading the advantage, until Chris Adams was handcuffed to the ring ropes. It seemed like we were sure to gain certain victory, however, Toni managed to roll me up for the winning pinfall.

As soon as referee Bronco Lubich declared Chris and Toni the winners, Chris Von Erich opened the door to the ring cage. Steve charged at him, so Von Erich slammed the door on his face.

The young Von Erich sprinted towards Chris Adams, to set him free from the cuffing. Once free, Adams nailed Steve with the Superkick, launching him from the ring to the outside of the cage.

With me alone, I was handcuffed to the ring, which could allow Toni to get her long-awaited revenge. The fans went wild as she grabbed at my scalp, seemingly ripping out chunks of my blonde locks.

"No one touches my hair!" I screamed as the good guys celebrated with the fans.

It was the last time that there would be any interaction with the two warring couples on television. By September, the USWA had stopped promoting in Dallas due to a legal dispute between Jerry Jarrett and the Von Erich family. As a result, the feud came to an abrupt halt, despite Chris having some strong ideas to continue it.

Although the angle was cut short by promotional fallout within the USWA, the finish to the ex-wife storyline came to a satisfactory conclusion.

For months, we had built up the heat by gaining unfair victories and, when there was nowhere to run, the Adams couple successfully came out on top at the end.

I will forever remember my time working the ex-wife storyline in the USWA with great fondness.

There was so much creative freedom for us to experiment with our characters and everyone had a desire to make the shows as fun as they could be. Devoid of the politics of the major promotions, it was a great place for a young star to flourish and learn the business.

But most of all, I will cherish the angle as it allowed me to work with so many wonderful people.

Having being friends with Toni and Chris for years, it was fun getting to work with them in such a high-profile situation, and we even brought my friend Laurie into the mix. I also got to make some new friends during the storyline, from Percy Pringle to Chris Von Erich and, of course, 'Stunning' Steve Austin.

With the USWA ceasing operations in Texas, the World Class brand was revived at the Sportatorium in shows promoted by Kevin Von Erich, where Steve had formed a tag team with 'The California Stud' Rod Price. I had fun managing the pair of them.

Rod Price, former WCCW wrestler: "I was introduced to Jeanie while tag teaming with Steve at the world famous Sportatorium. Wow - what a place to wrestle. I was new and still cutting my teeth in wrestling. I didn't know too many people, but Jeanie was in our team so I would have talks with her. She was a '10' if I ever saw one. She played her part to the tee! I also knew that Steve had his eyes on her, so I didn't make my conversation long. I liked and respected Steve and Jeanie. There was enough stress on us just being in the business; learning and working on making ourselves better, along with the self-promotion; that it didn't take much to tip the boat. I was asked to start going on the circuit from Dallas to Memphis, which was then the USWA circuit, I turned it down."

As WCCW returned to Dallas, Chris Adams partnered with a promoter called Tom Lance, to run some shows under the banner of L&A Promotions. In the meantime, Jerry Jarrett placed the emphasis of the USWA in the state that he had promoted for years: Tennessee.

Although the impetus of Chris' focus was with L&A, he really pushed for Jerry to offer his protégé some bookings, and I told Jerry that I would make some appearances for his show if he gave Austin a chance. Despite being penniless, it was clear that Steve was committed to improving himself as a performer. He had really developed in the short time he had been a wrestler.

Jerry Jarrett, former USWA promoter: "Jeanie was a valuable box-office talent, so I began booking her in our Tennessee territory. In those days the talent based in Tennessee would ride in our tour bus to Dallas for the Friday night show at the Sportatorium and then back to Memphis overnight for Memphis television. Jeanie was a real pro and never complained about the long trips back and forth between Memphis and Dallas…. Steve developed quickly and Chris began a campaign for me to take Steve to the Tennessee territory so he could get experience. Steve could only wrestle once a week on the Dallas end; because the show promoters didn't want to pay for an unknown talent that could not sell tickets to the events. Jeanie began putting in a good word for Steve too."

With Chris' promotion needing some names to fill his events, he asked if I would work a show in Louisiana for L&A. Even though the trip would take me away from Jade and the day-to-day running of Genies, I agreed to go as a favour to Chris. I had hired a nanny who was able to take my business enquiries, and Chris said I should keep my costs low by sharing a ride with the boys. I called Steve, who told me he was travelling with Bronco Lubich, and he offered for me to travel with them.

As colleagues, Steve and I had become quite close. But as we made the journey to Louisiana, I had noticed a change in the way he was looking at me.

In his eyes, I could see that he wanted us to become much more than friends.

With 'Stunning' Steve Austin, 1990.

9 ROMANCE BLOSSOMS

On the night we arrived in Louisiana for Chris' show, Steve and I went out for dinner.

We had been working together for months, but now that we were alone, he wanted to discuss something that had been pressing on his mind for a while.

He pulled my chair in toward him, and looked deeply into my eyes. We then kissed.

Whenever Steve was around me, he was so humble, and I liked being in his presence.

He had been subtly complimenting me for a while, but there was tenderness in his demeanour as he clarified his intentions.

I was initially surprised to discover that Steve had actually suppressed a crush on me for months. He already had a long-term girlfriend, but our kiss never felt awkward. It felt right.

Holding hands, we walked back to the motel, and he kissed me again before I returned alone to my room.

The next morning, I saw Steve, and we both smiled at each other. We had finally become more than colleagues, as our fondness had blossomed into a clandestine romance.

As we started to get close, Jerry Jarrett had recognised Austin's ongoing development as a star, offering him some bookings in a number of shows around the Tennessee area.

While working the circuit, Steve moved into The Congress Inn motel in Nashville with some of the crew. I joined him for a few of his earliest appearances for the territory, including his first Memphis television match against Danny Davis.

Jerry Jarrett, former USWA promoter: "I have no idea if the romantic relationship between Jeanie and Steve began in Dallas and that was the reason Jeanie began pressuring me to book Steve in Tennessee, or if the relationship began on the overnight tour bus trips to Tennessee, but love was quickly in the air…. Those were exciting days to be in the wrestling business and I'll always be grateful that Chris Adams introduced me to Jeanie."

I was grateful that Steve had secured the work in Tennessee, even though it meant that we were unable to see each other quite as frequently. He asked if I would stay with him in Nashville, but it wasn't possible to raise a child with the money being offered in the territory. I also had an obligation to my employees at Genies to ensure that the business was running on course.

When I returned to Dallas, I noticed a few unopened envelopes which had been mailed to the house. They were from Steve. He had taken the time to write me love letters each day, and in some cases when he had no money, he would scribble kind and romantic messages on the backs of old receipts or any paper he could find. He would even call me whenever he could, even if he had to reverse the charges via call-collect. He even developed a sweet pet-name for me; Cha Cha the Blonde Sheep.

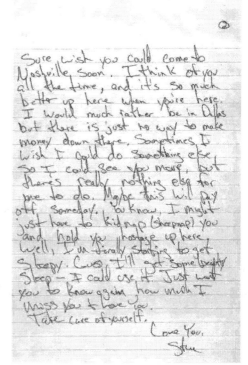

Letters from Steve, 1990.

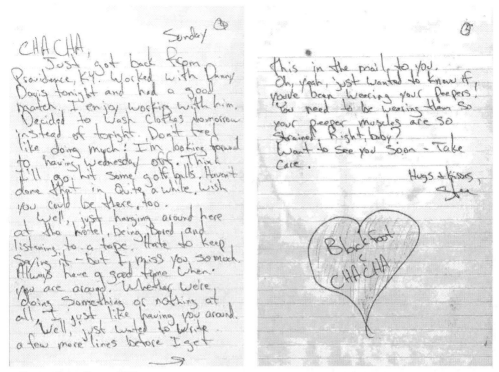

Letters from Steve, 1990.

In some of his letters, Steve had told me that he was naturally jealous, but it seemed sweet that he would want to protect me from the advances of other men.

I saw his discomfort when he visited one of my telegram appointments, even though he was hugely supportive of my career. Sometimes, he would get concerned if I spoke to any of the other wrestlers, which I thought was cute as it showed that he really cared about me. One day, Jeff Jarrett had asked if I would like to go for dinner, and it agitated Steve, who wanted to take our relationship to the next level.

By October, we had started to express our relationship physically, but I finished with Steve, after he had been unable to end his relationship with his high school sweetheart, Kathryn Burrhus.

To make matters worse, under the pressure of his family, he felt obliged to propose to her. After popping the question to Kathy, Steve came over, and asked if he could continue to see me. Shocked at the notion, I told him that he couldn't.

Undeterred, Steve continued to contact me, writing me frequent letters while he was on the road, and calling me each day, whether I was at work or at home. He had become upset that I had rejected him after learning of his engagement.

On Saturday 24th November 1990, he called me in a panic, as he felt he had no way out of his impending marriage. Later that day, Steve and Kathy tied the knot.

Steve explained that he felt obliged to get married out of a respect to Kathy, but said that he eventually wanted to marry me. There was a certainty in his voice that, one day, our relationship would be known to the world.

For weeks, I had tried to keep him at a distance. But after he continued to pursue me, I relented. We started seeing each other again, splitting our time between my house in Dallas, and his motel room in Nashville. Meanwhile, Kathy was stuck at home in Denton. I felt sorry for her, but I had become so close to Steve that I chose to ignore my conscience.

If we were in Dallas, Steve would usually want to leave the house, as the constant stream of calls and enquiries redirected from the Genies business line would be non-stop. Knowing he was not really able to afford to eat well in Tennessee, I would regularly pay for us to visit the Pearl Dragon, a Chinese restaurant that was local to my house. Steve would sometimes feel bad that I had to pay, but I told him not to worry. I was getting joy from doing something that I knew meant the world to him.

I also wanted to treat myself to something nice, and I decided to go for a breast augmentation surgery that I had considered for months.

As Steve returned to Tennessee, I would find little cards that he had hidden all over the house. It was such a warm, loving gesture. Even though he had very little money, he always tried to show me he cared by saving for romantic cards. It made me want to spend yet more time with him.

Cards left hidden for me to find around the house from Steve, 1990.

Whenever my work commitments would allow me to take some days off, I would fly over to Nashville and stay with him. We would play putt-putt golf, go to the movies and explore the city.

Steve had told me that he was barely scraping a living, and he had lost about ten pounds of weight in the time I arrived. Sometimes, he was surviving on a diet of three potatoes a day, occasionally with tuna if his pay allowed.

His old Hyundai car was barely managing to run and Steve was still using an old pair of Chris' boots to wrestle, even though they were falling apart and only being held together with worn strands of athletic tape. He was too proud and hated asking for help, but I was happy to offer him support whenever I could. After asking if he could borrow some money to buy some wrestling boots, I gave him the cash to buy a brand new pair as a gift.

Without the luxury of expendable income, Steve had being getting used to making his own entertainment and showed me a game which he had been practising. He would set up an empty trash can at the end of the room and would throw three empty beer cans at it. Whoever would get the most beer cans in the bin would be declared the winner. Steve said he had become a master at it, and he felt he was unbeatable against me. He then showed me a different way of throwing the cans. Once I picked up the technique, Steve lost one game. Flustered in defeat, he told me he never wanted to play again.

But it seemed his frustrations didn't really stem from losing the game, but were more centred on the fact that his career was not allowing him to make a decent living.

Penniless, Steve became increasingly demoralised at the pittance he was earning in his bookings. More often that not, he would only break even from the journeys between shows, but it was vital he paid his dues in order to improve.

Down on his luck, Steve received a call from the promoter Ed Watt. Running a show out of Dallas, Watt offered him a guaranteed sum of $100 to appear. Having struggled to pay for his own gas, or even food, the booking provided a lifeline to Steve, and he was thrilled to accept.

Unfortunately, the show conflicted with one being presented by L&A Promotions. Presuming that Steve would have been available to work for him, Chris pleaded with him to cancel on Ed, and promised to equal the amount being offered. Having given Watt his word, Steve told Chris that he couldn't and that he needed to establish himself as a reliable performer for every promoter as he needed the work. He could not afford it if the word had spread if he cancelled at the last minute.

Chris was offended at Steve's response, and reminded him that his loyalty should have been to the person who broke him into the business.

Feeling like he owed Adams for breaking him into the business, Steve picked up the phone and called Ed.

Uncomfortable, Steve humbly apologised, and told Watt that he had double booked himself. He hated lying, and felt guilty about letting down Ed, but felt compelled to do so to help out his mentor.

After pulling out of Watt's card and working for L&A, Steve received a fraction of the agreed sum and was paid a mere $40 for the appearance.

Depending on the income to make ends meet, Steve called Chris to clear up any misunderstanding. Unfortunately, there was not a mistake, and Chris told Steve to accept the amount that he had been given. All protests of the broken promise had been ignored, before Chris angrily put down the phone.

It was a betrayal of trust that would not be forgotten by Steve. He distanced himself from Chris, who had been cheating a number of other performers on their fees during his run as a promoter.

Despite the fallout with Chris, the career of Steve did not receive a setback. In fact, he was starting to reach the main event level of Jarrett's promotion.

By February 1991, Steve had impressed audiences in a series of matches with Jeff Jarrett for the USWA Southern Heavyweight Championship, and had also performed against enduring Memphis legends Jerry Lawler and 'Superstar' Bill Dundee. With his profile being elevated towards the main event scene of the territory, he had being getting positive reviews for his work, and received the 1990 Rookie of the Year Award in the March 1991 issue of Pro Wrestling Illustrated.

With the amplified exposure, it was not long before Steve found out that one of the two major wrestling promotions was showing an interest in his career.

By the spring, Steve had received a golden opportunity, which he was happy to accept. After months of struggling with his finances, he had been given a mid-level offer to join WCW. In comparison to his per-night agreement in Memphis, the secure contract provided a fortune to him. He would start work in May 1991.

Founded in 1988, World Championship Wrestling was created as a result of the changing industry of professional wrestling. It was formed when the media mogul Ted Turner purchased Jim Crockett Promotions, a family-owned business which operated in an expanse of regions throughout the southeast states. For years, wrestling had been one of the highest-rated shows on the Turner Broadcasting System network, but an accelerated expansion into new markets had forced JCP into financial difficulty. Crockett's attempt to compete with the World Wrestling Federation had failed, but Turner was committed to keep a strong presence of pro wrestling on his primary channel, the TBS Superstation.

With the backing of a major media conglomerate, WCW was immediately recognised as a viable competitor to the WWF, as it opened a front office in Turner's CNN Center, in downtown Atlanta, Georgia.

Moving to Dunwoody, a short drive from the Atlanta office, Steve was excited to work for Turner. But he was also saddened that I needed to remain in Dallas to run Genies. Despite the miles between us, we still managed to speak on the phone every day, and he would fly out to see me whenever he could get the time off his new routine.

My house in Dallas was like a second home to him, a retreat from his hectic schedule with a national promotion. Providing WCW management with my home number as a second point of contact, I received a call when he was at the gym.

It was Magnum T.A., a former wrestler who was working as a senior booking assistant within the promotion. He was really polite, and said he was looking for Steve, but I explained that he was not at my house.

Just as I was expecting to end the call, Magnum enquired about my English accent, and what I did for a living. I told him that I ran a company in Dallas, but had previously been Steve's valet in both the USWA and for the resurrected World Class promotions. He was surprised, and admitted that he had not really watched any tapes of Steve's matches in Texas or Tennessee.

Magnum asked if I could send some tapes of my interviews and matches, so I did.

After viewing the tapes, Magnum phoned me at the house and asked if I could attend the next show at the Center Stage Theatre in Atlanta, where WCW was scheduled to record a few weeks' worth of programming. Unfortunately, it was too short notice for me to arrange childcare for Jade, or the appropriate shift cover at Genies, so I had to decline. Nevertheless, Magnum wanted me to meet Dusty Rhodes for an interview on 31st May.

After retiring from a full-time career that took him to the top of the wrestling industry, Dusty was the main booker involved in the day-to-day running of the company. After boarding a flight to Houston, I was picked up at the airport by Steve. He drove me to the Sam Houston Coliseum, the arena that WCW was running that night. He led me to the backstage area, where I met Dusty for the first time.

Dusty was really warm and after a brief discussion which only lasted a few minutes, he asked if I could start immediately. Around the time I was being interviewed, Steve had been paired up with another valet named 'Vivacious' Veronica, but I was not even aware of that when I was offered a job that I hadn't actually pursued.

When I told Steve all about Dusty's offer to employ me, it delighted him. The prospect of me working as his valet meant that we could be on the road together every day, but I knew that I needed to get my business in order before I joined full-time.

Being on the road, I knew it would be impossible to run Genies remotely. I had to accept that there was insufficient time to train someone to run the company, whilst I was performing in other states. As a result, I gave up the business I had started from scratch to be with Steve. It was a big risk, but I wanted to be with him.

There was no time for me to sell the house, so I placed it on the rental market. I relocated to the same complex as Steve, in a three-bedroom apartment that could allow Jade and her nanny to join us without delay.

Before we moved, I went to see Chris, to let him know I was due to start in WCW with Steve. He was angry that he had not been consulted on our intention to work for Turner, and said that he should have been given the opportunity.

I could understand Chris' frustration, since he was the driving force of the ex-wife angle which had made stars out of Steve and me. But instead of being supportive of the mother of his child and his standout pupil, he was bitterly jealous.

When the dust settled, I went along for my very first WCW TV taping on 3rd June at the Boutwell Auditorium in Birmingham, Alabama. Steve and I couldn't continue the 'ex-wife' storyline feud without Chris and Toni, so it no longer made sense for me to use the name Jeanie Adams. It was bland and no longer had any relevance, but I hadn't really given this any consideration when Dusty called to see me.

"Hey Jeanie, have you got yourself a name?" he asked in his unmistakable lisp.

"Well, no, I haven't really thought about it. What would you suggest?" I murmured.

"From now on, you'll be called Lady Blossom!" he proudly announced.

Lady Blossom? I hated the name but with no alternative, and the fact that I did not want to upset the booker on my first night in, I was stuck with it. I later learned that the handle was due to my ample bust, which was apparently 'blossoming' from the dress I was wearing that night.

Arriving as Lady Blossom, 1991.

Although I never cared for my name change, I managed to keep some facets from my previous valet role. I continued to be adorned in luxurious revealing evening gowns, which I just loved picking out to wear. Best of all, the organisation wanted me to be an even bigger bitch on-camera. I would be far less verbal in my assaults but, rather, a silent-but-deadly siren.

I was told that my first appearance would instigate a major run for Steve, as he was scheduled to win the WCW World Television Championship from 'Beautiful' Bobby Eaton after my interference would help him win the match.

At the time of my arrival, there were already two other female stars working in the promotion: Missy Hyatt and Terri Boatright. We all got on really well, and with Toni no longer around me it was nice to have some other females to help me feel welcome backstage.

Missy worked as a ditzy interviewer, host and commentator on a number of WCW shows. She and I had actually first met during her World Class days in Dallas when she was managing her then-boyfriend John Tatum, well before I considered a career there.

When I first arrived in WCW, Missy was such a good friend to me. She took the time to show me around, and even recommended local hairdressers and clothes stores. She was in a relationship with the young actor Jason Hervey, a star from the hit coming-of-age drama *The Wonder Years*. The two of them would rollerblade backstage like a couple of teenagers. I was even invited to attend one of Missy's birthday bashes in downtown Atlanta. I'm still close to Missy, and she remains as much fun as she was back when we first met.

Missy Hyatt, former WCW wrestling manager and announcer: "Jeanie was cool enough to allow me to pull a rib on Steve Austin. The night that Steve Austin was scheduled to win the WCW TV from Bobby Eaton, I hid the title before the match. Steve was frantically looking for the title out of fear that his first major title was going to be scratched off. Jeanie stooged that I hid the title, so I tossed the title at Steve and said 'Welcome to the Biz, Kid'. I think if I did that in 2015, all I would earn is a bunch of stunners from Steve. Thanks Jeanie for stooging on me."

Terri on the other hand had initially worked as make-up artist for WCW, but had since been operating as an on-screen character under the name of Miss Alexandra York.

Her adopted persona was that of a laptop-carrying whiz who led an evil alliance of corporate sell-outs known as the York Foundation, formed of babyface turncoats Terrence (Terry) Taylor, Richard (Ricky) Morton and Thomas (Tommy) Rich. Financed by shrewd stock market investments, she played the megalomaniac figurehead of a corporation who used her riches to try and buy success in World Championship Wrestling.

In reality, she was a really sweet girl, who was dating Dusty's eldest son Dustin. Trying to escape the shadow of his famous dad and forge a legacy of his own, Dustin Rhodes was really showing some promise and fire in the ring. He was working hard to prove he earned his place on the roster and he was determined to overcome the accusations of nepotism made against him by some of the industry's veterans. As two girls who were both in relationships with rising stars, Terri and I had a lot in common and we loved to hang out backstage, talking about our dreams for the future and other girly chat.

I was seriously impressed with that first taping, and compared to those held at the Sportatorium it was a serious change. Gone were the days of sitting crammed into a tiny office; WCW talent had separate dressing rooms with private showers, catering, make-up, agents and crew on hand to take care of everything and it was all so organised. The professionalism completely blew me away and I was really struck by the quality of the whole presentation. I was even taken aback by the green ring-jacket of the company's top star, Sting, which was an amazingly ornate and beautifully crafted item in itself. Why that's stuck with me I'll never know, but seeing the care taken in the production of a wrestler's ring wear alone made me realise that absolutely everything was of such a high standard.

Backstage, Steve was blown away to be winning the title from Bobby as he was a veteran worker whom we both admired. Eaton was renowned for his selfless ring style, and had finally been given a run with a singles championship after years of working in tag team competition, as a member of the famed Midnight Express. We ran through the match and I have to say that Bobby was one of the most genuine and nicest guys I've ever met.

Bobby was so professional and took the time to go through absolutely everything I was going to do in the match. Nothing was too much bother and he was so patient, really helping out too by holding my hands into the rehearsal. On the show, he really sold the finish when I went to scratch his eyes, which was the cue for Steve to win the match and the championship.

Bobby Eaton, former WCW wrestler: "I enjoyed getting the chance to work with Steve (Austin) and Jeanie, or Lady Blossom as she was known to fans, right off the bat when they came to WCW in 1991. We had a lot of fun with their first few matches in WCW, when Steve ended up beating me for the WCW World TV Title. Jeanie was always kind and treated me with much respect when I was around her and I hope she felt the same about me."

So within a few short weeks of working for the promotion, 'Stunning' Steve had won the TV Title and it was partly due to his evil new valet in her debut appearance.

It was not a bad way for the pair of us to make a first impression in WCW.

As well as the surprise of us being pushed up the ranks so quickly, an even bigger one came to me on the car journey back from that first show.

Steve asked me to marry him.

The proposal really took me off guard.

"But, what about your wife? Are you getting a divorce?" I asked.

Steve reassured me, telling me that Kathy was a devout Catholic and had specifically gone to the Catholic Church to request an annulment. He said he wanted for us to get married as soon as the annulment came through. Between our new careers, plus living next door to each other, we were around each other constantly.

Of course, I said yes.

After months of being held apart, we were now finally together, and truly happy.

With Steve as the new WCW World Television Champion, 1991.

10 THE TOLL OF THE ROAD

With Steve and I together again, our careers were rapidly taking off in WCW as we were booked to a strong start. Although our day-to-day existence was basically travelling and wrestling, Steve and I had lots of fun on the road.

We got to see so much of the country, and many of its most unique, offbeat and historic landmarks.

During one stopover in Milwaukee, Steve wanted to see the infamous Oxford Apartments, where the notorious serial killer Jeffrey Dahmer had dismembered and murdered his victims. Dahmer had just been arrested and it was a huge news story. Steve always maintained his curiosity of the macabre, and he was really keen to visit this real-life 'House of Horrors'. We went there after an evening's card, but as we looked at the apartment block it had a sinister aura that cannot be conveyed in words.

I got totally spooked and insisted we drove away in a hurry.

When we drove between venues we would spend hours sitting listening to the radio and just taking in the scenery from the windscreen, absorbing miles and miles of Americana. However, as our mileage increased, the novelty of touring soon faded. A sense of adventure was being replaced by overwhelming exhaustion.

This was our travel itinerary for just one week from 12th-18th August 1991:

Roanoke, VA to Gainesville, GA (395 miles)
Gainesville, GA to Anderson, SC (80 miles)
Anderson, SC to Fayetteville, NC (279 miles)
Fayetteville, NC to Chattanooga, TN (493 miles)
Chattanooga, TN to Chicago, IL (604 miles)
Chicago, IL to Milwaukee, WI (92 miles)
Milwaukee, WI to Danville, IL (236 miles)

It equates to 2,179 miles. Or to put it another way, it would be like travelling the entire length of the UK two-and-a-half times over, and is just 501 miles shy of a coast-to-coast drive across the USA. On top of the travelling, we had to eat, sleep, perform, spend time in the gym and find time to do all the other essential day-to-day activities as well. Often, by the time we got to TV tapings, I was so tired that I would fall asleep backstage.

It was a tough transition as I adapted to the unrelenting physical and mental pressures of life on the road. Until you have lived the life of a touring performer, it is hard to understand the strain that it puts on your mind and wellbeing.

If we were flying, we usually had a 6am departure time, requiring a check-in by 5am which necessitated that our rental cars needed to be returned prior to that as well. It meant that we would often be getting up at 3am in order to check-out of our hotel. As our show from the previous night would finish late, by the time we found somewhere to eat, we usually were not able to get to bed until at least midnight, which just left under three hours until we had to get up – and this was on a constant cycle.

I dreaded each of these early morning struggles as I tried to manoeuvre through the airports with my handbag and a couple of cases containing all my evening gowns, matching shoes, make-up and accessories. I could never comprehend how the wrestlers could even function after taking the sheer amount of physical punishment that they took in the ring.

It is because of this gruelling schedule that substance abuse became so prevalent in the industry. Once we were on the next flight all anyone wanted to do was catch a few hours' sleep and so one drug of choice was Soma, a muscle relaxant which is usually used to treat musculoskeletal conditions, but it was used by many to provide a short sharp fix to get some sleep. Although it effects are short-lived, it's also highly addictive. I used this drug frequently just so my body could get some rest. As the only female who travelled on the house show circuit, I too was starting to succumb to the self-abuse and medicinal quick-fixes that made it easier to endure the grinding routine.

As well as Somas, Valium was another favoured drug to give the body some rest. Hand in hand with these were drugs needed to combat their effects, in order to shake off the lethargy. Then there were steroids used by some of the talent to keep in good shape and these were frequently washed down with alcohol, painkillers and even recreational drugs.

Before long, the body of a user can't function on its own. It needs drugs in order to sleep, wake-up and function on a day to day basis. It takes away control of how the body operates. As a result, even the smallest of activity is dependent on a chemical fix.

It can become the start of the long, slippery and painful descent into addiction.

As soon as we landed, it was time to get the rental car, drive to the hotel, go the gym, then to the arena and on and on it went.

Fatigue wasn't the only thing which wore down the body on the road; many were also dealing with the physical effects of being in the ring.

Sam Houston, former WCW wrestler: "It's such a hectic pace that you just have to keep going. It's a driven profession, because the moment you can't go then someone else lower down the level is ready to step in and take your place. So there's a lot of pressure to maintain and that's the biggest problem."

In order to maintain a career in the business, many stars would fall to substance abuse in order to stay at peak performance. Taking bumps night after night resulted in bodies that were constantly wracked with aches and pains which were treated with other drugs.

I also became increasingly aware of a stream of 'mark doctors' who became more visible on the scene. These were crooked doctors who would prescribe drugs such as Vicodin and Xanax in exchange for backstage passes, or even autographs for their kids.

It was frightening how easy it was to get hold of drugs on the road, and although I wasn't consuming them on the levels that some others were, I was now starting to crave them to cope with the arduous lifestyle of the business.

Standing in an arena full of screaming fans, knowing millions more are watching you on TV around the world, is an amazing natural high and there's nothing like it. But it could not compensate a loneliness and intense emptiness that I was also experiencing as a mother being hundreds of miles away from her child.

I was starting be overcome with an extreme sense of guilt for not being around my daughter. I felt so empty being on the road and having to leave Jade in the care of someone else. I missed her immensely when I was away, and my only comfort came from the knowledge that the work away from home would provide us with a better and more secure life in the future.

Coupled with the separation anxiety, I was now starting to become unwell, and had started vomiting at the beginning of almost every day. The months of stress and exhaustion had finally caught up, and it was now taking a physical toll on me. I could not wait to get some much-needed rest.

Whenever Steve and I got a few days off it was time to just go home and unwind. He would catch-up with paying his bills and walking his dog, Abby, who had been brought up from Dallas. All of the precious free time I had was spent with Jade.

Sadly, this relaxation would soon end and it was time to pack our essentials, and reluctantly hand Jade back to her nanny as we prepared to go back on the road again.

Despite the rigours of travel, the summer of 1991 was an interesting time for those who worked in the promotion. Ric Flair, who had been the enduring World Heavyweight Champion of WCW, and its forerunner Jim Crockett Promotions, had abruptly left the company after an irreconcilable dispute with the Executive Vice President of WCW, Jim Herd. On top of that, with Sid Vicious having already departed for an opportunity with the WWF, Stan Hansen returning to Japan and Nikita Koloff intending to take some time away from the promotion, it was clear that there was a dearth of upper level heels to work with the company's shining heroes.

It seemed that there was a huge financial investment being made into the production values of our shows to compensate, making the product seem more sleek and professional on the surface. Additional money was being spent on lighting, pyrotechnics and visual effects and there were rumours of contract negotiations with some of the top drawing talent of the WWF, which was still dominating in the mainstream as the industry leader.

Making my way into the ring before one of 'Stunning' Steve's title defences, 1991.

Meanwhile, some of the brightest new stars from the smaller territories were being acquired to freshen up the promotion to make it even more exciting. Even a few of our old colleagues from the USWA were also starting to join the company including Cactus Jack and Matt Borne, who was now repackaged as a rugged lumberjack called Big Josh.

Another star had been campaigning to join the Atlanta office, and had sent in some tapes to impress the booking team of WCW. I was backstage at a house show, when Dusty asked to speak to Steve.

Dusty explained that Chris Adams had been looking to continue the ex-wife storyline in WCW, and suggested the company could start with the ideas that had never been used in the angle. The material that Chris had sent over really impressed Rhodes, who wanted to see if Steve was open to resuming his on-screen feud with Chris.

Having been performing in WCW without any hands-on guidance from the booking team, I had missed Chris' direction, and I felt that his presence could be a real asset to the team.

Steve, however, felt differently. He told Dusty that he wouldn't work with Chris again, and explained that the angle had been run into the ground already. Deep down, I knew the real reason for Steve's refusal to work with Chris. Holding a grudge over the broken promise on pay, he had grown to resent him and would never trust him again.

Dusty accepted Steve's input and kindly informed Chris he wasn't required due to a surplus of recently-hired talent.

In that year alone, WCW had brought in an array of new talent, and there was a real buzz that the company was moving in the right direction. Steve and I were delighted when the first edition of WCW's monthly publication reached newsstands, as we featured in an article which focused on the top stars to join the company.

Bill Apter, former senior editor of WCW Magazine and Pro Wrestling Illustrated: "It was always a pleasure to pose Jeanie during my trips down to World Championship Wrestling. Jeanie was a photographic pleasure, always willing to stand any long amount of time I needed to get that perfect shot in the studio. Always smiling and eager to work with me she was just fabulous."

Steve was finally making waves with his hard work, and we had some fantastic matches with some great opponents, many of whom were also looking to rise to the challenge of filling the voids left by those who were no longer around. For a hungry young athlete, it seemed that the promotion was really building towards its future. For fans, it resulted in some outstanding matches between some of the finest new stars.

Gary Michael Cappetta, former WCW ring announcer: "When Stunning Steve Austin and Lady Blossom arrived in WCW I was hopeful their debut signalled a change in the direction of the promotion. Such a handsome couple with impressive ring skills and electric chemistry would be a marketing bonanza if properly presented and carefully cultivated. Elevating this adorable, yet devastating duo to main event status was surely inevitable as long as the private agendas of the company's decision makers did not conflict with their certain success.

With time, instead of utilizing their gifts to headline events, Steve and Jeanie became a solid mid card draw. While their contribution to the show greatly enhanced each event, I thought they never were given the opportunity to rise to a position that their talents commanded."

I loved standing behind the curtain with some of the talent to watch the events, but Steve was becoming increasingly protective and hated the thought of me mixing with the wrestlers. In the USWA, I had already seen a glimpse of his jealousy, but I also thought it was quite sweet as it showed that Steve still really cared about me. I reassured him that he would never lose me, but he wanted me to stay in a separate dressing room at each show and he would insist that I stay there until it was time to go out for our match. Sometimes I would nip out to get a coffee but Steve's face would turn as he never wanted me anywhere near the boys.

Although this worsened my sense of isolation that I was already feeling from missing Jade, WCW remained an exciting place to work once it was time to perform. The shows were often played to seemingly packed houses all across the country and the atmosphere in the arenas was electric.

With Steve as one of its champions we were positioned right near the top of the promotion, but the man at the very peak and the perennial face of the company was the charismatic sensation Sting.

Sting's image seemed to be on everything: from our tour posters and Galoob range of action figures to clothing, gadgets and soft toys. You could even buy kids training shoes with his unmistakeable scorpion logo on the treads! He generated so much energy and excitement from the crowds with his dynamic style of wrestling, and had a loyal army of young fans that he sweetly referred to as the 'Little Stingers'.

So many people who have followed professional wrestling will have their own unique memory of Sting; however I will always remember the date of 25th August 1991 as *The Great American Bash* tour reached its climax. Being held at The Omni in Atlanta that night was a tournament to crown a new United States champion. For a pair of relative newcomers to the company, Steve and I were so ecstatic that we were going to feature in a main event at the promotion's flagship venue to face its top star, a man who would become known as 'The Franchise of WCW'.

It was our dream that came true; this was the night we finally realised that we had made the big leagues after years of hard work for smaller promotions.

There were dozens of near-falls throughout the match, which brought the audience to a fever pitch. It appeared that 'Stunning' Steve was finally going to win after unloading with The Stun Gun, his finishing move at the time. I jumped with joy onto the ring apron and embraced Steve before telling him to pin the painted warrior from Venice Beach, California. I stayed on the edge of the ring, looking out to the crowd and gloating that the match was over. I could not hear the bell ring, but I was sure the match was finished as all I could hear was an enormous, collective roar.

Realising that Sting was behind me during a match at the Omni, 1991.

I could sense that Steve was coming back for a celebratory hug, so I reached behind me and went to flirtatiously play with his hair. But this was not the long locks of Austin, all I could feel were short spikes in the palms of my hands. I turned around, and discovered it was Sting! He flexed his muscles as I screamed in surprise while the capacity crowd went nuts. The match was still on, Steve rushed over in frustration to grab him from behind, and roll him up. 'The Stinger' quickly reversed the move to get the three count, winning the title and sending the fans home happy.

Steve and I would often talk about that match, which was the highlight of both our runs in WCW. As a fellow wrestler, Steve remained in sheer awe at just how over Sting was with the fans that night, and we both agreed that he carried himself with the class of a real champion. But most of all, I was taken by just how sweet and gentle natured he was, firstly as a dad to his children, and then as a good friend to us both.

We were soon getting rave reviews for our work, and the match with Sting gave Steve a conviction that he could perform at a main event level on the biggest stage WCW could provide. In matches with Barry Windham, The Yellow Dog (a masked 'Flyin'' Brian Pillman) and 'The Z-Man' Tom Zenk, he was determined to show WCW management that he could face a seasoned veteran without the need to be carried in order to have a thrilling match. We both knew that we had been given a lucky break caused by the departure of others, and that we were being awarded opportunities that would have been otherwise rare.

The company was in need of headline talent, and Steve was on a mission to prove he was one. As Steve's confidence grew in the ring, he was already being entrusted as someone who could work with a diverse array of talent in the ring to help establish them as viable stars in the promotion.

The flamboyant rookie Johnny B. Badd (Marc Mero), second-generation Florida veteran Mike Graham, the undervalued but dynamic 'Jumpin'' Joey Maggs and the rough and ready Big Josh all faced Steve in his defences of the World Television title.

We were also involved in matches with tag team stars, such as Todd Champion and Firebreaker Chip, collectively known as The Patriots, and both members of The Young Pistols, Steve Armstrong and Tracey Smothers, who each faced Steve in their rare forays into singles competition, as did Rick Steiner, a fan favourite who needed to be kept visible while his brother Scott was nursing a torn bicep injury. Even Robert Gibson, who had just split with Rock 'N' Roll Express teammate Ricky Morton, returned from a devastating knee injury to challenge Steve for the Television Championship.

Tracy Smothers, former WCW wrestler: "After WCW hired Jeanie and Steve, Dusty loved them and put the TV title on them straight away. He put Steve over all the middle and underneath babyfaces, and he had great matches with everybody. To this day, people come up to me about my match with Steve that is on YouTube. Steve was regarded as the best heel in the biz... Steve and Jeanie were always a class act and I was honoured to share the ring with them."

The World Television title was unlike any championship in professional wrestling. It was primarily defended during episodes of the syndicated programming of World Championship Wrestling, and we were able to do some really creative things with the concept.

Frequently, our main event defences of the belt would be scheduled to have a short duration, dictated by the limited time remaining on WCW's television shows.

This was not usually long if we were last on the card.

If there was restricted time left on the broadcast it allowed us to create immediate heat from the start of each match and foster a sense of urgency as the challenger tried his best to win against the clock. The drama would only heighten as ring announcer Gary Michael Cappetta counted down the time remaining before the match would be declared a draw.

In wrestling, the event of a draw results in the gold staying with the champion, and this even applies when there is a disqualification, regardless of the winner. Dusty loved using the idea of a challenger getting screwed out of the title by virtue of a disqualification win. His justification was that it made a series of rematches viable as we toured on the road for our non-televised house shows, and could allow Steve to face some worthy challengers without damaging the credibility of either man. He felt that it could solidify Steve's status as champion without him winning clean in the ring.

As Steve's reign with the championship flourished, I started to increase my level of physicality in his matches. We were experimenting with new ideas and inventive ways for Steve to be disqualified in order to keep the title. Despite many of our matches ending with the same result, we wanted to keep the finishing sequences fresh. Our aim was to preserve Steve as a truly vile cheat, who would stay the champion under the smallest technicality of the rules, but without making him seem desperate or weak.

Most of our disqualification losses were caused by my interference, but only once the referee caught me injecting myself into the match to give Steve an illegal advantage. One of my favourite methods of interference was to jump onto the back of Steve's opponents and either claw at their faces with my nails or try to choke them. This would usually occur late in the match as Steve would be lying prone on the mat, becoming increasingly vulnerable to a loss. With my petite figure, and most of Steve's opponents being well over six feet tall, it was not easy to do a standing jump whilst wearing heels and then attempt to clamber up their huge and sweaty frames.

In a televised match with Ron Simmons, we used this spot in the finish, but after Steve was disqualified he charged at 'The All American' while I was still on his back. Ron moved at the last second, and Steve collided with me in the corner, with the fans erupting as he knocked me senseless. It was one of the few times on television that I was seen to be taking a bump, but it was something that I had started to do with frequency on house shows up and down the country.

A bump is an inside term that wrestlers use to describe each time they take a fall to the floor, whether from a slam or strike, or anything that leads to them collapsing on the mat. Bumps are often taken for granted by wrestling fans, but years of doing it can really take its toll on the human body. There is no real way to fall without feeling any sort of pain. When I started taking bumps, I wasn't given any training, I was just asked to go out and do it. If the fans could not see Steve lose his title, they prayed that the wicked witch who caused them to be cheated out of their hero's victory would at least get her comeuppance after the match ended.

In one match in Sioux City, Iowa, I would take a bump after Dustin Rhodes dropkicked Steve onto me, almost crushing me flat. In another, I was thrown off the ring apron and landed backwards onto the ringside mats after being clobbered by Tracey Smothers. Each time I would take a bump, I was not aiming to express it by over-the-top theatrics; I wanted it to look like I was critically hurt. Management were becoming quite impressed by my bumping, not because any of my falls were particularly spectacular, but due to my subtle embellishments. I was credibly selling the pain each time I landed.

When I would return backstage, there were a few times that Dusty appeared anxious, he was concerned that I had sustained an injury. We laughed about after he realised I was just doing my best acting job, but he did start to notice a minor annoyance that he felt was hampering my work.

Dusty observed that after each bump, my hands would immediately grasp my skirt to pull it down and protect my modesty. It was something that I had been doing without thinking, and I knew it was a subconscious reaction borne out of my natural shyness. The reserved Brit inside of me explained to Dusty that it would not be ladylike for a woman to expose her knickers to the world. He smiled, but told me that I should ignore the temptation to protect my image, and continue to concentrate my efforts on expressing the pain from a fall, not save myself from the embarrassment of accidental exposure.

I tried my best to heed Dusty's advice, but it was difficult to fight my instinctive movements. No matter how hard I tried, I couldn't help but sort my dress. Backstage, word soon spread of my bashful demeanour, and some of the wrestlers took great delight in ribbing me during the matches, especially P.N. News and Big Josh. In one match, Josh intercepted me as I tried to slap him, lifting me up over his shoulder in a fireman's carry. Completely powerless, I could do nothing to fight back as he lifted up my dress, and paraded me around ringside, as the crowd were exposed to my revealed bottom. The audience laughed, but it was not the way I wanted our contests to come to a close each night.

By the fall of 1991, we brought a new finish that would recur in our matches. Rather than run my usual distractions and physical interference from ringside, I started to take a pair of brass knuckles which I had hidden within my evening gown, underneath my bosom. With the referee's attention drawn elsewhere, I would pull the knuckles out and hand them over to Steve so that he could use them on his opponent.

After knocking out his foe, he would then quickly hand the weapon back over to me, where I would conceal it before the ref had any idea of what had happened. It seems like a fairly basic concept but it was a trusted formula that we knew would get heat with the fans, especially as the referee would not be able to check where the foreign object was being stored, which only served to wind up the crowd even more.

We were next thrust into a short programme with P.N. News, a burly heavyweight who was given the moniker of a street rapper. He would come out and rhyme to the crowd before the match and get them to join in, and had been a frequent opponent of Steve in a number of tag team matches, with a variety of partners on both sides. The most famous of these was a wacky Scaffold Match at *The Great American Bash '91* in Baltimore which was the first time both Steve and I ever featured on a pay-per-view event.

Steve and P.N. News met again during a 7th October TV taping filmed at the Centre Stage Theatre in Atlanta, and once more, we sneaked a victory after I passed Steve the brass knuckles, allowing him to wrap them around his fist before he floored News with a stiff knockout punch for the win.

With Steve victorious, we rejoiced in the ring only to be interrupted by an enraged Dustin Rhodes who interrupted our celebration. He tried to explain to the referee that Steve had yet again cheated with a weapon which was hidden inside my gown. Naturally, we vehemently denied this, and dared Rhodes to validate his protest and prove to the referee that we had cheated in the match. A frustrated Dustin backed off, realising it would be improper for him to place his hand down the dress of a lady.

Moments later, Madusa arrived into the fray and stepped through the ropes with the intent to confront me. Having recently returned to the United States from a tour of Japan, she was another newcomer looking to make an impact in the promotion. She then did the unthinkable and delved into my dress, revealing our secret weapon and exposing it to the crowd.

After being provided with tangible evidence, the ref promptly reversed his decision, awarding the match to News by disqualification. Once again, the result allowed us to keep the title, while allowing the challenger to claim he had not been beaten. The aim of the finish served to solidify fan interest in future rematches held at house shows across the country.

Paul Neu, former WCW wrestler P.N. News: "I remember working with Jeanie and Steve a lot including a really great match in North Carolina that ended up running to a time limit draw. Jeanie was always such consummate professional when it came to wrestling and although we didn't spend a lot of time socialising away from the job, I do remember she was always so happy and would have a smile and a friendly 'hello' for everyone."

The disputed finish of our TV match with News also created a fresh issue with Dustin. This led into our second and my final pay-per-view appearance at the *Halloween Havoc 1991* event, held at the UTC Arena in Chattanooga, Tennessee. I still get lots of comments and mail from fans about the glittery red-sequined dress I wore to that card; however it was Steve and Dustin who stole the show that night. They had an epic and bloody match that illustrated that the two young stars of WCW could rise to the occasion when the spotlight was on them, wrestling to a fifteen-minute time limit draw that raised both their profiles.

Steve really wanted to impress during the big show, and felt it was essential that he was seen to excel without the constant interference of a valet. His new aim was to establish himself as a strong individual character without anyone at ringside stealing his heat.

Meanwhile, I had removed all of the bumping spots I had been taking in previous matches as I was no longer willing to take any unnecessary physical risks to my body. My mind was far from the unfolding drama in the ring that evening. It was completely centred on the future.

I had just been given some unexpected, but wonderful, news.

Our lives were about to change.

11 FAMILY COMES FIRST

My WCW career had only started four months before I discovered that I was expecting a baby. Radiant with happiness, I was overwhelmed as it served to remind me on the value of family. Meanwhile, Steve was hesitant in sharing the joy of the coming of our first child. He was a man riddled in conflict.

Although he was amidst the final stages of a marital annulment with his first wife, Steve was ridden with a deep guilt stemming from his inability to tell his parents that his relationship with Kathy was over, and that it had been for some time. Furthermore, he felt even more ashamed to tell his parents that he had pursued me during his marriage, out of fear that it would disappoint them.

The pregnancy gave Steve no choice. It was now time for him to muster up the courage, and he pledged to tell Ken and Beverly about this secret relationship that he had been actively hiding.

The log cabin at Villa Rica, Georgia.

As we contemplated how he could break the news to his family, Steve remained steadfast in his assurance that he was still intent on getting married to me at the earliest opportunity. We both agreed that with a baby on the way, that it was best to start house-hunting to accommodate our new family. It was not long until we found the cutest little log cabin in Villa Rica, just a ten-minute drive from Douglasville, Georgia. Flanked by acres of land, the lodge was also a mere half-hour drive from WCW's offices in downtown Atlanta, and it was the perfect property for our changing needs.

When we got back to work, Steve and I could not wait to tell our friends and colleagues about our impending arrival, regardless of the reaction. I had been slightly anxious that we might get reprimanded from management for not divulging any plans to get pregnant, but everyone seemed delighted.

I was relieved that the company was supportive of our pregnancy. Steve had worked so hard to establish himself as a reliable talent, and he had already expressed how he disliked having someone with him at ringside. In truth, he preferred to keep the heat of the crowd to himself. I knew that my leaving would allow him to forge his own path without any distractions. But most importantly, I realised that my maternity would give me the chance to spend much overdue time with Jade.

Terri Runnels, former WCW wrestling manager Alexandra York: "I have such fond memories of Jeanie when she and Steve arrived at WCW. She was always so very sweet and gracious with me. She and I would eventually end up talking about our pregnancies and little girls more than wrestling or the impending show!"

It had been an interesting few months on the road, but I felt exhausted, and I was relieved to be ending my tenure as Lady Blossom. On November 19th, I made my final appearance at the *Clash of Champions XVII* television special held in Savannah, Georgia, in another match between Steve and P.N. News. There was never any storyline created to explain that I was departing, and with no fanfare, my career in wrestling came to a close.

When I remember my stint as a performer during the early days of World Championship Wrestling, my feelings are divided.

In some ways, it was the highlight of my career as an on-screen talent within professional wrestling. Its syndicated programming gave me international exposure on worldwide television, and I had pictures and posters in globally-available magazines. Fans would wait outside the arenas and at the hotels for autographs and photos and I was really humbled by their love.

I felt genuinely blessed to have had the opportunity to work with some outstanding and creative people, both behind the camera and in front of it, many of whom went on to achieve amazing things within the industry.

By the early nineties, American wrestling was also becoming really hot in the United Kingdom, and the ITV networks, which used to broadcast the old *World of Sport* shows was now transmitting episodes of *WCW Pro Wrestling* in most of its regions. People back home could once again see little Jeanie Clarke from Southend appearing back on British television every week, albeit under a different name and truly wicked persona.

But as glamorous as the life of a touring performer may appear on the outside, trying to make a living by going town-to-town was anything but glitzy.

It was an unending succession of late nights and early mornings, punctuated by gruelling travel, cheap motels and, for me, a rekindling with an abuse of substances with which I had only flirted during my early twenties.

Most of all, being on the road reminded me that I had never really experienced a settled family life, or ever found a place that I could truly call home. It reminded me of a childhood consumed by finding temporary hideouts in which to find solace and retreat, as I lived in fear of abuse from my mum's drunken partners. As the memories of my damaged childhood started to return, they exacerbated the agony I was feeling from being apart from Jade.

As a child, I had been forced to accept the absence of my mother's love, and I was afraid that my time on the road would affect Jade. I would never want her to resent me for being away, and it tore me apart knowing that I had accepted a travelling job which would prevent me from watching my daughter grow.

Missing her intensely and, with the blooming of my maternity, I realised it was now time to say goodbye to my career in wrestling and embrace the joys of motherhood.

I was finally off the road.

It was a time to focus on raising my family, and create something for my children that I never truly had: a home.

Our nanny went back to Texas, and I could once again experience the joy of looking after Jade as we settled into our beautiful new house.

I was really enjoying being a full-time mum and taking a long overdue break from work as my maternity bloomed. It dawned on me that I hadn't really had a chance to unwind for years. I had been so busy running my business in Dallas, and my life had become even more hectic as I transitioned to the role of a performer on the touring American wrestling circuit.

It was nice to kick back and relax, but despite being pregnant I soon found myself decorating, landscaping the garden, planting flowers and riding around our land in our new four-wheeler.

On the precious days that Steve had off we would spend most of our time having fun. Between working on the house, we filled our days antique shopping for vintage Coca-Cola signs from the fifties, hanging out at our favourite restaurants and bars and we even started playing darts at a local pub with our friends.

As most of the WCW roster lived in Atlanta, we already had lots of friends in the area, but we were quickly making friends with our neighbours. As soon as we relocated, I was keen to foster my family with a sense of community.

I was set on turning our new house into a home.

Meanwhile, Steve's original hopes for stardom without anyone by his side were not to be, despite my time as his wrestling valet coming to an end.

His career had taken a new direction as he was paired on-screen with a new manager, Paul E. Dangerously. Dubbed the 'Psycho Yuppie from Wall Street', Dangerously was an obnoxious character intent on destroying WCW and was portrayed by the brilliant Paul Heyman.

Paul E.'s evil masterplan was to enlist an elite squad of rulebreakers into his stable, The Dangerous Alliance, with a pledge to injure the company's most beloved heroes and force them out of action.

It was an angle that made an immediate impact with the unveiling of former WWF headliner 'Ravishing' Rick Rude as the first member of the Alliance at the WCW *Halloween Havoc '91* pay-per-view show. Madusa had joined Dangerously in a similar valet role to the one I had been playing before my departure, proclaiming herself as 'The First Lady of WCW' to the annoyance of the fans who had adorned Missy Hyatt with that title. By November, the team grew to include WCW World Tag Team Champions Arn Anderson and Larry Zbyszko, the newly-turned fan-favourite Bobby Eaton, with Steve rounding out the group as their ferocious young lion.

As Steve was still in the midst of his lengthy reign as the WCW World Television Champion, Paul would often declare him as the 'Best Wrestler on TV Today' and 'The World's Greatest Athlete' during their interviews in order to establish his value to a group which was largely comprised of top veteran stars.

As the premier heels of the promotion, The Dangerous Alliance would continue to dominate WCW programming for almost a year. By joining as a member, Steve was able to become a regular fixture of its main event scene.

By the spring of 1992, he had been embroiled in feuds with all of the top stars, from mainstay talent like Sting, The Steiner Brothers, Ron Simmons and Barry Windham, to the returning Ricky 'The Dragon' Steamboat and Nikita Koloff.

Steve revelled in his work, as he was booked in a mixture of singles and tag team contests. With a new shorter haircut, he really shined when he was pitted against Barry Windham in a hot feud for the TV title, dropping the belt on April 27th and regaining it four weeks later in Chattanooga, Tennessee.

Although he was excelling in the ring with the very best WCW had to offer, there was one confrontation that Steve had been avoiding for months.

By the summer, our due date was rapidly approaching and Steve still hadn't told his family that we were together, not to mention that we were impending parents. I felt that it was strange that he never called them, as it didn't feel right having their grandchild without them knowing.

I urged him that they should share our wonderful blessing, and with our baby scheduled to be born via a Caesarean section on 7th July, he finally gave in and called his mum the night before the birth.

I was sitting next to him as he finally took a deep breath and picked up the phone.

"Mom, I have always respected you, but I haven't told you something. I've been seeing a girl and she's pregnant," Steve sighed as he grovelled into the receiver.

"When's this baby due?" his mum calmly asked.

"Tomorrow mom," he replied.

There was a long pause from the other end.

"Is this girl Jeanie?" his mum eventually enquired.

"Yes," he succumbed.

Steve immediately booked his mum, Beverly, a last-minute flight to Atlanta so that she could be there for the arrival of his first born child.

I had never felt so nervous in all my life. Not only was I giving birth but I was also going to finally meet the 'mother-in-law' for the very first time.

Steve had already told me that his mum was close to his first wife, Kathy. Beverly cared for her like a daughter, and was so disappointed when that marriage did not succeed. I felt awkward and I had an intuition that she wouldn't like me.

But none of that mattered. There was no time for me to dwell on the uncertain, as I was quickly whisked away to the theatre. It was time to have our child delivered into the world.

With Steve at the hospital, I gave birth to a 7 pounds and 7 ounces baby girl we called Stephanie Britt. I beamed with joy as soon as I glanced upon her.

I only saw her for a few brief minutes before the medical staff told me they had to stitch me back together, but I vividly remember that Steve stayed next to me and held our baby in his arms as I was put to sleep.

I faded away, but my smile remained. Our new arrival was perfect in every way.

I could not wait to wake up to our new family.

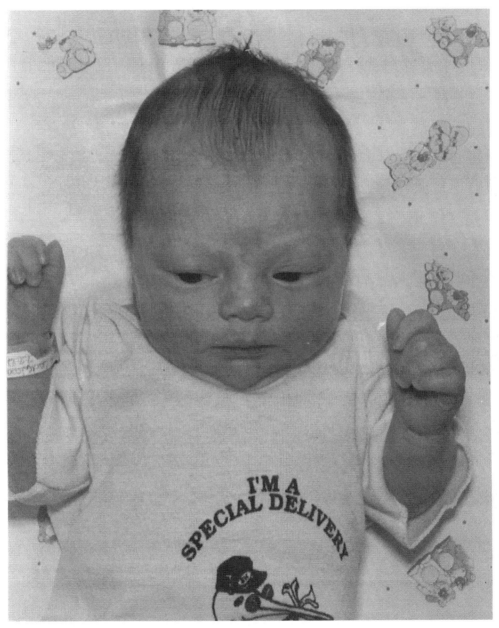

Baby Stephanie Britt in the hospital, 1992.

12 IN HOLY MATRIMONY

When I finally woke up in the hospital bed, I was alone and scared.

Although drowsy, I was experiencing a great deal of pain from the surgery and my baby daughter was nowhere to be seen. I asked for Steve, but discovered that he had left the hospital to go out shooting with Rick Rude.

Jade holding her new little sister Stephanie in the hospital, 1992.

The nurse told me my daughter was okay and was resting in the nursery, which was a huge relief, but I wanted to hold her in my arms.

I was so thrilled when Steve returned with Jade and my neighbour Ann to bring through baby Stephanie so I could finally embrace her, surrounded by family and my closest friend.

When we got back home, I realised that there had been a drastic regime change in Georgia which was starting to threaten the security of family life we had worked hard to create. I could sense something was unsettling Steve whenever I looked into his eyes. He was a man defeated.

A new head of state was in charge, a bespectacled bully with a burly frame and Deep Southern accent. This abrasive character would micromanage everything, intimidating many with a coarse my-way-or-the-highway attitude.

Given that it was the summer of 1992, many of the wrestling fans out there are going to assume I am describing 'Cowboy' Bill Watts, the no-nonsense alpha male who was appointed to lead WCW as its Executive Vice President of Wrestling Operations. Well, I'm not. I am trying to illustrate an accurate depiction of Steve's mum, Beverly, who came to stay with us for a short while after Stephanie was born.

I felt incredibly uncomfortable around Beverly, but I knew she was here to stay. I tried my utmost to appease her increasing demands.

Initially, I was so excited about meeting Steve's mum, and I really hoped to develop a lasting friendship with the grandmother of our child. When Steve and I first started dating, I had pushed him to allow me to meet Beverly. But when I did, it was evident from the onset that there was an animosity towards me based on her pre-conception that I was the wicked home wrecker who stole her little boy away from Kathy.

She would never accept my word that it was Steve who pursued me and there was a lasting resentment that never truly faded.

Beverly also had very rigid ideas on how to raise a family. She was deeply critical of every aspect of my homemaking, from the feeding of my children, to housecleaning and cooking. Even my sense of fashion was scrutinised, as she frequently made comments on my choice of clothing. She would often leave in a huff if things were not done her way, and I could not handle being the focal point within such a judgmental atmosphere. It drove me to tears and I even felt forced to leave the house and stay the night in a hotel.

When Steve finally managed to contact the hotel, he reached out to me and pleaded that I come home. He explained that his mum could often be challenging, but I just had to find a way to deal with it. He assured me Beverly was leaving soon and our lives would be back to normal.

I went out to clear my head but returned later that day. As soon as I got back, Beverly came over to apologise for driving me away from my own home. I could still tell she had a problem with me but, for the good of our new family, I was keen to bury the issue and so I hugged her.

When Beverly left after three weeks, it finally gave us a chance to truly bond as a family. Steve loved being a new dad, as he would spend hours cradling Stephanie. Jade was also amazing with her, and I could tell she really enjoyed playing the big sister.

Within the warm envelope of our lovely little log cabin, we suddenly had such a happy and loving lifestyle. It was the perfect environment for our young family.

Over the next few months, I rarely got the chance to go to Steve's matches. Instead, I stayed at home as a full-time mum and homemaker. This suited Steve too, as he preferred to keep a distance between his family and working life.

By 1993, Steve had moved into the tag team ranks, as he started to team with 'Flyin'' Brian Pillman. They rapidly progressed from a makeshift duo to the number one team in the division. Steve still had a desire to be recognised as a singles star, but Brian came up with some really neat ideas for them, and they got over huge as The Hollywood Blonds. The fans loved to jeer the arrogant pair who would goad their opponents with camera-winding taunts, outrageous actions and despicable double-team cheating.

It was not long before the Blonds would capture the gold, winning the Unified NWA and WCW Tag Team Championships from Ricky 'The Dragon' Steamboat and Shane Douglas at a taping held on 2nd March of that year. Steve had loved working with Steamboat in the months prior, as part of the hot feud between Sting's Squadron and The Dangerous Alliance. This eventually led to a thrilling match for his Television Championship at the *Clash of Champions XX* in Atlanta, in which 'The Dragon' took the belt.

Originally, Steve was demoralised when he was paired with Brian, fearing it would stall the progress of his solo career. In truth, it was the chemistry of The Hollywood Blonds that pushed him to the main event of the promotion.

In the second week of March, most of the top talent in WCW had been sent overseas, as the company presented *The Real Event* tour of the United Kingdom and Ireland. As a result, the domestic circuits of house shows were built around the Blonds and their defences of the titles against the former champions. The team were on a mission to excel, and prove to the front office that they could carry any shows they headlined against their challengers.

That week, the kids and I were faced with a huge challenge of our own back at the cabin. A destructive hurricane blizzard, dubbed by the American media as *The Superstorm of 1993*, had ripped its way through a large expanse of the east. Originating from the Gulf of Mexico, it tore through to the States and even all the way to Canada and Cuba, leaving a trail of carnage and claiming over three hundred lives. Georgia was ravaged by whiteout conditions, and our family was left with no power to the cabin as the conditions worsened.

As I clung to Jade and Stephanie to ride out the heavy winds and snow, our neighbour J.L. arrived at the door.

J.L. said that he was not going to leave us, and he went on to tell us that he had set up a spare room at his family's home, which was also fitted with a wood-burning stove. He pledged to cook us a really nice meal on the stove, which would also keep us cosy until the storm had passed. We were so grateful that his family immediately thought of our welfare as soon as the electricity to the street had dropped. Meanwhile, I feared for Steve's safety as the storm gained intensity.

Each night, I would wait with anxiety for Steve's phone call. I needed the reassurance that he had made it to shelter unscathed as the snowstorm continued into the Carolinas, where he had been booked to perform that week.

Shane Douglas, former WCW wrestler: "The matches that Steve, Brian, Ricky and I had in WCW are still some of my best and favourite matches. We put absolutely everything in to them. It didn't matter if there were 2,000 people in the building, or 20 people, we would tear down the house night after night.

Here's an example of how we would perform no matter what. In 1993 there was this huge blizzard and we were wrestling in this small town four hours' drive north of Atlanta, right up in the mountains. When we got there, they had been waiting three or four days for this terrible weather to hit. The whole of the Eastern seaboard had about three or four feet of snow, and I'd never seen snow like that before.

I'm driving up to the venue and making stops for gas or food and all the stores were empty! I mean it was like it was the apocalypse and people were just getting all these provisions. I couldn't understand it though, as I'd never known snow to hit like that in Atlanta before. As we got to the venue there wasn't a snowflake on the ground. As the first match was taking place I went outside to call my wife and it had just started snowing, but only a regular kind of snowfall.

Anyway after a few more matches it was the interval, and I could hear all these cars starting up in the parking lot and driving away. There were a few more matches and then Steve, Brian, Ricky and I went on dead last. And when we went out I counted from the apron and there were just 24 people left in the building. And we went out and did about 52 minutes and those fans who stayed got a great match. We ended up being snowed in for six days! But that's just how it was with us guys; we would always put on a good show.

There was an NWA tradition that the world title went on last and the tag team title was the semi-main event. At that time, Sting was taking on Vader for the world title, no disrespect to either of those two great workers but they couldn't do what we did. We would take the fans on a real journey in our matches and after a while it was hard for that main event to follow what was basically a 55-minute wrestling clinic and so for the first time in NWA history the tag match was the main event and the world title was the semi-main event.

I'm not bragging, but we all had such admiration for each other in those matches and all of us were all so competent that we never had any messed up matches."

Regardless of the venue or the size of the crowd, Steve and Brian were continuing to steal the shows in their series of rematches against the former holders of the crowns. It seemed that they were destined for big things as they gained increasing notoriety in their matches with a wide range of contenders.

Throughout the summer of 1993, the Blonds faced a diverse array of teams in their defences of their tag titles; from the returning stalwart 'Nature Boy' Ric Flair and any combination of his Four Horsemen partners Arn Anderson and Paul Roma, to the flashy athleticism of the youthful duo of Marcus Alexander Bagwell and 2 Cold Scorpio. They were defeating everyone in their path after each of their challengers had experienced a 'brush with greatness'.

While the Blonds were tearing it up on the road, I continued to get the support and company from my neighbours. Together, J.L. and his sister Ann created such a warm environment for Jade, Stephanie and me, and they were like a surrogate family to us. They knew I was missing my fiancé, so we used to host these really fun pay-per-view parties at the cabin. J.L. and his wife Gayle would bring their three sons, Darren, Scott and Nathan, while Ann and her husband Clifford would bring their son Jonathan. We would get pizzas, soft drinks and beer to the house, and watch 'Stunning' Steve every time he set foot in the ring.

I accepted that Steve no longer wanted me around the ring as his valet, but I still wanted to be at his side. As I watched him perform on the small screen, my heart was with him at each event, cheering his every move.

As autumn was approaching, I got a call from Jerry Jarrett. He pitched an idea for me to return to the USWA under the name Nanny Simpson, managing Brian Christopher and participating in a series of mixed gender tag matches similar to my previous run in the Memphis office. After discussing the idea with Steve, we turned down the offer. He was wary of Jarrett's intentions, and our time as a family together had become increasingly rare.

Whenever Steve got time off we would spend time with the kids. Even though we didn't see much of each other we remained incredibly close and both of us were so content with our happy little family unit.

With Jade and Stephanie bringing so much joy to my relationship with Steve, it reminded me on the importance of family, so I flew my brother and mum out to spend time with us.

The time spent with my mum was invaluable. As a child, it was a daily struggle to cope with her alcoholism, but she had made a real effort to clear herself of her addiction.

I wanted her to provide the love to her grandchildren that she could never give to me, and I yearned for her to be a part of my life again.

Seeing her so healthy and lucid healed many wounds. It created a new start for the both of us.

As if things could not get any better, Steve got the message that we had been waiting almost two years to hear. The annulment of his marriage to Kathy had been concluded.

We could finally start to make plans for our wedding day.

For so long, Steve and I could not truly express our commitment to each other and formalise our mutual love. With his annulment to Kathy, there was no longer anything holding us back. We were looking ahead to the celebration of becoming husband and wife.

It seemed we could finally revel in the joys of arranging our wedding. But it was not long before Steve's mum interfered.

His first marriage to Kathy had been a big church ceremony, so Beverly insisted that he should opt for a significantly lesser service this time. She would persist until we conceded that we would just hold a small ritual at the house, and she even asserted that I should wear a suit to the ceremony in place of a dress.

My childhood dream of a big plush wedding was not to be, but it didn't matter. The most important thing was that Steve and I were making a commitment to each other and our family.

I made no hesitation to visit the local church, the Dorsett Shoals Baptist Church in nearby Douglasville, to book the pastor for our nuptials.

When I met the pastor, Tom Kaplan, he spoke to me about his personal journey in finding God. He explained he had turned away from the Jewish faith from which he was raised after finding his true calling with Christianity.

"Can I book you for a wedding at my house please," I said extending my hand to him.

"Hold on a minute, we need sit down and talk about this," he said with a calm authority.

The pastor seemed quite surprised at my forward approach, but I was invited through to his office. He motioned at me to take a seat.

"So Jeanie, where are you at spiritually?" he asked me from across his desk.

Tom sat and listened as I discussed my faith, starting with my underprivileged childhood in Southend. I even recalled the story about being sent home from school for incessant crying as the whole class watched a film called *King of Kings*. I revealed that it was the first time I felt truly connected to Jesus Christ, after I witnessed the undying compassion for others that he embodied.

For me, the meeting with the pastor was refreshing, as I was able to discuss my life and convictions with someone who seemed genuinely interested in my beliefs.

"I can see that you're a Christian Jeanie, but what about your partner? Is he a Christian?" he asked as he leaned into his chair.

It suddenly dawned on me that Steve and I had never talked about the concept of belief to any extent.

Whenever I would discuss my faith with Steve, he was usually dismissive. I could tell that it forced him out of his comfort zone, so I never pursued the issue.

Tom explained that we would both need to come to the church for counselling, emphasising that he needed to establish Steve's views on spirituality. This was an essential process in order for the pair of us to be wed in a Christian service. He also said it would also be nice if we attended the church on a Sunday so he could see the ongoing commitment we were making to God as a couple on the road to matrimony.

Later that night, Steve and I spoke about my meeting with the Pastor. I asked if he would support the suggestion for counselling at the church.

"No way!" he declared, glaring at me with bewilderment.

When I went back to see Tom for the first session I was too embarrassed to tell him the truth and explain why Steve was not there. I suggested that his chaotic wrestling schedule prevented him from attending, but asserted that I was happy to start the counselling process on my own. I claimed that Steve would join us as soon as his schedule would permit him to do so.

"Well, let's start," Tom smiled.

A few days later, I went back to meet the staff at the church, and we started chatting over coffee and cake. From that day something just clicked, and I started to enjoy learning about the Christian faith.

I would intently listen to Tom's sermons on a Sunday and, after he had finished speaking, I would leave to study up on the Bible. The next day I would bombard him with questions on faith.

It interested me so much that I soon started a Bible study group so I could share my love of the teachings of Christ.

Regardless, I still couldn't convince Steve to come along with me. I knew he never entirely approved of my rediscovered faith, or liked any of my new friends at the church, but I was happy and content. It gave me a renewed sense of purpose when he was on tour.

When Steve returned, I could no longer quell my feelings towards our wedding. I stated that I wanted to be married in the Church, surrounded by friends and family.

Speechless, he simply stared at the floor shaking his head, but he agreed.

I was no longer going to suppress my faith to suit Beverly's hopes for a house marriage, and I was glad I stood my ground to be wed in the church.

It was originally Steve's idea to get married but, instead of celebrating our union, it sometimes seemed that he was just keen to get hitched any way he could.

I could tell that he was not exactly enamoured with the thought of being baptised, but he acquiesced, knowing that it would give me a marriage I dreamed of since childhood.

Steve always maintained that it didn't really matter to him where or how we were wed, but he knew that the church had become such a large part of my life. He told me that he did have some mild Christian beliefs but, most of all, he just wanted to be married.

I was surprised at Steve's change of heart, but I figured that he had probably endured a lifetime restricted by Beverly's stringent instructions. I sensed that he was actually relishing the idea of proving something to his mother with an overdue defiant act. The baptism was Steve's way of proving to his mother that he was his own man. He was now in control of his own life.

On 12th December, Steve and I were scheduled to be baptised together in preparation for our wedding the following week. Although this was a large step in my personal commitment to Christianity, it was a day that I will mostly remember for all the wrong reasons.

As Steve and I ushered forward for our immersion, he lost his footing and ended up slipping. He fell headfirst into the pool of water and became completely soaked.

In all of the years I had seen Steve perform as a wrestler, I can honestly say that it was the most spectacular bump that I ever saw him take. He became incredibly flustered as he struggled to find his footing, emerging fully drenched. Once he got up, I looked at his dripping face, trying to suppress myself.

I could hold it no longer, and burst into fits of laughter. It wasn't long before everyone in attendance was sharing in the hysterics. Nobody could believe what had just happened.

Leading up to our baptism, Beverly had made it clear that she objected to the service. We were mildly disappointed that she refused to attend, so the cacophony of chuckles from Steve's wet tumble were more than welcome.

Our wedding had been set for 18th December 1993, which was also Steve's birthday.

In the run up to the service, Jade was so happy to be a bridesmaid, and she looked forward to the big day with great excitement.

My other bridesmaid, my neighbour Ann, helped me plan the wedding. We arranged it all, from the flowers, to the music and everything else that would make the day so special.

Sadly, Beverly bore a grudge since I nixed her idea of a home wedding. She refused to bring any of Steve's family to the wedding other than her husband Ken.

It was such a shame for Steve, and I felt bad for him.

My family all flew in from England and, with my stepfather Fred Wallace giving me away; I arrived at the church in the most beautiful white dress.

As I slowly walked down the aisle and towards the altar, I caught sight of Steve and smiled. He looked so handsome in his tuxedo. It was a huge relief that the service went without a hitch and the both of us had a lovely day.

I still have the videotape of the ceremony and it gives me warmth whenever I view it.

Steve and I were just so happy to be finally married.

We had already started to create a loving home for our children, but we were now, truly, a family.

Getting married to Steve, 1993.

13 INJURED PRIDE

After the wedding, our lives seemed to be going the way we wanted. Steve and I had created a loving base in Georgia, and our children, Jade and Stephanie, were both healthy and happy.

Steve's dreams of singles stardom were finally coming true. Nine days after our wedding, he was booked on WCW's final pay-per-view of the year, *Starrcade 1993*. It was the night that he would be crowned the new WCW United States Heavyweight Champion by ousting his long-time ring rival Dustin Rhodes in a two-out-of-three falls match for the title.

He was relieved that his career was finally going the way he wanted. He had been concerned that internal politics were the reason that The Hollywood Blonds had disbanded, but he was now starting to climb the upper ranks of WCW as the solo performer that he always wanted to be.

Once again, his efforts were being recognised by the office and his future with the company was looking promising. In the years prior, the holder of the United States title was considered the number one contender to the holder of the WCW World Heavyweight Championship. With hard work, Steve was certain that it was only a matter of time before he would get his chance to lead the promotion.

Beyond his ascension as a talent, a number of internal changes within WCW were also having a positive impact on our lives.

Eric Bischoff, who I only knew as a backstage interviewer when I first joined the promotion, had since been appointed to lead the management of WCW following the resignation of Bill Watts in the spring of 1993. Eric had started to restructure the finances of WCW in an effort to make it profitable, and one of his first decisions was to drop a significant portion of the non-televised events promoted by the company.

By the summer, he ceased the touring house shows which he identified had been making losses for the office. This actually meant that the contracted talent would work lesser dates but take home the same guaranteed income.

Another change that Eric instigated was the relocation of the company's television tapings to the Disney/MGM Studios near Orlando, Florida. The crew would record multiple weeks' worth, and in some cases months' worth, of programming from this location, which resulted in a massive reduction in the production costs for the shows. Unlike the strict backstage environment that Watts had enforced, Eric encouraged the wrestlers to bring their families to the event. The Disney tapings provided a fantastic opportunity for us to visit Steve at work, as once the recording had finished we were able to explore the rest of The Walt Disney World Resort. It was a magical family experience as we delighted Stephanie with the parades and attractions of the theme park.

We were now able to spend more time as a family. Steve was working a lighter schedule, yet it did not affect his salary. Many of the stresses caused by touring were now alleviated, and the rigour on his body had been drastically reduced.

At long last, our family had received the greatest gift of all: time together.

Steve and Stephanie at the Disney/MGM Studios in Orlando, 1993.

It was important that we allowed Jade to see her dad, even though he was rarely in contact with her. In the years since we had moved to Atlanta, Chris had broken up with Toni and was in the process of a divorce. Having sustained a serious beating at the hands of Chris, leaving her with a broken nose, their marriage continued to deteriorate. After enduring repeated incidents of his chronic womanising, Toni eventually gave up, and was driven towards a relationship with Kerry Von Erich in the last few months of 1992. Unfortunately, she would suffer further heartbreak. Kerry committed suicide on 18th February 1993.

After splitting with Toni, Chris had started a new relationship and seemed happy again.

When he eventually came to visit Jade in January 1994, he was accompanied by his new girlfriend Brandi Freeman. The couple announced that they were four months pregnant. Steve still held a grudge with him, but any frictions the pair had were not visible during the visit. In fact, Chris' stories of his recent wrestling tours of Israel had Steve in fits of laughter.

We had discovered a great balance with Steve's working life and essential family time. He cherished our children, and he never seemed to be too busy for them, even when he was on the road.

Whilst on tour, Steve's body was struck by a bad case of gastroenteritis, and he was forced to come home. After he was cleared of his ailment, which inflamed his stomach and intestines, he went straight back to his performance schedule.

Within a few days of his return to work, Stephanie started looking off-colour. Still a very young infant, her condition deteriorated at a rapid pace, and she became quite ill. As she was continuously vomiting, I became worried so I took her to see the doctor. I was informed that a large fluid intake and dosage of antibiotics were needed to treat the infection. As a precaution, she was admitted to the hospital.

Steve and Stephanie at the log cabin, 1994.

I called Steve to give him the update that his daughter was ill. I reassured him that Stephanie was going to be fine, but he felt powerless being on tour at another city. Immediately concerned, he needed to see her, and drove at least six hours just to be at her bedside. It was important for Steve that his daughter saw him too, and that his family knew that no distance would ever prevent him from coming home for his family. He stayed with her as long as he could, even though he would have to drive for a full day to make it to the next show. It was an act of kindness that I would never forget.

But I should have expected that from Steve, as he was always so caring towards the children. He loved to play games with them, have fun on the trampoline and take them out for fun rides on the four-wheeler. Happiness seemed to be something that radiated from Steve. He was a loving father, and he seemed really content in his role within WCW as he continued his reign near the top of the card.

Even though I had not worked with WCW since the fall of 1991, I still saw some of the old crew. Steve and Brian Pillman had become really close since their days as a tag team, and Brian would often visit the house with his wife Melanie.

We occasionally had dinner with Dustin and Terri, and frequently arranged play dates with their daughter Dakota. Even Magnum T.A., who was responsible for my career break in Atlanta, came by the house to see the family when Stephanie was a baby.

Terri Runnels, former WCW wrestling manager Alexandra York: "[My daughter] Dakota and Stephanie enjoyed playing together whenever we went out to their home in Villa Rica. I always thought it was interesting that an English rose landed so deep in the country in Georgia, the juxtaposition of those two locations and all that it entails is very interesting! I have nothing but fond memories of times with Jeanie."

For a young family, our community of friends in Atlanta provided such a nurturing environment where each of us could live our dreams. It would take an unstoppable force to change our joy.

By the summer of 1994, Hulkamania was running wild throughout World Championship Wrestling. The man who had been the biggest star in wrestling for over a decade, Hulk Hogan, had just signed the most lucrative contract in the history of the sport to join the promotion. He was the recognisable face leading the WWF during its national expansion, and his widespread appeal enabled the company to push its business into international markets. After leaving the WWF in 1993, Hogan had since crossed over into other forays; however Eric Bischoff was keen to position him as the new face of WCW in an attempt to increase its brand awareness within the mainstream media. But there was a huge shift in the culture of the company upon his arrival.

Hulk would make his in-ring debut for the company at the *Bash at the Beach 1994* pay-per-view as he was immediately thrust into the main event to challenge Ric Flair for the WCW World Heavyweight Championship. That night, Steve was also in the biggest match of his career, as he was set to face Ricky Steamboat in a defence of his United States title.

Steve and Ricky always had a great chemistry in the ring during their time together in the promotion. In fact, Steve would often cite Ricky as the greatest opponent he had ever faced. It was a rivalry that had transcended the singles and tag team ranks.

With the celebrity of Hogan promising to broaden the market of WCW, Ricky and Steve were looking to put on a classic match in front of the larger audience that had been attracted to try WCW for the first time.

They excelled, putting on a twenty-minute match that stole the show. But it didn't matter. Regardless of what anyone did to elevate their game at the event, the night was all about Hulk. In his first match with the company, Hogan beat Flair for its top prize.

Backstage, there was a realisation that Hogan would not be moving from atop the promotion anytime soon, and word spread that he had secured a binding clause for creative control into his contract agreement. In other words, if Hulk did not approve of a match or storyline proposed for his character, he had the right to outright refuse it.

Hulk was an outsider joining the promotion. Concern that Hogan would trust very few of the existing WCW talent changed the dynamic of the locker room.

It was not long before an influx of former WWF talent joined the ranks of the Atlanta office. This would inadvertently result in the most humiliating night in Steve's professional career.

After a long championship reign lasting nine months, Steve finally dropped the U.S. title to Steamboat at the *Clash of Champions XXVIII* special. They were scheduled to have a rematch at the ensuing *Fall Brawl '94* pay-per-view from Roanoke, Virginia.

One of the reasons that Steve loved working with Ricky was due to his unselfishness in the ring, and would make him look good by selling his offence. It was a rivalry which enhanced both men.

However, on the night of *Fall Brawl*, Steamboat could not defend the title due to a back injury he had sustained in a previous match. Nick Bockwinkel, a wrestling great from the glory days of the AWA, was now working for WCW as an on-screen Commissioner. He declared Steve the new champion, on the provision that he defended the title that night.

As Steve protested, 'Hacksaw' Jim Duggan stormed down to the ring waving the stars and stripes of the national flag. Duggan was a veteran star who had been one of the more outlandish characters employed by the WWF during the late eighties and early nineties. Defeating Steve with one move, he squashed him in rapid order to lift the strap in a match lasting a degrading nineteen seconds.

The efforts of Steve's first reign were now forgotten. At a mere five minutes, his second marriage with the belt was the shortest in wrestling history and his only defence of it was a joke.

After his rematch loss at *Halloween Havoc 1994*, Steve was disappointed to learn that there were no plans for him to be featured in the company's forthcoming pay-per-view schedule. At the *Clash of the Champions XXIX* live television special a few weeks later, he again lost to Duggan within moments of the opening bell, this time by disqualification when Vader ran in and attacked 'Hacksaw'. With a new contender laying down a challenge for the belt, it fully removed Steve from the title picture.

The impact of three successive high-profile defeats devastated the credibility of 'Stunning' Steve Austin. For three years, Steve had been a mainstay talent for WCW. He appeared on each of its television specials and pay-per-view shows, and worked hard to maintain his position in the upper tier of the promotion. But now, the importance of his role had diminished.

It was clear that Steve's singles career in WCW was in decline. Humiliated in a sudden spate of televised losses to more ex-WWF stars, he knew that there was no chance he would headline anytime soon. WCW was now solely interested in banking on established ex-WWF wrestlers, with no succession plan for the development of its hungry, younger talent.

The increased media interest on WCW was not being used to spotlight its existing stars or create new marquee attractions. Its cards were filling up with talent that the WWF had pushed in the eighties.

For the first time, Steve appeared despondent.

He was starting to usher away from any conversation relating to his career. In fact, his internalised frustrations grew to the point that he was no longer comfortable having his family around the business.

Any future family trips to let Stephanie see her dad work at the Disney/MGM Studios would come to an abrupt halt. Steve was starting to feel ashamed of his position, and his face looked truly defeated when he would come home from work. All he wanted to do was escape.

I knew he was unhappy, so I was generally filling my time trying to make our house as comfortable as it could be for his return.

A bit of light-hearted fun was brought into our lives by way of a new business which, amazingly, spawned from Stephanie's first birthday. She had become a huge fan of Barney, the dancing purple dinosaur from the popular children's television show *Barney & Friends*, and we were scouring the stores for merchandise of her favourite hero. No matter where we looked, we could not find anything on the shelf. It seemed like Barney was selling out everywhere.

I felt a reawakening of the entrepreneurial spirit that encouraged me to open up Genies during my time in Dallas. After realising Barney's immense popularity, but dearth of associated merchandise, I figured that there was a gap in the market for a live-action version who could visit kids' parties. I knew that the interactive experience could really make a child's celebration feel special and personalised.

Purchasing a Barney fancy-dress costume, I placed an advert in the local press that the friendly dinosaur was now available for hire. We were inundated with requests from the onset, and it was not long before I was driving to homes all over the town, dancing and playing with the kids under my new alias.

It was not long before the demand for Barney was too high for one person to handle, so I even enlisted the help of my neighbour Ann. It was a really happy venture for the two of us, as we loved bringing smiles to children's faces each time we were called to a party.

Bruce, Gayle, J.L., Jade, Steve and I celebrate Stephanie's third birthday party with Barney.

On top of the Barney gig, I was still focusing on raising the children, and I filled up the rest of my diary by working on the garden and helping out at the church. I had just started a volunteer job teaching a Sunday school for children and I took the time to further absorb the scripture of the Bible.

For the first time since running Genies in Dallas, I had built a full life to keep me occupied while Steve was wrestling.

When Steve would come home, he started to become pensive around me. He kept everything inside, and would not communicate any of his career concerns which were clearly bothering him.

In an effort to lighten conversation, I decided to start talking about other subjects when he was around. As he listened, I could see his face turn. Steve had an ability to block out the world, distancing himself from everyone else in the room.

He would sit for hours and say nothing, but I almost felt guilty for not being able to reach out to him. Sometimes, he would give me the most vacant of stares, without saying a word.

His taciturn nature could be very cruel. My mind would try and make sense of what was not being said. The prolonged silences would force me to question if I had done something to upset him. I sensed that the quality of his home life was not enough for him to be content. Moreover, the love of his family was insufficient to counterbalance the emptiness he was feeling from the downturn of his career.

Persevering, I would tell him all about my life in Atlanta, and try to include him in an effort to stimulate a dialogue. But as I discussed my interest on the teachings of Christ his mood would change.

"Damn it Jeanie, you have more books than a preacher!" snapped Steve.

Tension had been brewing within him for a while, but he was now taking his career frustrations home with him. This intensified as a knee injury forced Steve off the road in December 1994.

Jade, who had previously maintained a good relationship with her new stepdad, was now coming into frequent conflict with him. He had no time for her rebellious antics and would often get very personal during his arguments with her. Entering her teens, she was at a delicate age, and I would express concern that he was crushing her confidence.

With Steve becoming increasingly irritable, he started to exhibit more reclusive behaviour as he continued to recuperate at the cabin. More frequently, he wanted to be left alone and would ignore our presence if we were in the same room. He could zone out for hours, and would then use drink to try and flush away his problems.

Luckily, the tension within Steve would pass, and we would continue to have fun in regular family activities.

When the girls were away, Steve and I used to go out to the woods and created many happy memories. One Christmas, he bought me a .38 Smith & Wesson Special, and we used to love shooting beer cans, and searching for treasure with our metal detector.

Another time, Steve asked if I wanted to go to the lake to try fishing.

It was a stocked lake, which was a hotspot for catfish, and he took along some worms. He taught me how to cast the bait using the fishing line and, sure enough, it worked.

It seemed that I managed to hook in a fish each time I threw the rod at the water. Reeling them in, one after another, I asked Steve if he would help remove my catches, and assist with the bait.

As I tallied a total of thirteen fish, I looked at Steve. Despite his determination, he had only managed to catch one the whole day.

We had a great laugh, but it was the last time he ever took me to the lake.

It was a nice distraction from the nagging pains of Steve's injury. He would miss over three months before returning to WCW in March 1995.

When Steve returned to work, there had been little change within the company and he remained disillusioned. Meanwhile, he started to develop a reputation for his defiance towards company management. He became vocal on his criticisms on the direction of the promotion and its handling of talent.

He wanted to know where his career was heading. It was suggested that there was going to be a reformation of The Hollywood Blonds, and plans were being put in place to recapture the magic that had been created by Brian and Steve two years prior. This time, the change to the tag team ranks was being welcomed by Steve.

He had been forced to accept that he was going nowhere as a singles competitor. Although a backward step, the guarantee of regular work in a featured tag team at least meant his job would be secure.

Two months passed, and The Blonds reunion had still not materialised. As his impatience festered, Steve was informed that he was being sent by WCW to work for New Japan Pro Wrestling under a talent trading agreement between the two companies.

Steve took the news of his Japanese booking as an insult and he was convinced that the overseas tour was a punishment for his internal criticisms of the product. WCW must have deemed him expendable. Usually, the company only sent over talent which was not critical to its shows. Most of all, he felt betrayed that none of the promises that had been made to him had been delivered.

The circuit of NJPW that June was an unmitigated disaster for Steve. During a match on the tour, the worst happened: he suffered a tear to his tricep. Due to another injury, he was unable to work yet again with an unknown period for recovery.

Requiring surgery, Steve needed to take the time to heal as it was his second major injury within a period of less than a year. As he was recovering, I flew my brother over from England and he stayed with us for a few weeks. Steve was not taking any chances with the rehabilitation of his body, and he seemed uninterested in joining my brother or me in any social activities when we would leave the house. When he was off with the wound to his knee, he was so impatient to be back on WCW's shows. This time however, he seemed unwilling to return before he was fully ready.

Tony Schiavone, who was working as an Executive Producer of WCW's television shows, called the house. He wanted to know if Steve would be available to attend the company's next round of tapings.

Miserable with his life, Steve refused to talk to the company.

On 15th September, he received another phone call to the house, while I was out with my brother.

This time, the person on the other end of the line was Eric Bischoff. We returned to find out that 'Stunning' Steve Austin had been fired from WCW.

A ninety-day injury rule had recently been incorporated into the contracts of all talent employed by the promotion. As a result, anyone who sustained an injury which would result in a three month departure from in-ring action could be terminated. It was a controversial clause that had already led to the removal of Ricky Steamboat and Harley Race from the roster. During the call, Eric noted that the company was exercising this right and thus ending Steve's agreement.

Our family were now victim to a change enforced by Bischoff.

Steve was incensed. His aggravation towards WCW had reached boiling point, and his fury finally needed an outlet.

He then got a call from an old friend who could give him one.

14 AN EXTREME DECISION

With no steady wage, and his future prospects within the wrestling industry uncertain, Steve was a man full of doubt when he received a call from his old friend and colleague, Paul Heyman.

Having acted as the on-screen manager for Steve under the name Paul E. Dangerously in WCW, Heyman sympathised with his plight. Paul had also been fired from the company in early 1993 following a dispute with its former head honcho, Bill Watts.

Aside from offering condolence, Paul also saw opportunity in Steve's burning rage.

In the years since his own dismissal, Heyman had been instrumental in redefining the sport of professional wrestling, offering an alternative product to a new generation of rabid fans. He had purchased the Philadelphia-based independent promotion Extreme Championship Wrestling, which was pushing a new brand of wrestling within the United States. Aimed at a mature audience, ECW was vastly different to the family-friendly WWF and WCW promotions which were vying for mainstream dominance.

It was a venture which celebrated its own sense of counter-culture, centred on intense (and sometimes controversial) storylines. Amidst some quality in-ring action, ECW placed an emphasis on hard-core violence and bloody brawling, sexual innuendo and innovative interview packages, which were often laden with expletives. Low production values and the use of recognisable music only served to enhance the gritty realism of its shows, providing an authentic and interactive experience for its growing fan-base.

Led by the creative genius of Heyman, the promotion was anchored by a hard-working crew of wrestlers and a small cluster of production staff, giving their all into each show and following their maverick leader with a cult-like obedience. As the reputation of the company grew, it created an underground movement which was starting to influence the major federations.

Most of all, it also celebrated the independence of its talent, allowing them to be experimental in their characters and promo interviews. Fostering home grown stars to find their niche, it was also a place for established acts to be reinvented or find a new calling.

Untapped potential was something that Paul had always seen in Steve. He lobbied for him to join the Dangerous Alliance in 1991, after seeing a raw value in him when he arrived in Atlanta.

Four years later, Steve was now being asked to join the revolution as the flagship star of ECW. It was a venue where he could vent out his career frustrations, and ridicule the establishment that he had endured for years. He was now a renegade talent in a rebellious promotion.

Paul sensed there was more beneath the surface of 'Stunning' Steve Austin. Together, they worked to accentuate the qualities of Steve's real personality. The aim was to create a new character that would finally play to his strengths.

Steve had made no secret that he had become disenchanted with wrestling during his latter days with WCW. He was an embittered talent in an era where ex-WWF superstars were deemed to be of the most value to the Atlanta office, regardless of the efforts of its loyal mainstays.

Renamed 'Superstar' Steve Austin, he was now cast in a role which suited him; as an embittered former star from a major promotion. His character was to be a wrestler at a breaking point, riddled with stress and bitterness stemming from years of being held back and never reaching his true potential.

Being held back is certainly something that Steve never experienced during his first appearance with the group on 16th September 1995. In his debut, he immediately took aim at Hulk Hogan, the star he blamed for his slide down the card at WCW.

In the closing moments of ECW's television show broadcast, the cameras frantically cut to a backstage altercation between New Jack and the promotion's top tag-team, The Public Enemy. Joey Styles, who was the host of ECW's weekly programming, sprinted to the back only to find a crazed Steve Austin, clad in a homemade version of the trademark red and yellow tank top and bandana worn by 'The Hulkster'.

Steve manically flexed his muscles and spouted the typical Hogan catchphrases before lampooning him and saying how tired his act had become, ripping off the shirt with disgust. He decried Hulk's gimmick, saying that it was lame and not enough to get the job done in a promotion like ECW. Styles was speechless as a truly wired Steve stormed off, and the episode came to an abrupt end.

His next appearance at the ECW Arena on 28th October was equally chaotic, as he was engaged in a wild pull-apart brawl with the reigning ECW Champion, The Sandman during his defence of the title against the young underdog Mikey Whipwreck. A few weeks later, Eric Bischoff was the next victim of 'The Extreme Superstar' as he dressed up in a jet-black wig and suit, impersonating his former boss with fervour and sheer vitriol in a hilarious backstage skit that again mocked WCW's ageing headliners.

Although he had not yet been cleared to wrestle due to the muscle tear, Steve had propelled himself into the main event picture with his interruptions of the company's top matches and by turning heads with his outlandish antics.

When he did eventually return to action on the 18th November, he was immediately pushed to the top, competing in matches for ECW's top prize from the onset.

Even though Extreme Championship Wrestling did not provide the same level of long-term security that his contract with WCW had provided, I was relieved that Steve had found an opportunity to find work so quickly after being released. It provided a boost to his self-esteem and it was clear he was having fun with his character.

I never had the opportunity to see Steve perform at any of Heyman's shows, as I had become quite independent with my full schedule back home. The Barney parties were still going strong, I was keeping busy with my church commitments, and the raising of my two daughters was making the time pass quickly while he was away.

When Steve returned from Philadelphia, he was a man with a renewed sense of purpose. With the reinvention of his career, it seemed that he had finally regained control over his own destiny. I hoped that he was now willing to communicate some of the discontent that had been brewing inside him for months.

Unfortunately, Steve never did share his innermost feelings, whether he wanted to express angst or joy. Instead, he simply wanted to convey a directive that would affect his family.

While he was away working for Paul, he had made a firm decision regarding our future.

"We're moving," he ordered.

I was in complete and utter shock; I felt truly blindsided by the decision.

For over three years, our family had gradually created the beloved home that I had always longed for as a child, and even as a young adult. I knew that Steve still harboured resentment towards WCW, but he never once told me how much he had been hurt by their decision to release him.

But this was the first time I had ever heard Steve express a desire to leave Georgia, and his conviction stunned me.

I felt so powerless that my fate had been decided, and I was saddened that he had not even asked for my input. I would have understood if he only told me that our home harboured too many negative associations with his former employer, but he would remain silent when I asked his reasons.

Because he never spoke, I felt wounded. Relocating seemed like such an extreme measure.

As I tried to get my head round the impending change to our lives, another was on its way.

Steve had received an offer to join the WWF.

15 A WORLD OF OPPORTUNITY

Spawning from the Capitol Wrestling Corporation, the World Wrestling Federation was founded in 1963 by promoters Vincent James McMahon and Toots Mondt. By 1982, the promotion had changed hands, as the young Vincent Kennedy McMahon and his wife Linda had bought out the assets of his father's company. Together, they set their sights beyond a primary operation of the New York area.

After an audacious national expansion of operations in the mid-eighties, the Connecticut-based World Wrestling Federation had reigned supreme as the undisputed market leader in the professional wrestling industry.

However, fortunes had changed for the Federation by the mid-nineties.

It was hurting due to a series of sex scandals and as a result of a costly trial with the federal government during an investigation into allegations of steroid distribution within the company.

It was not long before the bad public relations caused by the court case had a negative impact on the WWF's revenues. The promotion had suffered a downturn in attendance, and the inevitable reductions in pay forced some of the WWF's upper level talent to seek work elsewhere.

Meanwhile, under the leadership of Eric Bischoff, WCW had become a credible threat to the WWF's position, and both companies were vying for domination within the industry. The competition was intensified following the advent of the live *WCW Monday Nitro* show in September 1995, which ran at the same time as the weekly broadcast of *WWF Monday Night Raw* on the USA Network.

With heightened tensions between the two market leaders, the head-to-head ratings battle soon became known as the Monday Night Wars.

As many of the WWF's veteran stars had since fled to Atlanta, there were some gaping holes in Vince McMahon's roster. His response was to showcase fresh talent into the main event picture, branding them 'The New Generation'.

As one of the top stars in McMahon's locker room, Kevin Nash had been thriving under this youth drive. Renamed Diesel, he had left WCW as a lower card talent with limited prospects and within two years of joining the Federation, had held every championship within the company. Nash also wielded a lot of power backstage, and was part of a posse of five friends known within the industry as The Clique. The group (which was comprised of Nash, Scott Hall, Shawn Michaels, Sean Waltman and Hunter Hearst Helmsley) were infamous for pressurising the weakened company with demands on the creative direction of the product.

Kevin had maintained a solid friendship with Steve stemming from their time in WCW. As soon as he learned of Steve's availability, he recommended that McMahon sign him. During their negotiations, Vince had said to Steve that he was not offering him a spot with his company but, rather, an opportunity.

It was a bittersweet moment for Steve as he concluded his short but memorable run with ECW on 9th December, facing The Sandman and Mikey Whipwreck in his final appearance. But having found himself as a performer with Heyman, he was now ready to grasp the higher-profile role that was being presented by McMahon.

Although the WWF was the most famous wrestling organisation in the world, Steve was more than a little bit sceptical about Vince's promises. The WWF had a reputation for repackaging its new entrants, and moulding them into cartoon characters. Steve entered with a bit of a chip on his shoulder, knowing that he would no longer have the same creative freedom with his character that he had been given by Paul. Steve had really found himself as a performer in ECW and feared the worst as he prepared to make his transition as a WWF Superstar.

For a number of weeks on WWF programming, 'The Million Dollar Man' Ted DiBiase had been promising to bring in a new talent to the Federation.

By the late eighties, DiBiase had become one of the greatest villains in wrestling, but he was now performing as a megalomaniac heel manager after suffering a back injury that ended his career in 1993. He had been promising to scout the world and find a wrestler worthy of being declared his new Million Dollar Champion, an unsanctioned title he had originally brought to the WWF in 1989.

The time had finally come and, on 8th January 1996, Steve finally made his first appearance for the World Wrestling Federation. As DiBiase unveiled his new star, out walked Steve, complete with a new blonde buzz cut and green trunks.

Except it wasn't really Steve. The man appearing on our screens was to be known, simply, as The Ringmaster.

As soon as he was given the mic, The Ringmaster outstretched his hand to the camera, pleading with the audience to reach out to him because he was destined for success. As soon as I saw it, I realised it was a satire of the televangelists that Steve had been mocking when I was studying the various facets of faith.

It was the second time that I had witnessed Steve taking elements of Christianity into his character, as he had been using the title song from the Andrew Lloyd Webber and Tim Rice 1970 rock opera *Jesus Christ Superstar* as his ECW entrance theme.

Nevertheless, despite a passionate entrance, some of the frustrations Steve had experienced in WCW were starting to resurface within weeks of performing for the WWF. He felt that The Ringmaster gimmick had eroded the sense of identity he had finally found during his hiatus from the mainstream.

After all the years of scrambling to develop his own persona, he was now being forced to adopt a gimmick fabricated by someone else. To make matters worse, he was carrying Ted's old title belt, and using Ted's old finishing move, The Million Dollar Dream, a version of the Cobra Clutch sleeperhold.

It was clear from Steve's early WWF appearances that there was no vision for him to rise above mid-card status or be anything other than a vehicle for DiBiase's managerial role. McMahon viewed The Ringmaster as a 'mechanic', a solid in-ring performer who would be used as a utility to make stars, and not to become one himself.

Furthermore, DiBiase was generally handling most of The Ringmaster's interviews. Steve would often stress his displeasure; he had a voice of his own and did not want anyone else talking for him.

For Steve, his entry into the WWF had felt like a false start, and he sensed it was very much the opposite from an opportunity. Voicing concern about the longevity of his character, he explained that he wanted to take the gimmick in another direction.

One evening, we were sitting on the couch flicking through TV, and Steve's blue eyes slowly became fixed to the screen. He still harboured a fascination with the morbid, and he was captivated after stumbling on a chilling documentary about the sadistic contract murderer, Richard Kuklinski. The media had given Kuklinski the moniker of 'The Iceman', as he had frozen his victims to conceal their time of death.

I could almost see the wheels turning in Steve's mind as he was drawn to this callous, calculating serial killer.

'The Iceman' was the personification of sheer evil, and his no-frills approach in terrorising his victims without any sign of remorse hit a nerve with Steve.

He now had a vision for his character. Steve wanted to be wrestling's embodiment of an emotionless killer, a methodical figure who would get a kick from torturing anyone who stood in his way.

After calling the WWF front office, Steve explained his new idea, and how he envisaged the direction of his character. He was told that the marketing team would discuss his notion, and return with a suitable new handle which could replace his dreaded Ringmaster name.

We were astounded by the creative team's suggestions as they sent through a fax listing potential new names for Steve to consider. The team had taken the temperature element of the Kuklinsky precedent to form a series of names that would give Steve the lethal credibility he had been seeking.

As soon as we received the fax, Steve called Brian Pillman, and put him on the speakerphone. He read out the options that the Federation had devised for him.

"Otto Von Ruthless... Ice Dagger... Fang McFrost...," listed Steve, as he waited for Brian's response.

After a short pause, the pair burst into hysterics. They could not believe that these were legitimate suggestions from the Connecticut brain trust. But they were.

Within minutes, it was contagious. I was now in stitches simply at the cacophony of Steve's jock guffaws and Brian's raspy cackles. It was not long until the laughs faded and Steve was still stuck with the quandary. He was sitting at the edge of our bed, staring at the floor in meditation.

Being English, I did what we Brits frequently do when we are faced with a dilemma; I went to the kitchen and put on the kettle for a good old cuppa. I returned to the bedroom and put Steve's tea next to him and went about tidying the room.

Despite the tea being placed nearby, Steve never moved. Motionless, he just sat there without drinking a sip. I could tell he needed reassurance, so I went over to him.

"Don't worry, something will come up... Just drink your tea before it goes stone-cold."

Within a split-second, I turned round with excitement,

"That's your name! Stone Cold!"

With wide eyes, Steve looked up at me, grinning in disbelief. I could immediately tell that he loved the name. After weeks of hunting, he had finally snared the elusive identity that would give him a chance at stardom.

All he needed was the opportunity that he had been promised.

Having been stuck in the mid-card for months, Steve was still floundering in the World Wrestling Federation. The new moniker of 'Stone Cold' Steve Austin did not forge the immediate path to stardom that he had anticipated, but he was starting to feel comfortable in his new persona. He had changed his look; wearing plain black boots and trunks, he had shaved his head bald and was sporting a goatee. Outwardly, his demeanour had changed into a pure bad-ass tormentor. It was a brave change, a far cry from the glitzy 'Stunning' Steve Austin character that had led him to success in the USWA and WCW.

Moreover, he felt relaxed in his new environment, as the WWF locker room was filling with many familiar faces from his previous stint in Atlanta. Most of these talents were also hungry young stars looking to get to the next level, and Steve realised that he would have to be consistent in order to excel in his new role.

He had been assigned a series of matches with Savio Vega in the spring of 1996 leading into the *WrestleMania XII* pay-per-view, but something bigger was on the horizon for Steve. I was expecting my second child with him. When I told him about the pregnancy, he acted in a different way than I anticipated.

Frustrated, he seemed more concerned that the pregnancy was going to hamper his career, which was finally being given a second chance to develop after two years of faltering. I called Beverly to let her know of our exciting news, but she simply instructed me to understand the career pressures on Steve and be there for him. It was clear that I was not going to get the full level of support at home, so I would confide to my neighbours and church friends to find an outlet for my feelings.

I had been going to coffee mornings a few days each week at the church, which had offered such a supportive network for an expecting mother. While there, my interest in the Bible continued to reach new heights, and my increasing appetite for truth led to me studying all forms of faith in my personal search for God.

Meanwhile, I had started to notice some of the church patrons had been wearing Christian T-shirts. Stirred by an idea, I started to scour the Christian bookstores for a particular item that I had in mind. I decided that I wanted a shirt which proudly emblazoned the most famous verse from the Bible. The sheer thought of it filled me up with a joy I had not experienced since I had worn my cute duck-patterned dress as a child.

I could not find one anywhere, so I was inspired to craft it myself using a plain grey top and some black fabric paint.

Steve was home for a few days and we were at a bit of a loose end, so we arranged to catch up with two buddies from our darts team, Jim and Dee. We had heard that the Georgia Renaissance Festival was closing up soon, so they offered to pick us up and spend the day there. The festival is an annual fair held in Fairburn, a small city about twenty miles outside Atlanta down Interstate 85.

As soon as we parked on the grass field near the fair, Jim looked over and complimented my new tee which I was wearing that day.

Steve looked at the shirt with a puzzled face, and asked about its meaning. I explained that it was in reference to John 3:16, which is in many ways the definitive passage within the Bible. In one verse, it explains God's plan for the salvation of mankind through his only begotten son, Jesus Christ; the most elemental aspect of Christianity.

Steve paused to absorb my explanation for a few seconds before dropping the subject. His mannerisms and smug remarks had made it clear that he was starting to get agitated by my religious convictions, so I had stopped communicating the aspect of faith within my life to him.

We then arrived at the festival, which had a 16th century theme, and featured a variety of weird and wacky activities from the English renaissance period. We had a really nice day out at the fair, as Steve welcomed a break from the soaring demands of the WWF.

As WCW was establishing a firm lead with *Nitro*, the ratings war was starting to take its toll on the crew of the WWF. But an immediate necessity from within had also placed increased pressure on McMahon's mid-card talent to rise to the next level.

A void created by three of its major stars created a drive to groom new faces for the main event picture. Bret Hart had been the mainstay WWF Champion in the post-Hogan era of the WWF but, after losing the title to Shawn Michaels, had taken an extended leave of absence to film a television series. Furthermore, two other key talents within the roster, Scott Hall and Kevin Nash, had decided to finish up with the company and sign with WCW, which was now looking to aggressively expand its roster with marketable stars.

It would be the final night for Hall and Nash that would inadvertently create the foundation for Steve's opportunity.

On 19th May, at a major house show at Madison Square Garden, The Clique would give an unauthorised public farewell to two of its members.

Early in the event, the villainous Hunter Hearst Helmsley had faced Hall, who was wrestling under his popular Razor Ramon persona. In the cage match main event, the heroic Shawn Michaels wrestled his bitter nemesis Diesel, who was wrestling as a heel. Moments after the main event, Hall and Hunter entered the ring, and the four embraced in front of a puzzled crowd. Their actions, which broke the wrestler's code of kayfabe, overtly exposed the business as pure entertainment and created a backstage scandal for WWF management.

With Hall and Nash gone, the management decided that they needed to make a statement that such unsanctioned behaviour would not go unpunished. With Shawn positioned as the reigning flag-bearer of the company, this created a difficult predicament for McMahon. It was decided that Hunter, who was in the midst of a huge push towards the upper card, was to become the scapegoat. His planned crowning at the upcoming King of the Ring tournament in June had just been cancelled.

As Hunter saw his fortunes crumble with one loss after another, it was a match loss for Steve that increased his freedom as a performer.

Nine days after the incident at MSG, the WWF hosted the second part of the *In Your House 8: Beware of Dog* pay-per-view. Steve had found out that Ted DiBiase had decided to accept a role with WCW, and would be finishing up as his manager that night. The exit plan explained that Ted was to be banished from the WWF after Steve lost a strap match to end his television feud with Savio. The loss of Ted meant that Steve would no longer have anybody else doing his talking. He had his own voice and he intended to use it.

With no reason to remain lumbered with the strap or finishing hold made famous by DiBiase, Steve immediately seized the opening to freshen up his act. He introduced a new finishing move, the Stone Cold Stunner, into his evolving arsenal of no-nonsense offence. During interviews, his straight-talking Texan gravel was showcasing his quick wit to a broader audience.

Free from the hindrances that had curtailed progress in his first few months with the company, Steve was finally portraying a character that was closer to his real self. Moreover, the intensity of his solo performances had started to impress McMahon. Vince had made a decision; Steve would be the man to fill the slot previously earmarked for Hunter. The promised opportunity had finally arrived.

It was Sunday, 23rd June 1996: the night of the *King of the Ring* pay-per-view. With the spotlight on the tournament, it was Steve's chance to excel. After defeating his old colleague Marc Mero in the semi-final contest, Steve was rushed to an ambulance for over a dozen stitches to his mouth after a kick to the face tore open his bottom lip.

Steve had progressed to the finals, and was set to face Jake 'The Snake' Roberts for the throne. One of the biggest players during the golden years of the WWF's national expansion, Roberts had just returned to the company after spending four years wrestling across the world. A recovering alcoholic and drug abuser, Jake had become a born-again Christian. He had started to quote the Bible during his interviews, claiming that his faith had led him to sobriety.

However, the tournament had not been set to focus on the unlikely comeback of a veteran. It was the night for a hungrier, younger star to shine.

Adamant that his mouth injury would not curtail his efforts, Steve entered the finals with tremendous fire. Within minutes, he vanquished Roberts in rapid order to win the tournament. It was now his time to be declared the new King of the Ring.

Steve looked fatigued, but he was determined to make a statement. He trudged his way towards Michael Hayes, who had since joined the WWF as an on-screen interviewer called Dok Hendrix, to deliver his coronation speech.

Spouting fire from his swollen and bloody mouth, it was a post-match address that would gain infamy as the most memorable wrestling promo ever delivered.

Steve Austin post-match interview, WWF King of the Ring, 23rd June 1996, Milwaukee, WI: "You sit there and you thump your Bible and you say your prayers, and it didn't get you anywhere. You talk about your Psalms, talk about John 3:16... Austin 3:16 says, I've just whipped your ass!"

The fans erupted at the ferocity of Steve's controversial words. In his eyes, I could see such anger when he looked into the camera and spewed his feelings towards Roberts with such fury.

I realised immediately what had inspired Steve to reference John 3:16, but something else became very clear to me. Steve was making a statement that he would not tolerate anyone preaching the gospel. He closed his speech by putting the WWF on notice: Austin had arrived, and stated that it was only a matter of time before he was the World Wrestling Federation Champion. Uncensored, the voice that had been inhibited for months had just spoken, and it was used to make an impact beyond all imagination.

'Stone Cold' Steve Austin had taken his opportunity and maximised it. The world had just witnessed the conception of Austin 3:16, which would soon give birth to the highest-selling T-shirt in the entire history of professional wrestling.

Meanwhile, as Steve spawned a cultural sensation, I was preparing to deliver something far dearer to the world.

16 GEORGIA ON MY MIND

My third pregnancy should have been such a wondrous journey, a time to celebrate the joy of life creation. Unfortunately, I will always remember the autumn of 1996 as such a bittersweet season for our growing family.

I was so full of love, elated to be carrying a new child, but I had spent most of my third trimester packing our belongings to leave our settled home. At Steve's urging, it was time for us to leave, as he wanted to return to Texas. The mere thought of leaving really marred by pregnancy; I had developed such a fond attachment for the log cabin, but also the whole life we had established in Georgia.

Uncertainty had also crept into my life in another way. At the end of August, Steve and I had received a notice from the Internal Revenue Service stating that we owed the United States federal government a significant amount of unpaid back taxes. It was a complete and utter shock.

During the latter days of my management of Genies in Dallas, Chris had connected a hot-shot accountant by the name of Tony Cooper to Steve and I. Chris had claimed that Tony had done wonders for him, and promised he could turn around our finances as well.

Unfortunately, he did turn around our finances but in an illegal way. Unbeknownst to us, Tony had swindled the system by not properly filing our tax returns and pocketing a fraction. We were now faced with the huge stress in figuring out how to would manage this substantial debt. But no amount of anxiety could hinder the memory of my third labour.

With Steve running an arduous full-time schedule in the WWF, his mum Beverly had flown in to Atlanta. She had missed the birth of Stephanie but was able to see the arrival of her second grandchild.

Two weeks later than expected, my waters finally broke, and Beverly drove me to the hospital. I was in so much pain, I could hardly talk. Upon arrival to the maternity ward, I was given an epidural to numb the pain.

I was begging to see Steve. He had been wrestling in another town that night, and I knew he would have wanted to see his second child come into the world, but I was heavily in labour and accepted that my body had to give birth.

To my surprise, he arrived, just in time to see the arrival of his second daughter.

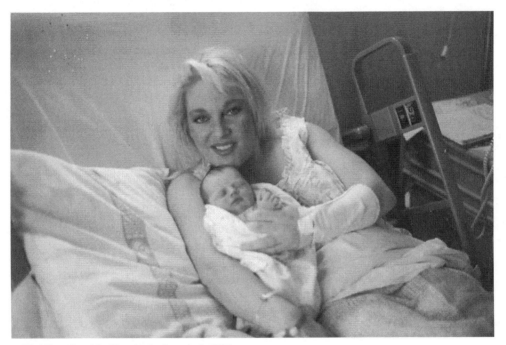

Holding Cassidy Skye in the hospital, 1996.

Born on 28th September 1996, our new baby completed our family. She was a glowing ray of sunshine into an autumn which had become increasingly bleak.

When Steve laid eyes on his new child, he doted on her with a tender affection and said the sky was the limit in her future.

It was only natural that we included that into her name, Cassidy Skye.

Within minutes, Jade and Stephanie came in to the ward to visit their new little sister, and we were soon joined by our neighbours J.L. and Ann.

After the birth, Steve could not hang around and left after a few hours in the hospital.

He was needed back in the ring, as he had been booked to wrestle Savio Vega the following daytime in a matinee card at Madison Square Garden, the prime venue of the WWF's operations in New York.

The next day, we received the largest, most beautiful bouquet of flowers. They had been sent by Steve's new bosses, Vince and Linda McMahon. I was so touched at the act of kindness. Two people whom I had never met had reached out to show support and love towards our family.

Despite the care and support of friends both old and new, there was little time for our family to relax.

With Steve back on the road, Beverly and I were making an effort to get along after I was released from the ward. Although I still never felt fully accepted as her daughter-in-law, she was thoughtful in helping me pack for the impending move and was a solid hand around the house before heading back down the road.

The ongoing problems that we were having with the IRS were preventing us from purchasing a home in Texas, as the collateral from our log cabin was insufficient.

Nevertheless, Steve was headstrong, and found a rental property situated on the outskirts of San Antonio. His uncompromising haste towards leaving was starting to splinter our family.

Now a teenager, Jade had acted out in rebellion at Steve's will to relocate, and aggressively refused to leave the house with us. Having settled and made a community of friends in her own life, she understandably wanted to stay in Georgia. We agreed that she could stay with one of her friend's parents for the couple of months that she needed to complete her school term.

Fully packed, we got into the car and prepared to drive away.

Our home in Georgia was a retreat filled with wonderful memories, and between our neighbours and church friends, I knew we were surrounded by a loving community who genuinely cared about our well-being. The undying kindness of my close neighbours J.L. and Ann gave me nurturing love that I had always craved in my unsettled childhood.

I wanted to celebrate the arrival of Cassidy with the closest thing I had to a family. Now that we were leaving, I knew that I wouldn't be able to.

It was inevitable; Steve would return to the road, and I would have nobody around to share in the joy of our new baby.

With tears streaming from my eyes, I waved goodbye to Jade and our beloved home. Our family were journeying out to the state where Steve and I had first met.

We were returning to Texas.

Our lives were turned upside down as soon as we arrived into our temporary dwelling in San Antonio. With Cassidy being under three months old and Stephanie still in her infancy at four years of age, I was finding it hard to create a homely atmosphere for our children.

The purpose of the rental was purely intended to be short-lived, and simply serve as a brief stopping point until we had agreed on a permanent location. With this looming in the back of our minds, we unpacked the bare essentials and never truly settled. All the items which would have made our house a home were still in sealed boxes stacked all over the garage.

It was the opposite of the stable environment that we had been living in for years. My loneliness would intensify as the increasing demand for Steve meant he was rarely around.

I was miserable, struggling to cope with the melancholy of a severe post-natal depression which had clouded my outlook on life. My despair had heightened to the point I was constantly tender and wallowing in a prison of my own emotions.

In this new unfamiliar town, I didn't have anyone to talk to and share my pain. With nobody to listen, I felt incredibly isolated.

By early December, we received a call that the sale of the log cabin had been finalised. Our move from Georgia was permanent, and the realisation that Jade was still there further saddened me.

My only consolation was the belief that our domestic situation was temporary, and we would soon all be together, looking for a new home for our family.

Despite the disarray caused by relocating, we continued to have so much fun whenever Steve was back from touring. We would go out, and spend as much quality time together as we could. Because we were new to the area, it became an adventure exploring the local sights and landmarks. We still didn't really know anyone in town, but it didn't matter. We had each other.

Whenever he would go back on the road, I would count down the days until his return.

In February 1997, Steve returned with an announcement. While we were still living in Atlanta, Beverly had suggested to him that we pick out a property in Boerne.

She had told Steve that she wanted her babies back in South Texas. He had since selected a property that he felt matched our needs, and his heart was set on the move.

I was stunned. The excitement and freedom of choice in finding the perfect home for our family had just been ripped away.

When we were looking for a house in Georgia, it was an inclusive process which brought us closer together. I was resentful that our family had not been included in the selection process for a home in which the children and I would spend the most time.

Furthermore, I couldn't understand quite how Steve could manage to secure the property, with our seeming inability to finance it.

Steve revealed that he had thought of a plan to ask the WWF to underwrite our mortgage, on the agreement that he would pay back the loan directly from earnings within his contract.

Without delay, he called McMahon to explain his unique request.

"How much of that fire-water have you been drinking Steve?" Vince chuckled.

Vince was sympathetic to our predicament, and once again offered support for our family.

"Thanks to you guys, I'll now be able to say that I own a property in Texas!" he joked.

Vince bought us the house, and we would be moving before the end of the month.

Although I was still annoyed that Steve had decided on a property without even letting his family see it, I was grateful that Vince had helped bring a sense of stability to our lives by securing us a house.

For the second time in three months, we were set to relocate into a new home.

Reclusively sited from civilisation, we drove for miles to view our new property.

It was the last house on the left of a long, secluded road. With only one neighbour, it was a desolately positioned Spanish hacienda, sited amongst stark trees and barren plains which extended as far as the eye could see.

When we entered our new abode, it had a chilling atmosphere to it, and with scorpions scurrying around the grounds, it was very daunting and rather scary. Sinister and spooky, even Steve named it the 'Amityville House', likening it to the dwelling from the 1979 horror movie *The Amityville Horror*.

Neither of us were particularly enamoured with the house when we first viewed it, but Steve was keen to conclude the sale and refocus on his career.

His momentum had skyrocketed, and he sought sanctuary in the solitude offered by Boerne. He wanted to live in an environment far removed from the media and the invasive enthusiasm of his ever-growing army of passionate fans.

Meanwhile, I was just glad that Jade had completed her school term in Atlanta and had moved back in with us. She quickly made friends as we enrolled her in Boerne High School.

Steve also sought solace in the prospect of hunting again, a hobby he had pursued for years. It gave him a sense of peace when he was not running hard to an exhaustive schedule.

His hectic travel itinerary and diet of daily physical punishment had escalated dramatically; he needed to regroup in the lead up to the biggest match of his life.

After returning to the company in October 1996, Bret Hart had been determined to show his worth, and prove he had not lost a step in the months that he had been away from the industry. He had wrestled Steve in months prior, with the original intention of using their matches as the lead up to Bret's lucrative return match with Shawn Michaels at *WrestleMania 13*.

However, the relationship between Bret and Shawn had vastly deteriorated, and their professional rivalry had escalated into a mutual personal dislike. In the weeks approaching *WrestleMania*, Shawn claimed to have suffered a knee injury that would prevent him from facing Hart in the ring.

Just like the opportunity that had arisen at *King of the Ring*, Steve would benefit from having to substitute for another wrestler. The decision was made for him to face Bret, in a Submission Match at the *'Mania* pay-per-view spectacular.

On the week of the event, Steve called with a really nice invite. He asked if I would accompany him during the weekend, and also attend a very special ceremony the WWF was hosting; The Slammy Awards.

It was such a wonderful night, and I had the chance to meet so many of Steve's new colleagues and their families. I spent an age talking to Shawn, but that evening gave me the chance to reconnect with my old USWA colleague Percy Pringle, who was now working for Vince as the manager of The Undertaker, under the guise of a mortician humorously named Paul Bearer. Anyone who ever met Percy will attest to his kindness. We pledged to keep in touch, and he became such a good friend to me.

Going into the match, Bret was the hero and Steve was the villain. But that night, the pair expertly told a story in the ring that repositioned both men on other sides of the fence.

For over twenty minutes, they went back-and-forth, furiously hitting each other with everything they had in front of a raucous Chicago crowd.

Towards the end of the match, Steve had been cut badly, and was locked into Hart's famous finishing hold, The Sharpshooter.

I will never forget the visual as Steve valiantly refused to give in, blood coursing down his face. It became one of the most iconic images in wrestling history. After a few moments, 'Stone Cold' passed out from the blood loss.

The fans knew he refused to quit, and cheered his gutsy performance.

As the match was concluded by special referee Ken Shamrock, a mixed-martial artist from the world of UFC, Bret continued his assault to a chorus of boos.

The circle was now complete, and both wrestlers' roles had been reversed with masterful precision. Bret was now received as the callous heel, and Steve was accepted as the hero; a lone wolf with a never-say-die attitude.

I was so proud of Steve that weekend. After years of hard work, he had finally made it. He was facing the biggest names in his profession, and more than holding his own. His star was shining bright.

The match with Bret that weekend had elevated Steve to the point where he was now viewed as the hottest talent in the company and it kick-started his hot on-screen feud with The Hart Foundation, a stable comprised of Bret and his brother Owen, their brothers-in-law Jim 'The Anvil' Neidhart and Davey Boy Smith, and Steve's former tag team partner Brian Pillman.

Steve might not have been the WWF Champion, but his cult fan-base had risen immensely to the point that he was gradually finding fame as a mainstream star. At live events, the wrestling ring would frequently resemble a miniature island within an expansive ocean of Austin 3:16 signs and T-shirts.

The demand for Steve was incredible as he was being groomed to reach the top of the World Wrestling Federation. In addition to his already gruelling events schedule, he was making an increasing amount of publicity appearances to capitalise on his soaring popularity.

As a result, he was rarely at home to spend any time with his family.

As much as I had a fondness for Texas, I still couldn't settle into the hacienda when I returned from the frenetic rush of the *WrestleMania 13* weekend schedule and after-party.

I was starting to miss Steve more than ever. Very much alone with the children, I had been unable to make friends in the remote town of Boerne.

As I was still reeling from the effects of post-natal depression, the detachment from any semblance of a social community was haunting me. There was neither a nearby church, nor an existing network of friends anywhere close.

Stuck at the hacienda without any company, I felt abandoned. Shutting off from the world, I soon found myself in a steady decline towards a reclusive existence.

For the first time, I was beginning to yearn for a means of escape from my living reality.

17 THE LONE STAR STATE

As I had been struggling to cope with the loneliness of life in Boerne, I was determined to find a social circle for the girls. I did not want them to grow up and feel trapped in the house, so I searched for a day care centre which could enable them to interact with other children. At the centre, I quickly became friends with one of the carers, a really lovely lady named Mary Hernandez. Sensing my loneliness, she understood my plight and had offered to help babysit so I could get out the house and form some measure of a life for myself.

Within weeks, I required a small surgical procedure to remove my breast implants which had been causing ongoing discomfort since my third pregnancy. In order to relieve myself of the agony from the operation, I had been given Vicodin, a pain relief medication. The pills did help me overcome the pain, but once the prescription ran out I quickly got another one, even when my aches had dissipated.

Vicodin gave me a sense of euphoria. It offered a quick-fix and it was an easy escape from the loneliness I was still feeling from the remnants of my lingering post-natal depression. By the summer of 1997, it became a daily habit, offering an aid to cope with the fatigue of the never-ending, scorching days in South Texas.

It was not long before I could not get through a day without craving more. With my body developing immunity to the pills, I was soon scrambling to find a bigger fix.

Ever since his time in WCW, Steve had been taking a legal drug called GHB to help him function. It was readily available from health food stores and had many uses. It could aid sleep, improve athletic performance, burn fat and could even provide an intoxicating sensation.

After finding Steve's stash of GHB, I decided to give it a try.

As soon as I tried it, the results were immediate. Despite being unsettled in my home, the intake of GHB made me feel incredibly relaxed. I reached out to Steve's contact at the gym, and ordered more.

When the effects would wear off, I would feel incredibly numb. I found that Vicodin could counter some of the numbness, so I started to interchange between the pills, discreetly mixing them when I was alone in the hacienda.

Panic attacks. These became commonplace as I increased my intake of Vicodin. Waking up in the middle of the night with high levels of anxiety, my body had no strength, my fingers seemed weak and my heart was thumping through my chest.

In desperation, I clutched to the calm persuasion of some more GHB to slow my heart rate. Each time that it happened, I could depend on it bring me back to a tranquil place where my mind and body needed to be. Nobody knew about my little secret.

But nobody needed to. My secret was not a problem.

It was my way of coping with the pressures of family life in a remote town in which I felt alienated.

Anyway, I was still very much functioning. I was able to look after the girls and my home was in order. Nobody would notice if I needed a little pill every now and then. And nobody did.

When Steve would come home from his commitments with the WWF, he also wanted to find some means of escapism. He needed to unwind, and would either ride around on our four-wheeler or sit around the house and drink. Frequently, he would head into the woods with his new friends Ricky and Sandra, who were avid deer hunters.

As the wait-at-home mother, all I wanted to do was to go out with Steve when he would eventually return. Unfortunately, when he did, he would journey straight out for hours on end or refuse to leave the house. Either way, I was stuck and felt abandoned.

But there was a way to cope with that.

If his tour had taken a larger toll on his body than usual, Steve would sometimes order Somas. These were a powerful muscle relaxant that was highly effective in managing the aches and pains that were caused by his punishing bumps in the ring.

It was not long before I had started to experiment with them. The Somas worked. They insulated me from the nagging pains we feel in our day to day lives. Of course, there were dangers in using Somas regularly. However, I was using them in moderation. I was still very much in control.

However, it was not long before I got a call that made me feel anything but in control. In fact, it was a call on 3rd August 1997 that made me feel absolutely powerless.

It was Steve, and he was calling from the hospital in a highly emotional state. He was choked up and sombre, and did not sound like himself at all. He had just wrestled a pay-per-view match with Owen Hart in East Rutherford, New Jersey, but something had gone terribly wrong within the execution of the finishing sequence of the match.

Owen had lifted Steve upside down for a tombstone piledriver. When performed correctly, the piledriver is a manoeuvre that elicits tremendous heat from the crowd, as it involves a wrestler being dropped headfirst to the mat. But there is a reason the move looks so unsafe; it really is dangerous.

Steve had not been elevated to the point that he could be fully protected when the move was performed. Owen then dropped downward, and the weight of both men came crashing down to the canvas, smashing the top of Steve's head into his neck with devastating force.

For moments, Steve just lay there. Motionless, and without any feeling below his neck, there was concern that he could be paralysed.

Owen sensed something was wrong, and mugged to the crowd to buy some time for Steve to get checked out. Trying to salvage the intended finish to the match and provide the desired result, Hart then fell backwards, allowing Steve's limp arms to make the cover and win Owen's title.

Steve was the new Intercontinental Champion of the WWF, but it didn't matter. What mattered was his health.

Like many, I had been watching the *SummerSlam* pay-per-view from the house and hadn't realised that the ending had not gone as planned. In Steve's matches with The Hart Foundation, he would often struggle out of the ring in a seemingly-battered state and, truth be told, I just thought the injury was part of the storyline.

After Steve gingerly walked backstage, he was rushed by an ambulance to the hospital. He was taken for an immediate scan to assess the long-term damage to his spinal cord.

Speaking to Steve was a sobering reminder of just how dangerous each manoeuvre in professional wrestling could be if not performed correctly.

For the first time, I heard true vulnerability in Steve's voice. He had an appointment scheduled with a neurosurgeon that specialised in spinal trauma, and Steve asked if I would accompany him. He didn't need to ask. Of course I would.

In no uncertain terms, the doctor told Steve that his injury was the worst he had ever seen, and that his career as a wrestler was finished.

Professional wrestling had become Steve's life, and he had just started to break into the prime of his career only to have it all stripped away.

I looked into Steve's eyes, and saw his face sink with disappointment. I could feel his pain, and I burst into tears.

"Crying will not do you any good," scowled the consultant.

I was taken aback by the insensitivity of the doctor. I knew how great a loss it would be for Steve to end his career under such unfortunate circumstances.

I could tell that Steve was not ready for such a setback. He insisted that he would get a second opinion before taking such drastic action as leaving the business, especially since he had finally found his niche and true calling as an on-screen character.

Further investigation was required to establish the best course of surgical action, so we both headed back to Boerne, where Steve's body could get some respite.

When we finally returned to the hacienda, the stress on Steve started to put a strain on our relationship. He was incensed at Owen for not calling him to check on his condition. Steve perceived that there was a lack of respect shown and he even suspected that there had been some malice to hamper his career and push him back down the card. Out of action for an indefinite time, I tried to make Steve's life more tolerable by trying to appeal to his sense of humour. We had shared a goofy connection from the minute we established a friendship, and I was doing what I could to make him laugh and distract him from the stress of his uncertain future.

Steve with Cassidy, 1997.

In the U.K., there was a famous children's comic strip, entitled *The Beano*, which I used to read every week. One of the main characters was the fastest boy alive, Billy Whizz. I used get pictures taken, in which I would pull these silly poses and faces in a running stance, and pass them to Steve. He would take one look, and crack up with laughter.

But I knew my jokes and attempts to get him to smile wasn't enough, and he started to become increasingly close with our new neighbours.

Steve started to spend a lot more time at Ricky and Sandra's house, and he found it to be a place where he could escape from his career and family. I had started to go there too, but there were some things I could not identify with whenever their discussions would drift onto various topics.

It was during these visits and social time together that I began to realise the vast cultural differences between us. I became unsettled as I tried to adjust to life in Boerne.

On 31st August, I caught a newsflash on the television. Diana, the Princess of Wales, had been killed in a horrific car accident in Paris. I was in shock at this dreadful news, and I cried.

Diana was a symbol of compassion and she had captured the imagination of the British public with her undying kindness. I had sympathy for Diana once the details of her loveless marriage with Charles were revealed. She was someone who had all the fame and fandom in the world. But for her it was irrelevant, as she did not have the love of her husband.

She was a lonely girl, trapped in a life that made her deeply unhappy.

Shaken by this tragic event, I went through to see Steve who was at Ricky and Sandra's house. I had tears in my eyes, and I told them what had happened. They could not understand why I would be affected by the death of someone I didn't know, and they laughed at me.

To them, Diana was just some chick who married a prince. To me, she was symbolic of something much more. The reaction of the three drove me to a sudden realisation; I was starting to feel like the odd one out in my life with Steve.

When Steve and I would visit Ricky and Sandra, I was starting to feel like the black sheep, as they only seemed to speak about two topics. Over and over, it got increasingly tiresome, but I was making an effort to be a part of the group and I still went through to visit.

All three were avid hunting enthusiasts. I always knew Steve was a fan of shooting from our time together in Atlanta. I have never stopped or tried to discourage anyone from doing what makes them happy in life, but the thought of killing animals for fun just was not for me.

I would bow out whenever the three would head off to go on one of their trips to snag some game, but tolerated it as I knew it was their right to do so.

There was one topic that I felt was not their right, or anyone else's to express.

It was not long before I found out that Ricky and Sandra were fiercely racist.

Whenever we would visit, they would constantly fill their conversations with the N-word and how they found Mexicans to be beneath them.

The word 'nigger' will always be an abhorrent slur from a shameful era in American history, and I could not stand to hear it being used so casually. I would voice my concerns about the use of such nasty dialogue, especially if they were around the girls.

Frequently, my pacifist reasoning was turned on its head and was used by the pair as a means to mock me. I was often ridiculed for my soft-nature and Christian views, which were amusing to them.

On one occasion, I expressed disbelief that the Ku-Klux-Klan had arrived in town and set up an enlistment drive for new members. When the topic was discussed, I was disgusted to find that there was not a shared derision of this extreme faction in Boerne.

When we had that discussion, I was just yards from the house, but I could not have felt further from home. For the first time in years, I yearned to be back in England.

To cope with my homesickness, I secretively swallowed a few more pills on top of my regular amounts in an effort to numb the pain. Slowly, my dosage increased to the point that I had started to become complacent in my domestic life.

I couldn't even bring myself to unpack many of my books and memorabilia that I took across from our move. All my belongings just stayed in a barn that was yards from the hacienda, locked away in storage. This added to my misery, as the house just stayed in the same state it had been as we arrived.

Steve's mum came over to check on us, and could tell that the house was in need of modernisation. She was an interior designer herself, and kindly got to work. In fairness, she made a real effort, hanging up curtains and wallpaper and in an attempt to make things more comfortable for us. Beverly was very good at what she did, and I was grateful that she made the effort, even if there was still an underlying issue between us.

It gave me a boost, and Steve and I started to resume our hobby of antique shopping, searching for vintage signs. We were starting to get closer again as his nagging pains were starting to heal.

Feeling physically better, Steve had sought a second opinion on his neck injury. He got the news he was desperate to hear. Within a few months, he would be able to return to the ring.

He called Vince, and a plan was put in place for his return. Instead of waiting until he was fully healed, Steve would make his return imminently. He could be used as an on-screen character who might not be competing in actual wrestling matches, but was still integral to a show that greatly needed strong characters to compete with WCW's star-studded spectacles.

McMahon was keen to use the legitimate neck injury as a means to enhance Steve's appeal, pitting him in confrontations against the corporation's officials. He wanted to make it seem that political obstacles were stopping Steve from returning to action, and bolster his underdog appeal.

By late September, Steve would resume his anti-hero character and became an even bigger star. Interrupting the WWF's programming, he dished out beatings to anyone who tried to prevent him from returning to the ring, including the management team who had stripped him of his newly-won championship for his own 'best interests'.

The fans saw Steve as an anti-authority figure, and cheered his on-screen rebellious attitude and out-of-control antics. The hiatus from the ring had been a blessing for the 'Stone Cold' character, as the demand for his return made him a red-hot commodity. Just as things seemed right for Steve in the WWF, tragedy struck.

On 5th October 1997, the World Wrestling Federation was preparing for its eighteenth *In Your House* pay-per-view, entitled *Badd Blood*. In the afternoon of the show, one of the talents hadn't arrived, and could not be contacted.

It turned out that it was Steve's old tag team partner, and good friend, Brian Pillman.

A call was made to the Budget Tel Motel in Bloomington Minnesota, where Brian had stayed the night before, to check and see if he had simply overslept or missed his flight. Brian's body was found motionless by one of the maids and was pronounced dead as soon as the ambulance had arrived. He was 35 years old.

For years, Brian had been one of the most promising talents in wrestling. He possessed a fantastic mind for the business, and was well-liked by most of his peers. Unfortunately, Pillman could never escape his own demons, which stemmed from abuse of multiple prescription and recreational drugs.

When the autopsy was completed, the coroner had discovered that Brian had developed a hereditary condition of heart disease; however there were significant amounts of cocaine found within his system.

As a result, his body was not given the chance to fight when he suffered the heart attack that, ultimately, ended his life.

Brian was respected as a wrestler, but moreover, he was widely known to be a caring father and was in the midst of raising three children and two stepchildren with his wife Melanie.

At the time of his death, she was pregnant, and carrying a child that Brian would never get the chance to know.

The death of Brian saddened us all. When Steve came home, he looked out a gold chain that he had received from him during their days as The Hollywood Blonds, and vowed he would never remove it from his neck.

Steve bottled up his feelings but I could tell he was in shock. He wanted to be alone, and journeyed into the woods.

It was hunting season.

His world had changed, and he wanted to focus his anger on a target that had become within reach.

18 LOSING IDENTITY

In the latter months of 1997, Steve set his sights on the top position in the World Wrestling Federation. The bitter departure of Bret Hart had created a void at the top of the promotion, and capitalising on the dearth of upper-tier talent, Steve had accelerated his return to full-time competition in the hopes of becoming the WWF's number one star.

As he returned to work, I felt increasingly isolated, and I was not fitting in as an accepted part of the Boerne community. However, a call from Steve gave me the shot in the arm that I needed.

Vince had scheduled Steve to face Shawn Michaels for the title at *WrestleMania XIV*, and the company had pulled a major publicity stunt by recruiting the infamous former boxing champion Mike Tyson as the special guest enforcer for the match. The event was scheduled for 29th March at the FleetCenter in Boston, Massachusetts, and Steve wanted to have me accompany him to the event.

With the boredom at the hacienda, I was relieved to get out for a few days. I treated the weekend as a little holiday, and felt like I had been let out of a cage.

Once I arrived, I was determined to have a good time, and spent a lot of time being silly with Steve and laughing. It was such a happy time, and everyone was so kind to us. I also got to see so many families of the WWF's talent roster.

We saw Jim Ross and his lovely wife Jan, who invited Steve and I to visit their home. I first met Jim when he worked as an announcer for WCW during my tenure there, but he was now working for Vince as his lead play-by-play commentator. I also got the chance to meet The Rock's wife Dany, who was such an elegant lady. We instantly clicked, so we sat and watched the show together. I was also thrilled to see Terri and Dustin once again, as well as Marc and Rena Mero, who were all working on the event.

I was pleased to bump into Shawn Michaels, who had been so outgoing and sweet during the previous year's show. This time, I was surprised at his demeanour. Something was off with him and he acted very distant. He was not his usual self and he never spoke to us during catering.

Two months prior, Shawn had sustained a serious back injury in a match with The Undertaker, but there had been rumours that he was resentful at the prospect of Steve overtaking his position at the top of the card.

At 7.00pm the show started, and it was a night I will never forget.

In the main event, Steve and Shawn finally squared off, with the added intrigue of Mike Tyson at ringside. Despite both wrestlers having nagging injuries, they put on a spectacle that deserved its status as the headline match on the company's biggest show.

After years of hard work, and repeated career setbacks, Steve had finally realised his dream after pinning Shawn for the three-count. He was the WWF World Heavyweight Champion, and had reached the pinnacle of his profession.

I remember waiting for him as he walked back through the curtain to lead to the locker room. He gave me the belt, and asked me to keep a hold of it for the rest of the evening. It was a very special moment for me, as I knew how much the title meant to Steve. By giving me the championship, he was letting me know how much I had meant to his career. It was such a kind gesture; he never forgot that I helped support him when he was struggling in his rookie year and had been at his side through all his battles to reach the top. I proudly carried that title, as we began to leave the arena.

Some of the boys ribbed Steve about dropping the belt to his wife as soon as he won it, but we were quickly ushered to a huge press conference which immediately followed the show. I remember sitting in the back area, waiting with Mike Tyson, before being called over to sit next to Linda McMahon. She could sense I was a bit cold, and put her jacket around me, rubbing my arms to give me warmth. Linda had a motherly kindness, and was such a comforting presence amidst this huge media frenzy.

All of the publicity paid dividends. The show was a massive success and, for the first time in over a year, the WWF had taken a lead in its ongoing ratings war with WCW. Within the company, there was a renewed confidence, and Steve was determined to lead the promotions resurgence and take it to unforeseen heights. The momentum was infectious, and it was such a thrill to be around the company that week.

But just as I was feeling the rush of excitement of the *WrestleMania* hype, there was a huge downer that I had to swallow. It was time to leave Steve on the road, and return to Boerne.

As soon as I got back, I felt caged again.

I continued to secretively pop some pills to mask the misery I was feeling at home, and had wangled a few prescriptions from various doctors. I was mixing Xanax with Vicodin and Somas, and moderately using GHB on top of that. It was a means to fill the void when Steve was away.

Wanting to distance the children from Ricky and Sandra, I virtually had no adult company in Boerne apart from Steve, the only exception being our babysitter Mary.

I really looked forward to Steve's return, as his schedule had worsened since he became the figurehead of the company. By the summer of 1998, Steve was performing in front of record-breaking crowds each night and was earning the astronomical money reserved for top sportsmen, but it didn't mean anything as we couldn't enjoy it together. I didn't care about our financial wellbeing; I was looking for his emotional support, as my life had started to degenerate without him.

Unfortunately, when he came back, he was smothered instantly by Ricky and Sandra who vied for his time. I became so jealous, as I felt there was now a third party in my marriage to Steve. More often than not, it seemed that he would rather spend time with them than his family.

Hoping to secure some much-needed private family time, I started to arrange a special birthday party for Stephanie, who was just away to turn six years old. I invited Mary and her children, who had become really good friends to my girls, and it had worked out that Steve would be home in time to share the celebration. Once Ricky and Sandra heard there was going to be a party, they asked if they could host it at their house, as they had a pool.

When Mary arrived with her children, there was an issue which simply disgusted me.

Ricky and Sandra did not want Mary's children to use their pool. In their bigoted minds, her kids were not Caucasian and, therefore, dirty. The pair went on to brag that they would sometimes pay a Mexican a paltry twenty dollars for a day's labour, to dig holes and fill them back up again, all in the scorching Texas heat and just for their sick amusement. Their comments were ignorant, and moreover, cruel.

I was appalled and could not tolerate their views any longer.

Although I was annoyed that Steve seemed to be spending so much time with Ricky and Sandra, it was only bearable because I didn't have to see them when he returned to the road. Steve's status as the top star of the WWF was providing him with even more opportunities beyond wrestling.

First off, a record label contacted Steve, and he was asked if he could be the face of a couple of compilation albums, each one containing his favourite songs within the genres of metal and country music. On top of that, he was getting offers from Hollywood, as requests for acting gigs were coming thick and fast to the house.

On one occasion, I received a really nice call from the television actor Don Johnson. He was the star of a hit police drama called *Nash Bridges*, and wanted Steve to do a few appearances on the show. I was thrilled for Steve, and became even more excited when Don asked if I wanted to fly to San Francisco and visit the set of the show.

I let Steve know about this new opportunity, and he immediately called Don to accept the recurring guest role.

Unfortunately, Steve refused to let me attend the production and it broke my heart. Only a few months prior, we had such a great time in Boston, but I felt that he had slowly become ashamed of me. Steve had always found it difficult to share his feelings during our relationship, so I could only speculate on what had not been said.

Feeling unwanted, I questioned every aspect of myself. After birthing Steve's daughters, my appearance had changed, and I pondered on whether my love was enough to sustain his interest in a life punctuated by gruelling tours.

Steve's life had become so hectic, and I started to feel like he was losing interest in me. Over the summer and into the autumn, the sparkle he used to have in his eyes whenever he saw me slowly faded. But I couldn't blame him. My depression and clandestine dependences had drained me to the point that I was not the girl he fell in love with, and I no longer had the same zeal for life as I once did.

With each passing day, I grew more worried that our marriage was heading for a bump in the road.

By October 1998, Steve's celebrity status continued to soar and he had become one of the few stars in wrestling to truly cross over into the mainstream consciousness. His immense popularity had continued to garner attention with the mass media, and he was set to be featured in an extensive article by the fortnightly publication *Rolling Stone* for their special New Year's double edition.

I knew how big this was for Steve, as the magazine usually reserved its focus on the elite names within the entertainment industry and popular culture. It was quite nerve-wracking as he was to be interviewed at the house, but I had taken a little bit of GHB to keep my anxiety under control.

Steve wanted to make a good impression with the reporter, so I went out to the shop to pick up some refreshments before he was scheduled to arrive. I got everything I needed and started the car.

My stresses were lifted, and I felt fully relaxed as I continued to drive home.

I don't really know what happened after that, I just know what I felt.

With a massive thud, my head bounced off the windscreen, and the car screeched along the road before coming to a sudden halt. The sedate feeling had led me to fall asleep at the wheel.

When I got inside, I was shaken and told Steve and the interviewer, Chris Heath that I had careered off the road after hitting a pothole on the road leading to the house.

Concerned, Steve took me to the side and asked if I had been taking GHB. I admitted that I had, and he shook his head.

Chris and Steve went out to look at the car. The wheel had buckled and there was a huge trail of rubber skidding. They both looked in awe that I had not been seriously hurt, and I could sense a realisation in Steve.

The two went back into the house, and concluded the interview. Chris was really complimentary to us during the latter half of the interview, and said we looked really sweet together before leaving the hacienda.

With the interviewer gone, Steve looked into my eyes and told me there could be no more similar incidents. He gathered up all the GHB he could find around the house, and flushed it down the toilet.

Frustrated, he walked off to see Ricky and Sandra. He wanted some space to digest what had happened and to simply release some steam.

When Steve came back, I could tell he had been drinking. He was slightly lethargic and kept looking at me.

With his head tilted, he smiled at me, but there was emptiness in his eyes.

"I used to be so in love with you," he slurred, before his eyes gently wandered to the floor.

Steve's remark was the overdue acknowledgement of what I had already figured; he no longer saw me in the same way that he once did. Like a broken Yellow Rose in the Texas Sun, his love for me had withered. Rejected, I yearned for company and to feel liberated from the marital stresses which were causing such turmoil at the hacienda.

I called my mum and asked if she would come with me on a trip to Miami. I needed to clear my head and rediscover the passionate soul that I once was. I had lost my fervour and sense of being, and I needed to be with someone who I knew cared for me.

I needed to know what it was to feel alive again.

When I got to Miami, I felt a huge release. I wanted to experience all I could on my short trip. I hired a sporty red Corvette, and drove along the coast, past the lines of gorgeous mansions and by the sunny beach roads sprinkled by palm trees and crowds of smiling, happy people.

That night, my mum and I were going to have a ladies night and go for dinner at a beachside restaurant. For the first time as an adult, I was able to spend long-overdue alone time with my mum. I had a reason to get all dressed up, and exuded a confidence that had been bereft from me in a while.

During dinner, I noticed some gradual flirtation from one of the male waiters.

He complimented me, and could sense I had enjoyed his continued attention. He asked if I was busy later, and if I would join him for a drink after his shift ended. I knew that it was objectionable to meet him, but his eyes drew me towards him. I agreed.

With my mum returning to the hotel, I had the drink with this mysterious gentleman from Brazil. Between the sounds of the ocean and the gentle breeze of the beach air, we danced under the soft glow of the moonlight. It was such a romantic setting.

Hand in hand, we decided to walk down to the beach and talked for a while. He was so attentive, and listened with such a calming demeanour.

We ran out of words, and he kissed me.

I knew it was wrong, as I was married to Steve. But this young, exotic man gave me a feeling Steve had not given me in months.

I felt desirable again.

When I returned from Miami, I just wanted to be noticed by my husband. After performing in the main event for just over a year, Steve was already starting to show signs of burn out as he ran hard to raise the standard of a headlining WWF Superstar. Injuries, coupled with wear and tear from the road, were taking a heavy toll on his body.

When he would eventually return home, all he wanted to do was rest his battered frame, or focus on studying his matches in order to improve and stay relevant.

He would watch tapes of his bouts continuously, and then replay them over and over again in order to pick apart what worked to elicit a hot reaction from the crowd. A diligent student of the game, he would also analyse the output of other top talent, to ascertain what made them special in the eyes of others.

Steve was no longer the outgoing man I had known for years and he was fully engrossed in developing the persona of his 'Stone Cold' character.

I yearned for us to spend quality family time together, but each time I reached out to him, he would shrug it off, because he needed to capitalise on the opportunities he had been given. Bitterness stemming from years of unrecognised hard work during his time in Atlanta would never truly dissolve from his mind.

Fully focused on his career, Steve became increasingly reliant on me to take care of business at home while he did his best to work hard and excel as the top star of the World Wrestling Federation.

On a recommendation from Vince, we decided to restructure our finances and appoint a new accountant to deal with our income and tax returns. I even travelled to New York, and met one of the partners of the firm before agreeing to appoint them.

Upon returning to my room, I got a call from Sue Aitchison, one of the senior assistants to Vince McMahon. She let me know that he was hosting a dinner and asked if I would like to attend.

Thrilled, I looked forward to getting the chance to go to a restaurant in the glitzy city, and it was even arranged that I would be picked up by a limousine. Along with Vince and Linda were my friends Rena Mero, who performed under the name Sable, and Mark Calaway, who wrestled as The Undertaker.

I was really enjoying a social night in the big city, and it was nice to be around such friendly people. We laughed as some of the talent shared stories of their time in the wrestling industry.

Then my phone rang. It was Steve.

When he found out I was with the WWF crew, he was incensed. He was annoyed I was out without his knowledge and he called Vince. Steve was probably concerned that others would see my induced state and wanted to conceal my embarrassment.

My one night in the Big Apple was cut short. It was time to return to Boerne.

When I returned to the stark misery of the hacienda, I needed to find an escape. I reached for some more GHB to numb myself.

From the time I had started taking the tablets, I had slowly built a resistance to the drug. My dosage had increased by three times from the amount I was previously consuming.

But as the intake increased, my fatigue returned with a vengeance.

One afternoon, I was woken up to the sound of Steve shouting and clattering around the house. He was enraged and had tears in his eyes as he reached for his rifle.

In the heat, I had passed out with the drugs, and had forgotten to tend to his dog, Abby.

Due to a previous incident, Steve's beloved pet had been kept away in a separated area from our children. She needed checked upon regularly from a mesh compound within our grounds that stopped her from running away.

Neglecting her, I had not realised that she had become ill.

When Steve went to check up on her, he was horrified.

Her tail had fallen off, and she was ridden with gangrene. He gently lifted her limp body and took it to the side.

Steve picked up gun as he put Abby out of her misery.

Knowing how much he loved his dog, I started crying. The GHB had overwhelmed me to the point I caused her to die, and it was something I could have prevented if I had been more alert.

I am still haunted by that day, and wish I could go back and save her. I had let Steve down, and wished I could erase the memory and start again.

A few weeks later, Steve came home from another hunting trip with Ricky and Sandra with an ultimatum. He was going to be clearing out a lot of the belongings that were kept in the barn, as he wanted to make way for a new beginning in Boerne. He told me that he was going to be torching everything that was left inside it, unless it was cleared.

Many of my belongings were kept in the barn. Steve knew that my modelling portfolio, early family photographs and my books on faith were stored there. Many of the items I had kept from my early business ventures were kept in sealed boxes. One day, I wanted to fondly look back on my life, and let the girls know about their mother's own career before their father became the biggest star in professional wrestling.

These keepsakes were the remnants of the girl before she met the boy.

I wanted to salvage what I could, but it was too late. Housebound by the sweltering Texas heat, my addictions had sucked all energy from my body. I would lay motionless for hours, weakened by unremitting fatigue.

Steve frequently reminded me to go through the barn, but I couldn't seem to muster the will to do so.

Devoid of strength, I pleaded to have the fire postponed. But there was no stopping Steve. In his eyes, he had given me repeated notice, and I had dismissed his request to clear the unit.

He arrived at the hacienda with Ricky and Sandra, who brought a digger and some gasoline.

Steve looked over at me with disappointment. In his eyes, he had seen that I had not bothered to retrieve anything from the barn. He needed to make a point, and he did.

Immobile, I sat from the hacienda as they ripped everything from the barn, and dumped it in a pile on our grounds. Without any compassion, the fire started.

My past was left in ashes, and there was little I did to resist it. The little girl from Southend-on-Sea no longer existed. She was just a memory. Underneath my skin, I was screaming. I wanted to function but my addiction was becoming hard to bear.

I was neglecting myself, and tried to find ways to shake off my melancholy. One day, I had been shopping in the local supermarket, and came across some hair dye. It had been months since I had went to the hair salon, and realised that my dark roots were showing. If I smartened up my appearance, it might give me the boost I needed to function.

I picked up a packet of dye, which was a nice strawberry blonde colour, and bought it. Once I got home, I put the product in my hair, and left it on before rinsing it off my head.

When I got to the mirror, I was aghast. It was far removed from the colour I expected, and was a luminous orange. I had to get the carrot tone out of my locks, so I headed back to the store to get some lightener.

The lightener didn't work. My hair was just a paler, thinner version of the previous tint.

To rid myself of the orange, I sourced some high strength peroxide. Bleaching my hair, I left it on for a while before washing.

I walked to the mirror to see how it looked.

The bleach had completely fried my head. All that remained were lifeless, frizzy strands of fluff above my scalp. Unhappy with how I looked, I made a decision.

I went to find Steve's clippers and shaved my hair.

When Steve got back that morning, I was still asleep, and laying on bed. When he got into the bedroom, he just stared at me, gaping in stunned disbelief. His wife was as bald as him.

"What have you done?" he sighed, as he looked into my innocent eyes with compassion.

I told him I had a bad experience dying my hair.

"With those big eyes and no hair, you now look like an alien," he painfully smiled.

After he asked what I was going to do, I told him I was going to get a baseball cap and a wig. He laughed. I felt comforted by Steve during the shock of losing my hair, and he even nicknamed me 'Spike' as a term of endearment when it started to grow again.

Considering how radical my appearance was from what Steve was accustomed to, he was very gentle with me. He seemed to sympathise with my plight.

Even though there was empathy, Steve was becoming increasingly concerned by my behaviour as a result of my use of GHB.

The following week, we were expected to attend Billboard Music Awards at the MGM Grand in Las Vegas, Nevada. Held on 7th December, it was a star-studded ceremony, featuring many of the top music acts in America. Steve had been invited to attend due to the popularity of his compilation album.

When we got there, I noticed Steve was walking slightly ahead of me during media interviews and any promotional spots that were being filmed. I realised that he perceived me as a loose cannon, and was worried at what this unpredictable wig-wearing vixen would do next.

Cautious around me, my husband was acting like he did not want to be associated with me. And it hurt. As the night drew to a close, Steve looked at me with pity. He placed his arm around me to comfort me. I looked into his eyes and smiled.

With his gentle embrace, I could feel that he still had love for me.

But I could see that his eyes were starting to look at me in a different way.

19 IN DARK DESPAIR

From the beginning of 1999, Steve had become distant and introspective. I feared that my unpredictable behaviour over the last year was driving him away from me.

I didn't believe it was in Steve's nature to cheat, even if he was thousands of miles away on the road. But various sources had called to tell me that Steve was now travelling with Debra McMichael, the new valet of fellow WWF performer Jeff Jarrett. I initially dismissed these rumours as fiction.

As problems were being reported in our marriage, we were smothered by the presence of Ricky and Sandra whenever Steve was home. They dropped by to share their latest complaint.

Ricky had been drinking an open beer while driving his pickup truck, and had been pulled over by Sheriff Hodges. Wanting to give him a chance, Hodges told Ricky that he was going to let him off with a warning.

"I like that Sheriff Hodges, he's a really nice guy," I said.

"I don't care if that Sheriff Hodges drives a Cadillac or has a college education, he is still a stinkin' nigger," Sandra barked.

Appalled, I raised my eyebrows at Steve and walked away from them. Stephanie and Cassidy were in earshot of the foul language, and I quickly ushered the children into the house.

Due to Steve's demanding schedule, our alone time as a couple had become increasingly rare, but he spent an increasing amount of time with the toxic pair. I had really become unsettled by their friendship with Steve, as he was spending more time with them than his family.

Within days of his return to work, an unnerving situation started to occur at the hacienda.

While Steve was touring, I had started receiving threatening phone calls late at night, frequently when I was alone in the house.

Unsettled by the altered voice, the caller would often tell me that my time was due at a specific hour. The caller was vague to the point that I was watching my back at all times.

I was terrified that someone was intending to hurt me, or worse still, kill me in front of the children.

Every night, I would get these calls, sometimes I would even be awakened by them.

The person knew my routine, and each of my movements. It was clear that I was being watched.

I feared that someone had overheard my outspoken views against the culture of racism in Boerne, and was trying to drive me out of town.

On Sunday 24th January 1999, I got another call. My time was to be up that night.

Frozen with fear, I paced around the living room of the house. The night was particularly dark, and there was a torrent of rain that was quite unusual in Boerne.

Distressed, I was shivering when I heard the rumble of a pick-up truck coming down the road.

The truck turned into the drive, and the beams of the headlights came closer and closer to the house. With the rays beaming through the windows of the hacienda, the vehicle stopped and the door opened and an obscured figure approached the door.

There was no way I was going to let myself be murdered in front of the children. I had to make a decision between fight and flight.

Determined by the maternal instinct to protect my children, I ran.

I was alone and scared, but I needed to lead danger away from the house.

Stumbling onto the ground, I scrambled to pick my body up, and ran to the gate.

I sprinted across the road, and hurtled myself over a fence, treading on a rattlesnake as I journeyed into the woods.

With rain pelting off my face, I could not stop. I was determined to get away from my stalker and journeyed into the thick darkness of the forest.

I could see beams of light in the night sky, flickering off the falling rain. I was convinced that there was somebody searching for me. But I would do whatever was necessary to prevent anyone catching me.

Exhausted from the running, I needed to hide. My sweater and jogging bottoms had soaked right through, and my face was being hammered by the icy downpour.

Finding shelter under a crooked tree, I ripped my skin as I scratched at my watch to remove it. I could not take the chance that it would reflect any flashlights, so I clawed at the wet earth with my nails, burying its glass face under the mud.

Crouching down, I wrapped my arms around my legs. Closing my eyes, I tried to shut off from the horror of the outside world.

The silence wouldn't last. Within minutes I could hear the abrasive cacophony of barking dogs.

Convinced I was being tracked, I had lost hope. It was only a matter of time before I would be found.

Dejected, I looked to the stars, and sighed.

As my eyes wandered upwards, I saw the tree offering itself to my hands. I had to climb.

Clutching at the timber, I ascended, making it high before resting myself on a high branch.

As I sat, I tried to get a better view, but my vision was obscured by tear droplets and heavy rain. I had to come up with an exit plan if the worst was to happen.

I could not allow myself to be torn apart by the hounds, or tortured and raped by their master. In these remote woods, there would be no witnesses, and I would have simply been reported as a missing person if my body had never found its way back to the hacienda.

If I was going to die, it would be by my hand.

I took off my sweater, and tied it around a nearby branch, which I knew could take the weight of a person. I was trembling in my bra, as I prepared to say goodbye to the world before hanging myself.

I closed my eyes, and would take in one last inhale. I prayed for God to listen to my desperate plea for help, and to show mercy to my soul.

Then there was a silence. It was a hush that I had never heard before. The rain had stopped, and the wail of the pursuing dogs had calmed, then faded.

I opened my eyes, and there was nothing. In disbelief, my wide eyes looked all around. There was no danger, and I was in amazed disbelief.

Gathering myself, I unwound my sweater, and followed the noise of a passing truck to lead me to the civility of the road.

Exasperated, I started to feel an incredible thirst. Cupping my hands into a nearby pond, I started to drink the water. It was rejuvenating, and I wandered towards the sound of the passing carriageway.

I turned the corner and noticed a familiar garden shop. I knew it was close to the hacienda, and knew my way back from the shop.

When I returned, the hacienda was empty. A message was left that Jade had taken Stephanie and Cassidy to stay with Ricky and Sandra, and had disrupted Steve's work during the *Royal Rumble* pay-per-view to call him.

Despite happening in the most remote setting imaginable, the tabloids had been notified of my sudden disappearance that night, and a story had been printed in *The National Enquirer* about my crazed run from my home.

There was never any interview with the press for my side of the story, nor had there been any mention about the death threat calls that led me to run.

The article was solely trying to smear my name, painting me as an unfit mother. I could not understand the motive, nor could I figure out who had tipped off the media about the incident.

Terrified by the repeated phone calls, I was driven by a maternal determination to shield the girls from sharing my threatened fate. I loved my children to the extent I was willing to accept the worst possible ending on my own.

When the story hit the papers, I got a call from Steve.

"What are you doing? Are you trying to ruin my career?" he asked.

He had grown concerned at my unpredictable behaviour, but the attention caused by *The National Enquirer* story forced him to ask what was going on in my head.

After a brief reprieve, Ricky and Sandra returned Stephanie and Cassidy to me, but my relief was short lived.

I received another call.

I needed to ensure the safety of the girls, so I took them to Mary's house. I was growing tired of having to put the girls through my misery, and I wanted them to be in the company of someone who cared.

Trembling, I checked myself into a hotel for a couple of nights. I hoped the distance would allow me to evade the fate that was promised by the mystery caller.

Increasingly paranoid, I vowed to get off the GHB which had been dulling my senses.

Even if the withdrawal symptoms heightened my anxiety, I had to become more vigilant if I was to survive the pursuit. I was still using other medication, but the GHB had altered my perception of reality to the point I was not as alert as I needed to be.

Shattered from a few days' inner reflection, and coupled with the drain of a self-imposed detox of the GHB, I returned home.

On the way, I drove to Mary's to pick up the girls. We had dinner together, and laughed before I put them to bed.

Stephanie and Cassidy fell fast asleep, and then it happened.

When I put down the receiver, I knew I could no longer run away.

Fragile, I sat and stared at the walls, hoping that the cloud of uncertainty would pass. But it didn't.

I was standing in the hallway, and a blinding light shone into the house. The walls were floodlit by a stark illumination.

Peering out of the window, I saw a black truck. It had driven all the way into our garden.

Rigidly facing the house, I realised it was hostile. For over ten minutes, it just stayed there, with its engine grunting.

Steadfastly decreeing that I was not going to be forced out of my house, I looked into the light, staring at the truck until it eventually turned and drove away.

There was only one way out of my predicament.

Knowing that I could no longer live a life filled by running away, I wanted the girls to grow a normal life, even if it meant one without their mother. There was no way my situation was going to improve and they could no longer be around the worry that was consuming me.

For months, I had tried to ignore the threatening calls and strange occurrences that were happening around the house. To ensure I was assessing my predicament with lucid thought, I even rid myself of numbing drug dependence.

But it was all in vain. I was now completely beyond hope.

I had picked up some tablets and cleaning fluids from the nearby convenience store, and returned to the house.

Walking to the kitchen, I was careful in my footsteps as I did not want to wake the children.

I quietly opened up the bottle of pills and swallowed them all.

I wanted to make sure I did the job right, and washed the drugs down with some detergent and disinfectant.

In my mind, I had finally done it. I had killed myself.

I felt an intense burning in my throat. It rapidly got worse, and I was no longer in control of my body.

Projectile vomiting, I went to lie down on the kitchen floor, before mustering up the energy to complete my task.

Life had clung to me like a disease, so I staggered into the hallway, towards the cupboard by the bedroom. It was usually locked, but I managed to get inside.

In the unit was what I had needed to find; a gun from Steve's collection. I reached down with my hand, and curled my hand around its grip, and looked into the barrel.

I pulled the trigger but nothing happened.

Desperate, the gun was supposed to be an escape from my living hell. I needed to find bullets. I turned on the lights and looked inside the cupboard, hurriedly shifting things that were in the way in search of some.

Frantic, I entered the bedroom, and started raiding the drawers of the bedside unit and nearby chest of drawers. I was adamant to keep looking, and continued the search. But I was becoming increasingly tired.

I started to fade, and drifted away.

Waking up the next day, I went to the kitchen to fix some breakfast and clean the mess I had made. Saddened by the evidence, I could see the trail of my despair, with scattered pills, vomit and a pool of detergent all over the floor.

I was scared at how I had been driven to the point of taking my own life.

The next day, Steve came home earlier than expected. Having thought about our last conversation, he wanted to come home and offer me support. He dropped a number of scheduled appearances, and arranged for Ray Traylor to fill in for his commitments at WWF live events.

His first action was to locate all ten of my remaining GHB bottles, and flushed them down the kitchen sink.

By leaving the drug around our home, Steve felt guilty that he had introduced me to it. I admitted to him that I had ordered the stash from his contact at the gym, but assured him that I had made the effort to get clean.

Steve wasn't going to take any chances. He remembered the car crash on the day of his interview with Rolling Stone, and requested that I no longer drive until he was certain I was clean. Conceding with his request, I relinquished my car keys to him.

As a temporary measure, Steve would arrange for Ricky and Sandra to help me on my trips to take the girls to school or to their nanny.

Over the course of his time off, Steve really tried to help me and doggedly wanted to save our marriage.

He spent the time to take the family out of the hacienda in an effort to help me get well, and he even cooked to ensure I was eating right.

It was not long before the front office made contact with Steve. They were aware of my problems, and wanted to know how I was doing. Furthermore, it was explained to Steve that the WWF were willing to send me to rehab if I needed professional help.

Without really asking me, Steve told them I was doing alright, and it wouldn't be long before he was back to work.

Although I was Steve's wife, I was starting to feel like a widow to the pro wrestling business. I knew it was only a matter of time before he would be back on the road, and I would be in the same position as I had been before.

It was obvious that our relationship was struggling but we were both uncomfortable discussing the issues as a couple.

More and more, if Steve became troubled with an aspect of our marriage, he would leave the room and call Jim Ross. They would talk for hours on end.

For a generation of fans, many will remember Ross as being the greatest announcer in the history of the business. In addition to his role as a broadcaster, he was employed by the WWF front office as the Head of Talent Relations.

Jim knew the value that Steve had to the company, and was always there to listen to his problems. Over time, they became very close.

The following week, I picked up the phone to make a call and briefly overheard Steve on the other line. He was again confiding to Jim about our increasing marital differences.

"You need to tell that young lady that she needs to stay in the kitchen," Ross joked.

Jim might have been trying to make light of the situation but I found the comment demeaned the horror of my addiction.

The next month, I found myself having a wry snigger when I discovered that Jim had published a cookbook and that he was looking to sell a range of cooking sauces too. I guess we all found out who really belonged behind the hot stove.

Regardless, I had known Jim quite well for years and he had always been a gentleman whenever we met. The truth is that I am glad that Steve had someone to talk through his problems.

He needed the support of a friend during a time that his home issues were impacting his ability to perform. The stress of being the company's top star alone would have broken many men.

Nevertheless, the phone call to Jim underlined what I already knew.

It was clear that neither of us could directly speak to the other about our relationship. Steve was now turning to the company to discuss his personal issues, shutting me and our family out of his life.

To an international television audience of millions of fans each week, Steve could produce the most intense and articulate interviews with a command of the spoken word that is rarely witnessed. It was ironic that he could not communicate his most basic feelings to his wife.

With each passing day, I felt that we were becoming increasingly detached.

My abuse of drugs stemmed from loneliness, and my unpredictable actions became a cry for help as I descended into addiction.

In a last-ditch effort to save the marriage, Steve identified the isolation of the hacienda as the source my decline.

He asked if I would like to move, and offered to show me a new gated community in San Antonio called The Dominion. We went to view a property within it, and it was beautiful. I told him I loved the house.

Steve wanted to commit to its purchase, and quickly laid down a deposit, but I told him I was not sure about buying it just yet.

Simply moving seemed hasty. I felt that there were issues beyond the home location that needed discussed, some of the core problems within our marriage had to be sorted.

Remembering his previous drunken comment that he once really loved me, it was an admission which had weighed on my mind for months, and really affected my self-esteem.

Damaged and vulnerable, I wanted to let him know how that comment had upset me. As a result of feeling unloved, I confessed that I had been driven towards another man during my brief visit to Miami.

I told Steve that I still had love for him, but I was no longer in love with him.

I hoped that if I could stimulate an argument, it would allow us to have the much-needed dialogue to save our marriage.

We had never communicated to each other about our feelings, and we needed to if we were going to change our relationship to make it work.

With counselling, and commitment we could. But Steve needed a break. He went off to see Ricky and Sandra.

By this point, I accepted that the pair would forever be a part of our lives, even if we moved. They had been a poison within our household. I resigned to the fact that I was better without my husband if it meant I would no longer be in their presence.

After taking time away from work to reach out to me, Steve felt he had done everything he could to try and salvage the situation. Frustrated by my inability to commit to the new home, he sensed it was time to give our marriage a break.

We decided to separate, and Steve moved in with Ricky and Sandra until we both decided what we wanted.

I was heartbroken for our children, as it was inevitable that their lives were going to change once again.

Our days as a family were numbered.

20 A FRACTURED HOME

It was not long after Steve had moved his mobile home outside Ricky and Sandra's that I got a visit from the police. I answered the door to be greeted by Sheriff Hodges and a female officer.

The female officer noted a complaint that I was a drug addict. She said that I was going to be taken away for questioning. Her demeanour was threatening, and she demanded that Hodges looked into my eyes.

"Look at her, she's in la-la land," she uttered with anger.

Sheriff Hodges was quick to pacify the situation, and asked if I was okay.

"Please sir, I'm gonna be fine. I am just tired," I explained.

Hodges looked at me and paused. There was a kindness and compassion in his eyes.

"Just go back and have a rest, get yourself well," he gently advised.

Meanwhile, the female officer started to get anxious, suggesting I should be arrested immediately, and she started to argue with her superior officer. It was odd that there was such urgency in her assessment, and it seemed as if she had a pre-conception of my lifestyle.

Her annoyance at Hodges was out of place, given his rank as the town Sheriff. It seemed as if she had failed to complete a task that she had been set by someone else.

Once Hodges spoke to me, I think he realised that I was also an outsider facing intolerance in Boerne.

Within a few days, I received a call from Sue Aitchison.

She told me that the WWF had become concerned with my personal issues and that they were going to source me a rehab clinic. The company was aware that I had developed a dependence on prescription pills, and I accepted their offer, but there was no further indication on when my rehabilitation would commence.

In the meantime, I vowed to maintain my promise to Steve that I would not drive. After the previous incidents caused by my abuse of GHB, he said that he had arranged for Ricky and Sandra to help by driving me to the nanny of our children whenever required.

The first afternoon of our agreement, Ricky and Sandra came over to pick me up in their truck. Despite being Valentine's Day, I was alone at the house as Steve was wrestling on a major WWF pay-per-view that evening.

When Ricky and Sandra arrived, they were strangely kind to me, and I got into their pickup, before we set off to collect the girls from Mary.

Except we never went to Mary's; they drove past her house and continued on the highway, even though I asked them why they didn't stop.

They continued to drive, speeding towards San Antonio. They started to laugh and mocked me. It became clear that I was being set up by them.

Ricky threw a beer can at me.

"Have a beer," he sniggered, as he tossed a second can off of me.

The pair continued to mock me, and wouldn't tell me where we were heading, as I pleaded with them to let me out of their vehicle. They seemed to get a sadistic pleasure out of my suffering.

I had promised Mary I would collect the girls from her, and panicked that they would wonder where I had gone.

As I begged for them to stop, they just drove faster, laughing at me until we reached an unfamiliar building in a suburb I didn't recognise.

They stopped the car, and went inside, walking purposefully towards a reception area. Shaking with fear, and worried for my girls, I followed them. I hoped that I could speak to someone about being taken to this strange place against my will.

I walked to the desk, where Ricky and Sandra were speaking to a lady about me. They told her that they were bringing me in, and I then realised I had been taken to a clinic.

172

The lady got up from her seat, and asked the three of us to follow her into an assessment room.

Instantly, she could see I was shaking. It was clear that I was afraid.

She looked at me and smiled.

"So, do you want to tell me what is going on?" she asked us, before directing her eyes towards Ricky and Sandra.

Ricky and Sandra started claiming that I was an out-of-control drug addict.

"Look at her, she's in la-la land," asserted Sandra.

Strangely, those were exactly the same words uttered by the female officer who visited the house only a few days prior.

The lady continued to listen, as the pair continued to aggressively declare that I should be admitted with immediate effect. They professed that I should be locked away, as I had gone crazy. They grimaced as they rudely pleaded their case, and continued to mock me in front of her.

After hearing their arguments, the lady turned to me and asked for my opinion.

Despite being frightened, I composed myself, and patiently explained that I had been taken to the clinic against my will. I told her that I had been taken away on the pretence of collecting my children from their sitter. I went on, to tell her that I had promised my babysitter that I would collect my children at a certain time, and I was not agreeable to being admitted into rehab by these people.

Ricky and Sandra had been drinking during the drive to the centre, and were exhibiting signs of being under the influence. On the other hand, I had remained calm and coherent during the discussion.

"Test her blood, go on, give her a test," Ricky demanded.

"Fine, give me a test, but I need to be home soon to collect my daughters," I firmly replied.

I knew that I had no illegal substances in my system, and any issues I had were caused by prescription drugs.

The lady said a test was not required, and realised that Ricky and Sandra had no power of attorney over me.

Ricky and Sandra were incensed. Their plan to have me detained had failed.

Aggravated, they led me back into their truck. They did not get into the pickup, and made a call on their cell phone.

A few moments later, I saw the flash of police lights in the rear view mirror. The police car pulled over next to them, and the officer started to speak to them.

They frenetically waved their arms, and went on a tirade about how I was a danger to society and should be forced into rehab, or arrested.

I watched Ricky and Sandra, as they got further enraged. I looked down into my hands, and realised I was still holding onto the roses that Steve had sent me before I was collected.

Opening the door, I walked towards the officer who seemed to be getting irritated by their demeanour.

"Excuse me officer, I am extremely concerned that I was supposed to pick up my children from my babysitter and have been brought here against my will. Would you please be so kind to give me a ride to my babysitter's house?" I politely interjected.

"I'm sorry sweetheart, I can't do that. Would you please take a seat back in the truck?" he asked.

He then went over to Ricky and Sandra, and instructed for them to return me to my babysitter's house.

Grudgingly, they drove me to Mary's and I got out of the truck. I knocked on her door, and she let me in to her house. I was so relieved; Stephanie and Cassidy were sitting in the living room playing with Mary's two daughters Jennifer and Michelle.

I started to talk to Mary, to explain why I was late, but turned around to see Ricky and Sandra.

They had followed me in to the house, and grabbed the girls. Within seconds, they took them away into the truck and sped off down the road.

I burst into tears, and called the police. Amongst my sobs, I struggled to explain that my children had just been snatched.

Hours passed, as I became increasingly frantic.

As the night sky darkened, the police returned to the house. They informed me that they had traced the girls to the address of Beverly Williams, the mother of my husband.

Ricky and Sandra's defence of the kidnapping was that I had become an unfit mother, and they were taking the children for their own good.

I called my lawyer to arrange for an urgent court order. It ensured that my children would have to be returned with immediate effect.

Moments after Beverly was informed of the order, I got a call from Steve.

"You know, it's really late for my mum to be driving. Would it be okay if she could bring the girls back in the morning?" he mumbled.

I agreed to Steve's request. Stephanie and Cassidy were to be returned to me by 9am.

It never happened. Concerned, I called the police again.

Hours later, the officers returned with the girls. They had been dropped off at Ricky and Sandra's house. Beverly did not even have the decency to take her grandchildren home to their worried mother.

A few days passed without incident, but then it happened.

The unsettling phone calls returned.

Whoever was behind the calls knew one thing; I was in a vulnerable condition, and near tipping point.

By March 1999, Steve had moved into an annexe property with a friend, as he prepared for his match against The Rock at *WrestleMania XV*.

A couple of weeks before the show, he arrived at the hacienda with Ricky. Steve said that he was looking to take away one of our couches in Ricky's pickup truck, while I was playing in the garden with Mary and our daughters.

As we were sitting on the grass, Steve reached to hug Stephanie, as Ricky went over to say goodbye to Cassidy.

In an instant, the two men lifted the girls and marched towards Ricky's pickup.

I sprang up, chasing towards the vehicle, as the girls were banging their hands in terror at the windscreen. I managed to get to the side of the truck, to try to open the door. With the driver's window down, I begged for Steve and Ricky to wait.

Steve strapped the girls into their seatbelts as I begged them to stop. Ricky smirked and spat in my face. The truck then sped off down the road.

With the shock of the girls being taken from me, I broke down on the street. Not knowing when I would next see my children, I was riddled with the horror of my two youngest daughters beating on the glass and screaming for their mum.

With Cassidy, 1999.

As I sat and cried with Mary, I was in such a shaken state that I could not even remember the moment when the girls were returned to me.

Regardless, the incident made one thing clear; I could never be alone with the children. After the girls were snatched from me a second time, I was consumed by a fear that it would happen again.

I wanted to be civil to Steve, as I was worried that they would be forcibly taken from me if he decided that he wanted to challenge me for their custody.

Any issues I had would need to be put on the back burner, and I decided I would have to conceal my prescription problems. I could not afford to seek help as it would afford Steve the opportunity to prove that I was an unfit mother to the authorities.

With our relationship beyond repair, it was only a matter of time before Steve and I instigated divorce proceedings. Although our relationship had taken us to the heights of fame, the world had become a much lonelier place for me. It drove me to the depths of despair before I accepted my problems with Steve were irreversible.

Once we separated, I sought a rental house in The Dominion, the gated community that Steve and I had considered as we tried to save our marriage.

I was broken by the misery of my life in Boerne, and even Steve looked drained when he announced our divorce on *The Howard Stern Show*. I hoped that the distance would do us both good, as it was important to remain amicable for the sake of our children.

I had already witnessed the effect on Jade as a result of her estranged relationship with Chris, and how confused and damaged it made her. It was important for Stephanie and Cassidy to have access to their dad, and each of my decisions were made with them in mind.

Within the divorce papers was a clause inserted at Steve's insistence.

The clause stated that I couldn't leave Texas with Stephanie and Cassidy for any period longer than three months, nor could I take them on holiday abroad without his written permission.

Steve knew that my judgement was impaired, and I was still too dependent with drugs to make a correct assessment of the terms that were being presented.

I just sensed that I could trust him as he had seemed so understanding throughout the process. I figured he just really wanted to maintain contact with the kids. I never fully agreed to the terms, but I felt compelled to sign. Despite feeling badly represented by my lawyer, it was my only way out of a loveless marriage.

On 5th May 1999, it was official. Steve and I had finalised our divorce.

After the divorce was finalised, I sat on the pavement beside the lawyer's office. Steve followed soon after, and seeing me there, he sat next to me and we put our arms around each other.

We shared a moment, as we realised that our nine year relationship had finally ended.

"You know, it was the business which broke us up," Steve said.

He was convinced that the time away, chasing fame as the Stone Cold character had torn apart his marriage.

"Actually, I think it was my addiction problems," I responded.

After we parted, I came to a realisation. It was neither the demands of the wrestling business, nor my addiction issue which was the sole reason for the demise of our marriage. It was a failure to communicate our feelings which caused us to drift apart from each other.

I remembered a comment from Vince McMahon, during a call when I had been discussing domestic issues between Steve and me.

"Jeanie, you are from two different worlds," observed Vince.

In many ways, Vince was right. Spiritually, culturally and in terms of what we wanted to achieve in life, Steve and I were two very different people.

But what had always kept us together, was our common goofy sense of humour, which Steve had once said was his main attraction towards me. When I think of some of the silly sense of humour and fun we used to share, it still brings warmth to my heart.

However, the greatest from our marriage were the two wonderful daughters he gave me, and I see them as a blessing every day.

Creating a fresh start for everyone was the best step forward, so I decided to collect the rest of my belongings and take them out of the hacienda.

I was in the process of moving my stuff when I noticed some clothes in the bedroom that weren't mine. I knew that another woman had already taken residence. In a similar way that our affection had blossomed when Steve was married to Kathy, he was already seeing another lady before our divorce had been finalised.

I received various hints that Steve had been travelling with Debra McMichael, one of the female talents who worked for Vince. But after we split, their bond had quickly developed into a full-on relationship.

Debra had led an interesting life. A former homecoming queen, she spent much of her adult life chasing glory. She chased a career in beauty pageants, before marrying Steve McMichael from the NFL's Super Bowl-winning team of the Chicago Bears. As her husband transitioned into pro wrestling, it was not long until Debra followed him in a non-wrestling role in WCW. They had divorced in October 1998, and she then fled to the WWF, where Steve Austin was its biggest star.

Strangely, I was not hurt in any way by Steve's new romance. I was just happy that he had found company so easily to help him move on with his life.

My main concern was that he would remain a good father to his children, and I fought to keep a sense of amicability so he could continue to be an integral part of their lives. But gradually the terms of the divorce were being used as a vindictive method of keeping a level of control on my life.

It was not long before Steve stopped seeing the girls and he swiftly put a halt on his contributions of financial maintenance. I needed to talk to him about who was paying tax for Stephanie and Cassidy, so I rang the house. Debra answered the phone and was irate as soon as she realised it was me on the other end of the line.

"Don't ever call here again!" she barked.

On another of these occasions, I had arranged to meet up with Steve to hand the girls over, but when I got to the meeting spot Debra was with him and looked noticeably outraged. I questioned why she seemed so angry, when she didn't need to be there. He told me that she had a very controlling nature and wouldn't let him out of her sight.

Her attitude explained Steve's absence. He seemed content to give his daughters the cold shoulder to stop any strain on his relationship with Debra. With no help from Steve due to his reluctance to upset his work schedule, or his girlfriend, I was finding it hard to cope.

Struggling, I told a doctor of my difficulties sleeping, which I claimed was due to the divorce. I was prescribed Ambien, a highly addictive sedative.

Due to its strength, I was told it is rare to overdose on the drug. As I was increasingly sedated, I needed help with the girls. I called my old nanny back, who came and lived with me up in San Antonio to help look after them.

Even though The Dominion was a gated community, I still had reason to be afraid. I would occasionally get a phone call, suggesting I was being watched.

One night, a caller had asked how I had enjoyed my margarita by the pool. Sure enough, that day I had drank one and the terror of being stalked had returned to my life. No matter how far I had tried to shake off the causes of my fear, there was a darkness that was following me around, awaiting my self-destruction.

Within a number of weeks of the call, my nanny's had confided in me that she felt that we were being watched. I asked Steve if he had paid anyone to follow me. He confirmed that it was Debra's idea.

I became anxious that there was a chance that Ricky and Sandra would return to snatch the girls, so I always wanted another adult around the girls and me at all times, whether it was my old friends J.L. and Ann, Linda or Dee. I was so insecure that I even paid for my mum and her husband Fred to fly out and visit.

Even though the marriage was over, I was still trapped as my movements had really been restricted by the divorce order. I could not leave Texas, even though Steve was not making any real effort to see the children.

In the year that I was living in The Dominion, Steve never bothered to call and only saw the girls about two or three times, despite taking a year away from wrestling to recover from the overdue surgery to repair his neck.

Although he hadn't regularly called to check up on his children, there was a time when Steve did ring the house. Having had a few drinks, he phoned to ask if I wanted to meet him late at night. As we spoke, he hung up the phone once he could hear Debra stirring in the background. If the fact that he was married to Debra was not enough to turn me away from him, I could never look at Steve in the same way after he tried to take the girls away from their mother.

But it was while I was at my home in The Dominion that I received another call I would never be able to forget. On 24th April 2000, I answered the phone to a frantic voice.

It was Chris Adams. I had never heard such desperation from him. He was hysterical and in an uncontrollable state. Between the sobbing, he scrambled for the words that could explain why he was so upset.

He had just been released from hospital, after a night he spent hanging out with his latest girlfriend Linda Kaphengst. They had been drinking and playing pool, before continuing the party at the house of Brent Parnell, where he offered her some GHB.

She collapsed on the floor and Chris lost consciousness too, passing out while slumped on a chair.

The two were later found by Parnell and it was some time before the emergency services were called. They were then taken out of the apartment by ambulance.

When Chris woke up in the hospital twelve hours later, he was told that Linda had died. Chris had given her too much GHB, and she overdosed. He was faced with a second-degree felony charge for causing her death, with a potential imposed jail sentence of twenty years.

Chris' was begging me for help, and he asked if I would meet him and go to Florida to hang out and help him clear his head. As much as I wanted to help Chris, I just couldn't do it. He had really changed over the years and I had become wary of him.

Crippled with the vices of both drink and drugs, Chris could be a dangerous, volatile monster when he was not sober. He had a violent side that could not be controlled. I knew that any association with him would give Steve the ammunition he needed to question my ability to look after the girls.

I was sad for Chris, and saw a reflection of myself in his downfall. We had both arrived in the United States with dreams for the future, but our American Dream had degenerated into a nightmare of paranoia, wasted promise and substance hell.

Before we ended our call, Chris did make one request that I would consider. He suggested that I move back to Dallas, a town which he promised would provide a better lifestyle for my family. Chris knew that I carried a fear in The Dominion, and wanted me to be free from my pain.

Dallas was familiar ground for me. I knew it well, had many friends there and had some wonderful memories in the city. Like Atlanta, it was a nurturing town bustling with opportunity, and the perfect place to raise the girls.

After thinking about Chris' advice, I gave Steve a call and told him I wanted to return there. He didn't seem to mind, and I looked forward to the prospect of moving.

But before I could go, I needed to find a way out of the drug hell in which I was living.

21 ESCAPE FROM REALITY

By the spring of 2000, I knew I was living on borrowed time. Having had health scares and losing manageability of my life, I sensed it was only a matter of time before my body would shut down once again, possibly with consequences from which I could never recover.

It was arranged that Steve would look after the girls for a fortnight, so I grasped the opportunity to find a way out from my addictions. With Stephanie and Cassidy staying at their father's house, I was able to source somewhere isolated, allowing me to focus solely on my health.

Due to my manipulation of the private medical system in America, I had managed to stockpile over two hundred Ambien pills. My dependence on the drug had since skyrocketed from several tablets a day, to a dosage of seven. It was clear that the doctor's advice that the drug was not addictive was a total untruth, as was his prediction that one pill a day would suffice. I needed to seek refuge in a place where prescriptions are managed by a national institution and not falter to the allure of a network of self-interested private medical professionals.

Travelling to London, I wandered into the Churchill Hotel. I had not called in advance of my flight to make a reservation, I just needed to get out of the States first, and improvise my recovery. Once I got to the reception desk, I was lucky. There was only one room left, but I managed to check-in without issue.

With my luggage taken to my room, I locked the door and started my self-imposed detox. There was not a moment to lose, and while I was still in a determined mindset, I needed to ensure that all temptation would be eliminated from my grasp.

I opened my bags, and placed all my bottles of pills in front of me.

"You can do it, you can do it," I kept urging myself.

I went into the bathroom, cradling the bottles in my arms and deposited them onto the top of the vanity unit. After lifting the seat of the toilet, I unscrewed the tops of the bottles.

One by one, I turned the bottles over and watched them drop into the pan, which slowly turned into a muddled pattern of white, orange and blue dots on the surface of the water. I stood back, and took a deep breath at the magnitude of my stash. There were at least four hundred pills there.

I needed to be strong, and I closed my eyes, as I pulled the lever on the cistern. With one flush of the handle, I watched the mouth of the toilet open itself and drink away the pills for me.

I had done it. After realising that I was in an environment without the triggers of addiction, I sat on the end of the bed content in my strength to overcome the vices which had seized hold of my life.

It was not long before the reality of my situation started to affect me. Shaking, I could start to feel the power of my withdrawal symptoms. As it sapped my strength, I had to lie on the bed, as it became harder to bear.

My senses started to feel heightened, and I was drawn by a scent of roses, and petunia. As the joy of the flowers slowly died, I coughed as the mustiness of cigar stench filled the room.

The room became stifling hot, and I struggled to breathe. Baking in the sweltering heat, I scrambled for the air conditioning control. I started to thump at the buttons as the heat became unbearable.

It was not long before the burning changed to a chilled iciness.

I tucked my legs into my chests, and wrapped my arms around them, as I started to shiver. The room was starting to become a glacier of freezing misery, and I went into the bathroom, to run a bath with warm water.

As the bath started to fill, I waited at the edge of the door and looked at the television in the bedroom. It was flickering, on and off, and I could sense a dark presence in the hotel room with me. I locked myself into the bathroom, and sat in the bath.

I heard a click, and within seconds, the lights went out within the room. Sitting in the darkness, my body fluctuated from being hot to cold, and within minutes, the lights went back on again.

Standing in the water, I was naked, and vulnerable. I looked into the mirror and screamed.

I could not see my own reflection. In its place was a hooded figure.

As I panicked, it remained still. It was staring at me through its withered and skeletal face with the blackest eyes.

"For unto thee, a child is born," growled the wraith.

A deafening, mechanical roar started to fill the room. I tore into the lock of the door, pulling at the doorknob in a frenzy to get out of the bathroom.

Running to the window, I looked into the night sky. It was filled with helicopters, circling the building.

At that moment, a fire alarm sounded. I reached for my clothes, and hurriedly put them on, as I made my way to evacuate the hotel. As I was running out, two men in suits restrained me, and forced me to return to my room.

Hopelessly frightened, I called my brother.

Phil wasted no time, and made his way to the hotel to pick me up, as I waited for him in the lobby. He knew what had happened. In my attempt to go cold turkey from the pills, my body and mind had gone into shock, and I was experiencing the delusions of drug psychosis from my withdrawal.

My brother told me that I could stay at his house in Canterbury, and needed to see a doctor. I was comforted by him, as he would look out for his little sister.

Over the course of several days, Phil showed great patience with me, as I struggled with the symptoms of my withdrawal. With my hands twitching, and my nose streaming from illness, I had not slept for three days. Despite weakness, I needed to make a run for it.

Getting off of the tablets was a mistake. But it was something I was keen to fix.

With no shoes on my feet, I ran out of the house. Seeing the madness of my addiction, I was pursued by Phil, who ran to save me from running into the oncoming traffic.

He easily caught up with me, and grabbing the sides of both my arms, he looked at me with a defeat in his eyes.

"I am so sorry Jeanie, but I am going to have to try to get you some help," he sighed.

As he tried to comfort me, an ambulance arrived.

I was driven to St. Martin's Hospital, and taken into a padded room with just a mattress inside it. In a delusional state, I felt a jab in my backside. It was a shot of Haloperidol, an anti-psychotic drug. It did not take long to enter my bloodstream.

Seconds later, I was out for the count.

Waking up, not fully knowing where I was, I learned that I had been detained under the Mental Health Act. In the opinion of the team who had evaluated my condition upon arrival, I was a danger to myself and those around me, and had to be sectioned.

I needed to stay until I was re-evaluated, but I became impatient. I needed to leave.

On a programme of anti-psychotic medication, I was starting to eat again, and my delusions had come to an end. Engaging with the psychiatrist who put a section on me, we had formed a bond as doctor-patient.

I knew I needed to appeal to his compassion to arrange my release.

Confessing everything, I told the psychiatrist all about the terms of the Texas order. I explained that I would need to return to the States as I was desperate to see the girls. I also knew that having a section on me would enable my ex-husband to attain full custody of Stephanie and Cassidy.

If that had happened, I would have been crushed. Even though I realised I needed help, I knew that nobody else could have loved my children as much as I did.

As I softly told my doctor of my predicament, he stood up and looked towards the window. Turning to the ceiling, he took a deep breath.

"Tell me how I can be decent," he sighed.

He looked at me and paused for thought.

"I see it in your eyes, go home to your children," he offered.

I had managed to find freedom, but I couldn't fully celebrate. I was still caged by my addiction. After flying home, I gradually resumed my old habits. By now, my body had stopped hiding the fact that I was a drug addict.

One June afternoon, I lost consciousness. My young daughters couldn't waken me, and they alerted their temporary nanny, Jodie.

Years of substance abuse had caught up with me. I had finally overdosed.

An ambulance was not in reach, so the call was answered by a nearby team from the fire department.

A number of weeks later, I was in the grocery store, and saw one of the firemen who had responded to the call. I was still in disbelief that I had overdosed and wanted to approach him with gratitude.

"Hi, how are you?" I asked.

He paused and looked at me. His eyes welled up as he slowly shook his head.

I was taken aback by the sadness in his eyes.

"Was it a close call?" I continued, wondering why he was so moved to see me.

"Yes. We thought we had lost you," he confided in a gentle whisper.

It was quite the realisation, to find out how close I had come to death. I needed some time to clear my head.

Steve asked if he could see the girls for Cassidy's birthday. As we shared joint custody of the children, I agreed to let him look after them that week. With some free time, I decided to spend a few days with their new nanny, Kym. I quickly became good friends with her, and she asked if I wanted to attend a party being hosted by a chiropractor who she knew well.

It seemed like a normal party, until I was asked if I wanted to take some cocaine. His girlfriend seemed to be getting annoyed at the attention he was lavishing towards me. I could sense she was uncomfortable, so I left to return home.

As I drove down the road, I was pulled over by the police and arrested on the suspicion of using drugs.

When the police had carried out a search, there were no drugs on my person or in my car. After being bailed out by Kym's mum, I arranged to meet my lawyer. The case was then dismissed.

After the arrest, I wanted a new start, and to finally move out of The Dominion.

I had been taken by a new scheme of houses that were under construction in Arlington, so I committed to the purchase of a property there. But until the building works were complete, the girls and I moved into a rented accommodation in San Antonio. It was an initial measure that I took to escape the surveillance which I was sensing within the gated community, before relocating us once again to the house of Kym's parents.

The support of Kym' family was astounding, and their nurturing home gave me the motivation I craved to wean myself off the Ambien. When I had been prescribed it, I was told that its strength was certain to prevent it from being abused. Developing a rapid immunity to it, I had tripled my dosage of the pill by early December. I decided to let my supply run out, and clear it from my system.

As Christmas was approaching, I was sitting next to Kym's mother, chatting on the couch. I stood up and felt strange. Grabbing for the sofa to give me support, my hand could not reach it.

I collapsed on the floor, biting my tongue, as my eyes rolled into my head.

I had lost total control of all my body functions, as my body started to experience convulsions on the floor. Bereft of the drugs, my body had started to shut itself down, as I had a seizure in the living room of Kym's parents.

And that's all I remember.

Hours later, I woke up hospital. I hoped that the New Year would be clear of any further destruction caused by drugs.

Once I got home, we packed up our belongings and prepared to move to Arlington. I hoped that the new house would give us some much-needed happiness. The previous summer, I had already received some wonderful news; my eldest daughter Jade and her boyfriend Derek Kutzer, were pregnant.

On 21st February 2001, Jade gave birth to her first child, the cutest baby boy named Blaise. I was so proud to be a grandmother, and I couldn't wait to visit my new grandson.

Not long after that, I got a call from Steve. He let me know that the WWF was going to be broadcasting its live Raw is War telecast from nearby Fort Worth on 2nd April, and asked if I would bring Stephanie and Cassidy. He said he had missed them and was keen to see his children given that he would be in Texas for the show. Since the divorce, the girls' time with their father had been a rarity, so I told him that we would be there.

Jade and my grandson Blaise, 2001.

When I told the girls about the show, they were thrilled. Bustling with excitement, they asked if they could make some signs to hold up in the crowd in support of their dad.

On the afternoon before the show, the phone rang.

"Hey, sorry to have to tell you this now, it's best you don't come. Debra's not to happy with it," he awkwardly confided.

I couldn't believe what I was hearing.

"Steve, don't do this. They're so excited they've made signs and really want to go. Don't upset the girls. Let me take them and we'll just sit in the audience. We'll leave straight after the show and I'll just tell them you couldn't see them as you had an injury. Anything, just don't let them down. It's too short notice to cancel on them, it's not fair" I pleaded.

There was no way I was going to crush the girls by stopping them from going to the show after weeks of promise. I told Steve that I was taking them, before we ended the call.

We arrived at the Convention Center, and watched the show. I let the girls know that their dad was busy, but they were just happy to sit amongst the crowd and watch him perform. They yelled and went crazy for their dad, as he faced The Rock in the centre of the ring.

The girls had such a fun time, and we headed towards the exit. On the way, we were stopped by one of the road crew. He recognised me and waved us over to him.

We started speaking and he asked us if we wanted to go backstage. Just as we were going to, we bumped into Paul Heyman. After his ECW promotion had filed for bankruptcy, Paul was now thriving as the primary heel commentator for the WWF.

Paul was so gracious. Having not seen each other in years, he led me to the backstage area, and opened one of the dressing room doors. It swung open, and we saw Steve.

Sitting on a bench, icing his knees, Steve had a blank expression when he saw us. He gave the girls a brief greeting but it was clear from his awkwardness that we were not expected. I let Stephanie and Cassidy give him a wave from the corridor, as we turned to leave.

We started to walk our way down the hall, and saw Debra. She frowned and started approaching us with anger, before grabbing a hold of Stephanie's arm.

"Come on, I'll take you to your father!" she snapped.

I snatched my daughters arm away from the grasp of Debra's bony clutches before we squared up face-to-face. There was no way I was going to back down from her volatile attitude.

"They've already seen him Debra. And by the way, do you have a problem them seeing their dad?" I retorted.

"Yes!" she barked. She turned on her heels and stormed into the locker room to see Steve.

I then realised why Steve did not want the girls to come to the show. He was so worried that our presence would enrage Debra, and would rather that our children did not come to the show at all.

Later that night, when Debra was in bed, I got a call from Steve. He wanted to apologise for his wife's actions, and continued to explain that she had been in such a rage that she had taken his rental car and drove away from the arena without him.

Stranded, he had to hitch a ride with his new on-screen associate Triple H. I shook my head, realising this debacle could have easily been avoided if Steve had just told Debra that his girls were coming to the show, regardless of her jealousy.

It was pathetic that a rare visit to let the girls see Steve had caused such uproar, and I knew the situation would not improve. After years of trying to make the joint custody of our children work, I resigned myself to the fact that it never could.

For two years, I had been forced to stay in Texas on the agreement that Steve would have access to the children. He knew I had struggled to get clean in the States, but had insisted that I stayed in the country so he could see them.

Since the divorce, he repeatedly let down our kids, and I was always left to pick up the pieces. I could not accept any more broken promises. Feeling I had lost all hope of a happy life in Texas, I found myself in a no-win situation.

I had made up my mind. I could no longer tolerate being trapped under the court order of Texas house arrest, and I needed to return home to England.

Stephanie and Cassidy, 2001.

But this time, I was taking my daughters with me.

22 GENTLEMANLY CONDUCT

In the two years since my divorce, my life had been dictated by an ill-advised agreement between Steve and my attorney. They established a court order for me to live under house arrest in the state of Texas. The aim of the settlement was supposed to guarantee that Steve would see his family on a regular basis.

But Steve rarely called to check up on his children, and seemed to be ignoring his family out of a fear that any interaction with us would upset his new wife. On a number of occasions, Steve would hang up the phone in the middle of a call to me, even if it was simply to ask how his girls were doing. This continued as the months passed, and it became obvious that Debra's jealousy of me would never fade while I was around.

It made the situation of sharing custody of the children together impossible. I knew that any attempt to reach Steve would only serve to stir up trouble in his new marriage, and the last thing I wanted was to cause any more hurt to him. It was widely known that he never wanted to get a divorce from me, but I was glad to see he had found someone with whom he could share the rest of his life.

Debra was aware that he had two daughters from his second marriage when she met him, but she still felt threatened by me. As a result, her selfishness and insecurity stopped two little girls from seeing their dad.

Our divorce agreement had failed in its objective. I had received no assistance to raise the girls, and the order was being used as a means to control me. There had already been attempts to portray me as an unfit mother, and I couldn't visit home, or take the girls for a brief vacation without expressed permission from my ex-husband.

At boiling point, I needed a temporary escape from the unsettlement in my life. The control of my destiny had caused me to suffer anxiety attacks, and I depended on one mechanism to alleviate stress.

Each time I would reach out to try and get off the pills I was abusing, I was prescribed even more drugs to counter-balance the cocktail I had been taking. Everyone knew that I had prescription problems, but it seemed that a game was being played until my inevitable self-destruction. I needed to be miles away from the familiar network of mark doctors who had been feeding me drugs to serve their own interests.

Nobody cared about the cesspool of addiction which had trapped me, and it was common knowledge that my issues had stemmed from loneliness and homesickness.

In the weeks following the Fort Worth incident, I had felt a strong yearning to return home.

Chris could sense I was discontented and started visiting regularly. He had recently gotten engaged to a single mother named Karen Burge. She was really warm and brought some much-needed love into Chris' life following the end of his wrestling career. The couple even offered to take Stephanie and Cassidy to the Six Flags theme park with his young daughter Julia.

Karen Burge Cole, former wife of Chris Adams: "When Jeanie and I first met, we became instant friends. Chris and I and my two children, Shea and Tyler and his daughter Julia would spend time at her house in Arlington. Shea remembers playing with Stef and Cassie. I recall Chris taking the kids to Six Flags. It was important to Chris to always have season passes to Six Flags."

After years of turbulence, it was nice to see Chris revert to his former fun self.

In early May, his parents arrived to visit and I offered them the chance to stay with me. It had been years since I had been around Jean and Cyril, and I looked forward to catching up with them.

One night during their stay, Chris came to the house with his friend Brent Parnell, who he called 'Booray'. It was a really fun evening, but Chris and Booray never knew when to stop drinking. They turned a family event into an exhausting booze binge.

Chris with his mother Jean and Karen's son Tyler, 2001.

Nevertheless, being around Chris' parents had made me realise how much I had missed England.

I wanted to fly across the pond and see my own family. I also believed that the rigidity of Britain's National Health Service could save my life.

I was certain that my daily diet of Vicodin, Ambien and Xanax would be reassessed, and a plan would be put in place to help me get well.

I wanted freedom from addiction. But more than that, I wanted freedom in my life. However temporary my stay would be, I just wanted to fly back home.

On 31st May 2001, I hurriedly packed a couple of suitcases and set off to Dallas/Fort Worth International Airport with Stephanie and Cassidy. I hadn't received anything in writing from Steve to permit our departure, but I knew that a call to him would only enrage Debra.

Once we arrived at DFW, I was terrified at the prospect of being followed and abandoned my car in the parking lot. I was in such a rush to get on the next flight, and ushered the girls to the gates.

As we boarded the plane, I looked out the window and sighed. I knew I would miss Texas, but I felt enslaved by years of having to abide to the law of Steve and Debra, and wanted to escape the scrutiny of watching eyes.

To save Steve from worry, I left a message on his voicemail so he would know that the girls were safe with their mother in England.

Ten hours later, I arrived in the United Kingdom. It seemed that I was finally free.

After taking a moment to savour my surroundings, we gathered our luggage and set off to stay with my mum. She had continued to remain sober from her alcoholism for years since getting married to Fred in 1981.

Fred and my mum.

I was in awe of how she had managed to get over her problems and regain control of her life. Having spent a childhood ashamed of my drunken mother, I started to view her as an inspiration. She was the role model who showed me that it was possible to get clean, and stay that way. I was so proud; she finally seemed to find peace in her life.

As a person who was struggling with addiction, it was so important to be greeted by someone who had overcome it. She will never realise the hope that she gave me. I believed that, one day, my life would change.

We went to stay at her house in Southend and even though it was going to be a tight squeeze with the three of us all sharing a bedroom, it felt far more liberating than being caged within the confines of the Texas court order.

My mum will never know how much she did for our family by taking us into her home when we returned to England. Free from alcohol and the threat of an abusive partner, her house was the secure shelter that I wished it had been when I was a child.

After we dropped off our belongings, we sauntered down to the beach. I wanted to take a long, peaceful walk along the seafront, and get a cup of good old English tea.

Meanwhile, Stephanie and Cassidy absolutely loved playing on the beach and at the amusements that I had frequented as a child.

I felt like my life had come full circle. All I needed was to find a way to wean myself off of my pills.

It was not long after my return to England when I realised that my stash of prescription pills were starting to dwindle. I knew that I could not allow myself to experience the shock of withdrawal, and set about finding a way to source some lower-strength pills which could lead me towards a drug-free lifestyle.

My aim was to gradually reduce my intake until I was ultimately clean.

Having tried to go the cold-turkey route which led to disaster in London and Arlington, I realised that I needed medical help. I made an appointment at the local doctor's practice, and confessed my addiction.

It was obvious to the doctor that I was gripped by my dependencies, and he set up a withdrawal programme for me.

Unfortunately, the programme was not enough for my cravings. Years of abuse had made my body resilient to the medication, and I craved more.

The withdrawal symptoms had returned. Not only that, they were worse than ever.

I needed to feed my craving, and searched for a private doctor. I made an appointment, professing to be a visiting American citizen, who wasn't registered with an NHS doctor. To reinforce my claim, I showed my Texas driving licence.

It worked. I had talked my way into another months' worth of pills.

My attempt at getting clean was short-lived.

The girls and I needed the space of our own home, but I could not commit to buy a property. Having stayed in the U.K. longer than I expected, I lived with a growing unease that I would get extradited by Steve.

And then, on 11th September 2001, the world changed.

As the World Trade Center collapsed, the confidence of the Western world had changed, and there was an inherent fear of air travel.

To my surprise, I got a call from Steve. Worried about the safety of the girls, he told me not to fly back under any circumstances.

Because we couldn't fly back to the States, I was worried that the girls would miss out on their education, so I enrolled them into a local school and sourced a rented bungalow near the seafront. Living at my mum's house had started to become difficult, and we found ourselves irritating her husband. Worst of all, Stephanie and Cassidy were afraid of him, and I knew we needed to find a place of our own.

We were beginning to be settled as a family in our new rental home, when my mum stopped by the house. As soon as I saw her whitened face, I could tell something had troubled her. Her eyes were glazed with shock, as she led me towards my couch.

"Sit down. I need to tell you something. It's Chris, he's been shot – he's dead!" she trembled.

I could not believe it. I had spoken to Chris only a few weeks prior, when he seemed positive that he could avoid the manslaughter charge that had loomed over him, even if it meant he would be deported from the States. He had married Karen on 25th August, and spoke of his dream of returning to England to open another wrestling school.

I heard my mother's words clearly, but my mind couldn't process the information. Surely it was a mistake.

Unfortunately, it wasn't. It was Jean who had called to provide the sad news.

As soon as the information registered with me, I fell apart. I wanted to know the circumstances which caused his demise.

Chris had been drinking with his friend Booray, during a visit to Parnell's mother's house in Waxahachie, Texas. They had gotten into a drunken argument which ended with the two of them brawling. But the fight continued to spiral out of control.

Blinded by rage, Chris had managed to get on top of Booray, strangling him on the bed. Gasping for breath, Parnell reached for a gun.

He hit Chris with the pistol, but there was no stopping him. As Chris continued to choke Booray, it resulted in a desperate act.

A shot was fired into Chris' chest. Tragically, his life ended at the hands of his best friend.

When I met Chris Adams, he was such a charming and funny guy with unlimited potential. He was a caring and sensitive individual who just wanted to be loved.

After moving to the States, Chris floated across many different independent promotions all over the country, but had never really found a home in any of them after World Class had shut its doors. His star rapidly fell, and years of fast living had caught up with him.

In later years, his face always seemed to be etched with worry. He was penniless, and gripped by a dependence on drugs and alcohol. After Linda died, his spirit was truly broken. By the end, Chris lost all the qualities he once possessed, alienating almost everyone who cared for him. He became a violent man and he died a violent death.

Jade needed to know that her father was dead, so I was next faced with the horrific task of calling her to break the news. Inconsolable, she just screamed and cried into the phone.

Not knowing where to turn, I called Steve. He didn't have much to say other than he expected it. Despite the news of his death, the resentment that Steve harboured for Chris never softened. I felt completely helpless but tried to reach out to assist Chris' family as best I could.

Because my Arlington home was vacant, I offered it to them in order to make the trip as comfortable as it could be, under the circumstances. Chris' parents Jean and Cyril, his brother Neil and his sister-in-law Niki all stayed there, and I arranged for Jade and a friend to go there too. A drinks reception was held at the house, and so many of Chris' remaining friends attended the service, including his old friend Kevin Von Erich.

Karen Burge Cole, former wife of Chris Adams: "We were only married for six weeks when he died. I remember at his funeral hearing someone behind me say that I was a newlywed widow. It was so sweet of Jeanie to let all of us including Chris' parents Cyril and Jean stay at her house the night before the funeral."

Depressed at the prospect of not having the chance to attend Chris' funeral, I desperately wanted to go back to Texas. But I couldn't.

Having violated the divorce order with Steve, I was certain that law enforcement authorities would be waiting at the airport to arrest me if I returned. I could not risk the chance of being locked away in jail and having the girls taken from me.

I went to see a solicitor to understand my legal rights. Even though Steve had not yet bothered to arrange my extradition, I was increasingly fearful that he would try to take away Stephanie and Cassidy, if given the chance.

The lawyer suggested that I should try to obtain a domestic court order to overrule the Texas one, in order to prevent an extradition of the girls. But he couldn't guarantee that the Texas order would not be upheld if I returned to the States.

With no guarantee of immunity, I wasn't going to travel unless I could get a formal agreement in place. The lawyer advised me to draft a letter to Steve, requesting that he agree to my return with no repercussions.

Cruelly, Steve refused to liaise with the English court or even write a letter to put my mind at rest. Even though I was thousands of miles away from Steve, he was still exerting control over my life.

As a result of Steve's stubbornness to avoid communication with the legal system, I was subsequently granted a Residence Order of the Family Court, which gave me sole custody the girls under English law.

It was not the resolution I was seeking from my custody dispute with Steve. I wanted the girls to grow up with regular visitation from father. Unfortunately, Steve could never agree to share our children, so I had to fight to stop them from getting ripped away from me.

No longer faced with the continual worry about being extradited, my house in Arlington was put on the market. I told Jade that she could clear the house of anything she wanted, and arranged for the remainder of my personal belongings to be shipped across the Atlantic.

With a heavy heart, I accepted that I could never return to Texas. I was determined to find happiness now that I was home in the United Kingdom. I set about purchasing a new house in Southend. We needed a permanent residence in order to bring some overdue stability to our lives.

There continued to be very little communication from Steve until his volatile marriage with Debra had ended in February 2003. Without her smothering influence on his life, he felt free to call me with a request. World Wrestling Entertainment (previously the WWF), were going to be producing a DVD feature on him. Entitled *The Stone Cold Truth*, he wanted the documentary portion of the disc to feature a segment on his relationship with his family, and asked if the girls and I would be filmed.

I agreed to be interviewed, and the crew filmed at the house and along Southend seafront. Between takes, I sneaked away to top up with pills. Embarrassingly, I returned in an impaired condition before the production team asked me their list of questions.

The following year, Steve returned to Britain for a WWE tour and stopped over in a nearby hotel in Southend. Finally, it gave Stephanie and Cassidy time to see their dad, and Steve and I were able to coexist in a civil way for their benefit.

For the girls' sake, I hoped that he would visit when it was not in the middle of a wrestling tour, so that they could get the chance to properly reconnect. Unfortunately, that never happened. When Steve was not contractually obliged to go to England, he never visited his children. Not once.

Nevertheless, despite my shortcomings, I did what I could to bring the girls up as best I could, but it became a struggle as my dependencies worsened.

Despite obtaining the Residence Order, I still harboured a fear that I would lose the children, and did what I could to keep them content. I was worried that if I confessed my addiction, I would be deemed an unfit mother. I couldn't bear the thought of them being taken away to live in the States.

Unfortunately, some of the decisions I made to conceal my problems were not in the best interests of the girls. I had often spoiled them with gifts and money to ensure they were kept content, but had neglected to teach them responsibility or the value of hard work. Even though I wanted them to be happy, I had failed in my duties as a parent.

As a result, the girls became a victim of my addiction. My life was becoming less manageable, as I began to take more pills in order to function. I even resorted to buying the prescriptions of other people.

At the start of the year, I had learned of the tragic passing of Chris' ex-girlfriend Brandi. She had died in January 2003 of an overdose, leaving behind her daughter Julia. Her death should have given me the wake up call to accept my own problems, but it didn't.

Then the worst happened. I ran out of pills, and my body went into shock. The debilitating physical symptoms of my withdrawal returned, as did the horror of drug-induced psychosis. I was crippled by fear as my hallucinations intensified.

Stephanie and Cassidy were still so young, and afraid.

Not knowing what to do, they called one of my friends for help. Upon arriving at my house there was only one course of action, to alert the emergency services. Moments later, an ambulance arrived to take me to the hospital.

For the next six years, this became a recurring incident.

My greatest fears were becoming a reality; the girls were rapidly losing their mother.

23 BREAKING POINT

For so long, I was worried that my daughters would be torn away from me. It was a paranoia that accelerated my downward spiral. As I was fighting to keep my two youngest children from being taken, my relationship with my first-born daughter was starting to deteriorate.

Even though I had moved to the United Kingdom with Stephanie and Cassidy, it was decided by Jade that she would remain in the States to raise her son Blaise with her boyfriend.

After they split, she continued to live in Colorado, but she frequently visited us in Southend. We went on a number of holidays together and we kept a close bond until she met Adam Bryniarski.

Bryniarski was a Coventry wrestler who competed in the States under the name Adam Windsor. They had chatted online for a few months before starting to date. Adam practised judo, and had claimed to know Jade's uncle, Neil Adams.

She fell deeply in love with him but couldn't understand why he would not let her visit his home in Florida.

A few weeks later, she called in floods of tears. It turned out that Adam was married to another woman and was still living with her.

My first instinct was to try and protect Jade, who will always be my little girl.

I invited her to come to back to Southend as I wanted to give her my support. Once she arrived, I let Jade know of my apprehensions towards their relationship, and told her that I did not really care for Adam's secrecy.

Perhaps I shouldn't have voiced my opinions, but I did.

Within days, Adam started sending roses to the house, and was pleading with her on the phone to be with him.

The situation was very reminiscent of how Steve and I started our relationship. I told Jade of my concerns that she might end up repeating the same mistakes that I had made.

Jade however was blinded by love and just felt that I had gone too far by interfering with her business. Being older, Jade was fully aware of the addictions which I fought to hide over the years. She viewed me as a mess, a mother who had failed to become a reliable role model for her and expressed that I had no right to criticise any aspect of her life.

Our disagreement over her new relationship was the final embarrassment for Jade and, at Adam's urging, she decided to cut ties with me.

Nevertheless, Jade and Adam continued their affair and later decided to marry in Coventry.

In the weeks leading to the ceremony, a policeman arrived at the door with a restraining order. It would prevent me from attending my first daughter's wedding. I was heartbroken.

It is incredibly sad how things turned out between us. Even though I was initially wary of Adam, I wanted Jade to know that I will always have love for her.

As my relationship with Jade fell apart at the seams, I was comforted by my friend Marti. She and her husband Dory provided me with so much emotional support during a difficult time for me.

Marti Funk, wife of wrestler Dory Funk, Jr.: "My family and my friend Jeanie went through some tough periods in our lives at a similar time. We both hit a low point with our respective problems, but she was always a thoughtful friend whenever we called one another. We hope she knows how much she means to Dory and I with her friendship and understanding. Someday we are going to hug and pray and give each other blessings for surviving the years of sorrow."

Just as I had lost a daughter, I heard some horrific news about Chris' ex-wife, my dear friend Toni.

Toni and I had remained close beyond our time working together in Dallas and I was incredibly fond of her. She was like a sister to me.

Sadly, her life had taken a turn for the worse under very familiar circumstances.

Toni had started taking prescribed medication during her time in the wrestling industry, which rapidly progressed to larger amounts and onto harder drugs. It escalated due to a mountain of personal problems stemming from her painful divorce from Chris, and the tragic death of Kerry.

Like me, Toni thought that running away would solve her problems.

Attempting to start a new life in Kentucky, Toni had since remarried, but could never rid herself of drug addiction. Her fix was a drug called OxyContin, a powerful and very dangerous narcotic that is time-released. When chewed, it discharges an overpowering hit all at once, up to three times its intended strength.

Even though I was paralysed by my own addictions, I kept in touch with Toni to offer all the support that I could muster. It saddened me when I learned that she had become so hooked that it caused her to divorce yet again and lose all custody of her daughter.

Just when it seemed she had lost everything, it would only get worse for Toni.

On 24th June 2010 at the age of 45, she died, leaving behind a son and daughter.

Once I learned of Toni's death, I was left with an empty realisation. Overdosing just like Linda and Brandi; Toni became the third girl linked to Chris who had passed away after being hooked on drugs, another example of the tragic legacy that he left beyond his own sad ending.

I was troubled that there was a chance that I would follow a similar path to Toni, and give in to the temptation of even harder drugs.

It would not be long before I would be faced with the choice.

As my mum had become increasingly frail, she was starting to need some assistance around the house. I would help her do the shopping, and when I would visit I started to see more of my sister Valerie. Despite being siblings, we had only sporadically seen each other since we were kids.

In the years since we lived together as teenagers, Valerie had struggled to survive her own deeply unhappy adult life. She had lost a child, had met a series of abusive boyfriends and needed an escape.

As her life completely fell apart, she became a regular abuser of heroin and crack cocaine. Her impoverished life was actually a saviour; her addictions had been reined in by her limited income.

After one visit in July 2012, I offered Valerie a lift home.

During the drive, she asked if I had ever tried crack. I told her that I hadn't and asked her what it was like. With my sister, we sourced some crack cocaine and our smoking of it became a weekly occurrence. It quickly spiralled out of control to the point where I needed to take it several times a day just to function.

I still cannot fathom why I decided to experiment with crack. It was the start of a dark journey into an abuse of recreational Class A drugs on top of my addiction to other pills. I had now fallen into an abyss which was leading me to an early grave.

Rapidly, I wanted a bigger hit. The insanity of progression led me to try Heroin.

By November the following year, I had completely lost manageability of my life and my recklessness was starting to be a danger to others.

In one instance, I had been driving and lost control of the vehicle whilst driving and had hit the curb, destroying the wheel. I stayed in the car, and just sat there, motionless.

I didn't even notice the tow truck pull up behind me as I was in a deep trance.

The tow truck driver led me out of the car as he arranged for the car to be impounded. After I stood up, I dropped down on my face, falling over with the grace of a tree. He suspected I was drunk, and called the Police.

While the car was impounded, somebody must have broken into it. There was not a sign of the stash of drugs I had concealed in the car's glove compartment, even though it was searched following my arrest.

I was taken into the station, but there was not a trace of alcohol on my system. I was quickly released due to a lack of evidence.

Crack had taken me to the point that I could no longer function. I had long stopped paying bills, cleaning the house and caring for myself or anyone else. Physically, I was a wreck. I would often go days without a shower, I had lost around thirty pounds in weight, and I became gaunt and ill-looking. I just didn't care. Instead, I holed myself up in my room, isolating myself from responsibility and normal life.

I feared the inevitable; it was only a matter of time before I would take a bigger hit than my body could handle, leaving my children without a mother. I had always resented my own mum for yielding to alcohol when I was a child.

I had become no better, an addict who was neglecting her wonderful children.

For years, I was torturing the children in my own, selfish way without even realising it. I was failing them as a mother and knew that they deserved better.

As the winter drew closer, the only thing keeping me going was the thought of seeing Stephanie and Cassidy together again. Stephanie had been living in Los Angeles since 2011, and was due to be home for the holidays.

By Christmas Day 2013, I just couldn't stand it anymore. I opened the door to the bedroom, where my daughters were sitting and watching the TV. They turned to me and their young smiles sank as they saw my defeated face, streaming with tears.

"I'm a drug addict. I need help. I'm sorry, but please help me!" I blurted in desperation.

The girls empathised with my vulnerability and could finally see me for the broken soul that I was. We all cried and hugged each other.

After sixteen years of denial, I had managed to utter the words that lifted such a huge weight from my shoulders. The guilt of sneaking about, lying and having secrets could now be over. It was painful burden for the three of us to share, but there was no other choice.

I had finally hit rock-bottom.

Once the weight of my revelation had registered, the girls were incredibly supportive, despite the shock. They immediately asked what I needed. I just told them that I needed help to keep me away from the drugs.

Stephanie and Cassidy put me under 'house arrest' and had me confined to my bedroom. I promised not to touch any drugs. This kept me away from doing crack, but I was still managing to use pills in the house.

They were keeping a close eye on me, taking turns to ensure that I stayed put. Years of concealing my addiction meant that I was well versed in being sly, so I started hiding my pills. When the girls weren't about, I would sneakily consume them to get my fix. I would frequently search in desperation for these scattered pockets of tablets, my muddled thoughts forgetting where I had hidden them. I was a pathetic mess, lying not only to my children, but to myself.

Sam Houston, former WCW wrestler: "Before long though, after taking the pills, you start to believe your own hype and believe you're a superman or you're the chosen one but you're just as susceptible to anything as anyone else. Because we're bigger people and because we have a better tolerance or that our metabolisms are faster we can consume more but eventually it all catches up."

A week later, Stephanie returned to the States, and I only had Cassidy to watch over me. It wasn't long before I took advantage, and smuggled some crack into the house. Cassidy caught me smoking it in my room and, after a series of broken promises, she eventually gave in and sought help.

She contacted the rehab clinic on 10th February 2014.

We had to face facts; there was no way I was going to beat this on my own, even with the love of my daughters.

I needed professional help, and it was now forthcoming. I received a call saying that my daughter was so worried about me. I was scheduled to get picked up the following day.

I could not have asked for anymore help from Stephanie and Cassidy. After accepting the truth on just how crippled by addiction I had become, they immediately tried to help me overcome it.

I was so blessed to have the undying care of the girls. They were my guardian angels. Persevering with their mission to save my life, I felt guilty as I did not believe I deserved another chance. In seventeen years, I had done everything possible to destroy myself, and just wanted an easy way out of my suffering. My mind started to dwell on some of my friends who had followed a similar path, but had been less fortunate.

I was haunted by the fun times and laughter that I had shared with Toni, Chris and Gino in Dallas, but memories were the only remnants of these three friends who had created such a happy time in my young life.

My mind then started to reminisce on other friends within the industry who had passed before their time, and the scarring grief felt by the scattered trail of broken families.

I felt the pain of Kevin Von Erich, the sole survivor of a proud dynasty, who had to say goodbye to each of his brothers when they had barely a chance to become men.

I remembered Brian Pillman, who met his demise when his wife Melanie was pregnant. He never experienced the joy of holding his son in his arms.

I could still feel the breeze of the summer wind against my hair the day that Rick Rude took me out for a spin in his new convertible. Although he appeared such a tough, abrasive ladies' man to the fans who watched him each week on television, the truth is that he was a loving father who was torn from his family far too early.

I thought of Davey Boy Smith, the skinny young lad I knew from his early days as a teenage competitor on *World of Sport*, who went on to become an international sensation who wrestled all over the world. I know in my heart that he would have given up all of the sacrifices he made to create a lasting legacy, just to spend one more day with his children Harry and Georgia.

I imagined the cries of Chris and Brandi's daughter Julia, who became orphaned after both parents lives unravelled at the seams, and all due to a series of bad choices.

All I could think of were the tears of these children, who had their parents taken away at a young age.

It drew my mind to my own children; Jade, Stephanie, and Cassidy.

I knew that it was only a matter of time before someone told them that their mother was gone.

I could not do that to them, knowing how they would feel. Their lives would be tainted by the question on whether they could have done something to help me.

They did.

I was determined to stop my family from crying those tears. I was determined to get clean.

I clung to the guilt of being one of the lucky few who had managed to survive my vices when so many others had faltered.

I owed it to each of my fallen friends to be their voice. In their names, I vowed to beat my addiction and share the story that they never got to tell on the crippling horror of drug abuse.

My mind had been willing for years, but my body had always refused the change. Even with all the will in the world, the severity of my crack addiction still led me to pursue it. I was living on borrowed time.

I knew that this was my final chance.

Although I was now going to receive professional help, there was still a daunting journey to undertake as I knew my drug rehabilitation wouldn't be easy. I was in such a panic that I even bought some crack cocaine on the morning that I was due to be collected. Trembling, I feared that I couldn't make the journey without it.

It was time to make the trip. A van pulled up outside my house and a friendly, warm man met me at the front door. I hugged Cassidy goodbye and we drove away to the clinic.

As we made our way up the motorway, I was already starting to get withdrawal symptoms. Once we arrived, my hidden stash was confiscated.

This was now it. I was checked in to the rehab centre.

After checking in, a lovely doctor talked me through the process. A team of experts had put together a withdrawal programme for me.

They had experience in the detox procedure, and knew how to treat the convulsions of patients with varying degrees of addiction.

My body was fighting hard against the drugs but the withdrawal symptoms made me so lethargic. There were times I wanted to give in, but I kept thinking of my daughters and how they would react knowing their efforts to help me had failed.

Not only was my body being challenged to battle addiction, my mind was as well. As part of the detox process, I was to attend group therapy sessions, where I would share my tales of addiction with other addicts in the centre.

The aim of these seminars was to understand the psychological and physical triggers of substance abuse.

Shane Douglas, former WCW wrestler: "So we were zigzagging half way across the country four nights in a row, but that was what was required and we did it proudly as we were making our way in the business, paying our dues as they say.

But as you do that it doesn't take a brain surgeon to work out the rigours of the business; the aches and pains, the pulls and strains, the breaks and bruises that you eventually need something on top to numb not only the physical pain, but the boredom of life on the road and being away from your family.

The problem you have in wrestling is by being an independent contractor; if you don't work, you don't get paid."

In my past, I had heard so many stories of how addictions had ruined lives. In the wrestling industry alone, I had seen the death and tragedy caused by drugs, and even heard sad tales of former beauties starring in hard-core pornography as a last resort to fund the mess they had become.

But seeing real people, talking about the loss of their jobs and families was heart-wrenching. It soon became clear that nobody in the therapy sessions were going to judge me or ridicule me for being an addict. It was a network of support, and talking through the burdens of the past was part of the healing process.

Another part of the healing process was the daily diet of assignments which we had to undertake. My first assignment was quite a benchmark for me. Our group was asked to summarise our life in ten pages and I suddenly realised the pain and tragedy I had experienced in my life. I broke down and cried.

In the treatment centre, I was told that one of the greatest joys about overcoming addiction is that I would get my feelings back. But it was also the worst thing about getting clean. Pains that were once subdued were coming back harder than ever.

The counsellor was so kind though and gave me a hug. I felt a lot of love and friendliness in the clinic, being amongst people who also suffered from the same affliction. We could all identify with each other.

I was starting to regain my health and strength and, within weeks, my body was finally clear of the drugs. I was a little wobbly, but I felt so fresh to have the substances cleared from my system.

With the programme slowly starting to work, I began to enjoy my surroundings. I had a lovely room in one of the houses that made up the clinic. There were beautiful views of the gardens which were full of flowers and of the fields with sheep peacefully grazing.

It was very tranquil and quiet and gave me a sense of inner peace.

As well as feeling a sense of mental peace, there was a marked improvement in my physical appearance. I no longer looked gaunt or washed-out, and I was noticeably healthier.

I soon had the added boost of a visit from Cassidy. In the short time I had been away, I could see that my little girl had grown into a level-headed young woman. She was still so young and I know that having a mum in rehab must have been difficult for her, but she was a real tower of strength, telling me to persevere and get better.

Even though I had a friend staying with her, I still worried for her coping around the house without me. But she never made any issue out of her circumstances; she was completely dedicated to making sure I was okay.

As Cassidy did not want to cause any undue stress to me, she did not let me know that Steve had found out about my stay in rehab from Stephanie. By February, he quickly arranged a one-way flight to stay with him in Los Angeles soon after the visit.

When I was told that Cassidy had left for the States, I was absolutely devastated. I blamed myself for her leaving, and that I had been selfish in not being there for her. I cried and I cried, believing that I deserved this agony for destroying our lives with my addiction to drugs.

Luckily, I was able to have phone privileges at the clinic, so I called Cassidy and Steve. I wanted to know she was okay living with her dad, who had been distant in recent years.

I promised Cassidy that I would continue to work at my rehabilitation at the clinic and that I would hopefully see her soon. She and Stephanie sent flowers and cards and they knew that this was the best place for me to get well.

By April, Cassidy called and said she was homesick and wanted to come back to

England. I spoke to Steve about the possibility of her coming home to Southend, but he was not happy about the suggestion. He was certain I would have a relapse, but agreed nonetheless.

Steve and I both worked hard during that call to be civilised to each other, for once we both agreed in the best interests of Cassidy. I booked her a flight home, she would return in the first week of May.

That July, Stephanie returned from Los Angeles too, and both of the girls visited me. I was so happy to see them, and they were allowed to stay in the next room for a couple of nights. Once again, we were all under one roof. I felt so comforted to have my family around me.

By August 2014, I had completed my rehabilitation and had remained fully clean for three months before leaving the centre.

I will always be grateful to the staff for saving my life after seventeen years of being gripped by the misery of substance abuse.

I was finally free from addiction. It was time to rebuild our lives.

Arriving home after six months in rehab was a hugely daunting experience. It was going to be a massive challenge to get back into everyday normal life. For six months, I had been confined within a safe environment, with a regular routine of therapy and tasks.

Once I returned, my first obstacle was to face the consequences of my actions whilst I was an addict. The house had fallen into complete disarray and needed sorting. It was very sobering seeing the mess and devastation caused by my neglect. It took quite a while to put everything right, but in a way it was very therapeutic, clearing out my old life and putting things in order for a new one.

At home with my daughter Cassidy, 2014.

As I was getting my house in order, I sifted through the vast amounts paperwork which had been left and completely forgotten about. Scattered amongst a backlog of ignored bills, were a collection of unpaid speeding tickets.

I contacted a lawyer for advice, who told me that I would need to go to court for an official hearing. He forewarned me that I had accumulated enough points on the tickets to warrant a one-year ban from driving.

It was a real wake-up call as to how reckless I had been when using drugs, but I was willing to accept the decision. I was just relieved that my negligence had not caused anyone to have been injured.

During the hearing, the judge was sympathetic to my situation. He listened as I recounted my battle with addiction and subsequent commitment to rehab.

The judge could tell that I was committed to staying clean, and gave me a reduced 28-day ban. I was truly grateful that I had been given a second chance.

I wanted to celebrate my recovery and so I put my house on the market.

Within three months I had a buyer and started to pack. I felt it was time for a new beginning.

Finally clean and with my daughter Stephanie in London, 2014.

Stephanie came home from Los Angeles to visit Cassidy and me, and her return was such a happy occasion. Travelling to London, the three of us saw all the sights. We spent the whole time smiling and laughing throughout her stay, and the girls found what they deserved; after years of self-denial, they finally got the mother that they knew I could be.

With over two years of remaining clean, I have worked hard to earn back their trust.

They know that I have become free from the shackles of addiction, and I look forward to more memories filled with laughter and love. Despite an unsettled upbringing, they have become two amazing young women and I owe my life to them.

Today, they are my best friends and we have a fantastic relationship.

207

Cassidy Williams, daughter of Jeanie Clarke: "When my mum asked me to include my feelings about the past, so many memories flooded my mind. A lot of which I didn't want to bring to the surface as our joint past remained in a closet for a very long time. My mother's addiction was obvious to me from an early age. Evidence of her drug use was easy to find and I would work tirelessly to get rid of it in any way I could, regardless of her reaction.

As the situation worsened, my sister and I grew closer but I still had to grow up fast. I often wondered whether contacting my dad would be a good idea but I always pushed it away, never thinking it was possible. From this point on, the situation was never any better.

By 2013, my sister had been living in LA for a while. During my time alone I had begun to notice things which I had never seen before, all of which pointed towards something worse than I had ever experienced, and all of which I blatantly ignored, due to my fear of the past.

Picking up on this caused my relationship with my mother to severely deteriorate. I began to be very hateful as I was unable to understand why she was doing this to herself and me. My sister was oblivious to this as I didn't want her to relive this situation as I was doing; however during her visit at Christmas in 2013 my mother admitted to her abuse of a Class A drug. My sister was heartbroken, as was I. Although we wanted to help, helping was all we had ever known.

By this point my sister had to leave and once again I was on my own. But after finding out my mother was still addicted, even though she had promised to get clean, I finally decided to take the situation into my own hands by calling a rehab to which my mother agreed to go to. She left the next morning.

After the rehab process had exited our lives, we started to bond again. Not as a mother and daughter but as best friends. I had finally begun to understand the meaning of her addiction.

Although it has been extremely hard growing up as my mother's child, seeing her deteriorate and having to cope with that from such a young age, I have never been prouder of her. Seeing how we have come through this and finally defeated that which has haunted us for so long has made me realise how strong my mother really is.

Mum, you are my best friend and seeing you finally able to laugh and smile is something I am so happy to be able to share with you.

I love you."

24 IN GOD WE TRUST

When I set about writing my autobiography, I promised myself one thing; that I would tell a no-holds-barred truthful account of my life.

In many ways, this was a chance at retribution. I have had some amazing experiences and wanted to share these joys, but I also made a number of bad decisions and needed to examine the reasons why I made them, in order to complete the healing process.

It is the pleasure and the pain in life that has given me my character, and it has given me tremendous strength through some dark times. I would like to thank you, my reader, for following me on this journey of discovery into who I am.

The level of support I had during the production of my autobiography was overwhelming. After getting a call from Steve Lynskey, a local talent agent, he made an enquiry whether I would consider doing a signing at a recent convention. I was convinced nobody would remember me, or be interested in learning about my life.

I eventually agreed, and I ended up being so glad that I chose to go.

One of the most amazing experiences for me during the writing of this book was the fact that I was able to meet so many great fans and a number of my former colleagues, all of whom offered support and seemed genuinely interested in hearing my story.

Adrian Street, former wrestler: "[My valet and wife] Linda and I first met Jeanie in California in 1982... She's really a lady who's been there and done that, on both sides of the Atlantic, when it comes to wrestling."

I am grateful for my time in the wrestling industry, as it has allowed me to connect to an audience during my personal journey. Even today, I get kind messages from fans and colleagues who fondly remember the wicked antics of my on-screen persona.

James Beard, former WCCW referee: "I'm sure most wrestling fans who watched World Class or WCW in the 1980s and 90s, especially of the male persuasion, have a particular image of Jeanie Clarke (or Lady Blossom, as she was called in WCW). That image, most certainly, has to do with her strikingly beautiful face and the image of her in a low cut evening gown standing at ringside as a distracting figure who gave her then husband, Steve Austin, an advantage at just the right time during his matches. But for me, when I think of Jeanie Clarke, the first word that comes to me is 'class'.

I certainly am not blind to Jeanie's physical gifts, but the Jeanie I know is much more than simply someone whose appearance was her only value. She is an extremely intelligent, business savvy and down to earth lady who is as sweet on the inside as she is beautiful on the outside.

Jeanie has seen and experienced the wrestling business from a very unique perspective. The two well known and significant relationships she had with Chris Adams and Steve Austin put her in situations with and around an elite class of talent from an era of wrestling that, in my opinion, was the most exciting time for the business. But, Jeanie not only saw it as someone who was in those relationships, dealing with that side of things, but as someone who actually participated in the business, as well. So, she understands and has experienced the wrestling business in more ways than most and she has a wonderful and interesting story to tell because of those experiences."

But although I have some wonderful memories, I was also saddened to lose so many friends who succumbed to the temptations that touring performers have to face.

Within a few weeks of beginning writing, I received a call from Ken Sowden from the British Wrestlers' Reunion. He asked if I would like to accept a Lifetime Achievement Award in recognition of the late Chris Adams' professional wrestling career on the 9th August 2015 in Kent.

I was thrilled to be offered his award at a ceremony held at The Bridges, a cosy tavern owned by British wrestling great Wayne Bridges.

On the big day, I felt like my journey in the wrestling business had come full circle. I reconnected with many names from the rich history of the UK circuit, from Mal Sanders, Steve Grey and Lee Bronson to Johnny Kincaid, Clive Myers and Colin Joynson. It brought back lots of wonderful memories from an innocent time in my life.

It was such an honour to accept the award from Chris' peers within the wrestling fraternity and around six hundred fans that beautiful summer day. What made it more special was that the plaque was presented by Tony 'Banger' Walsh, and that Jackie Turpin was also there to celebrate Chris' accomplishments and legacy.

However, after I accepted the award, I felt a great sadness which made the occasion bittersweet. Seeing Walsh and Turpin together, but without Chris, was the first time that it really sank in that Adams was dead.

With my friend Linda Hanley at the British Wrestlers' Reunion in Kent, 2015.

We were the Leamington Crew who used to travel to all the shows together during our stint in Joint Promotions. I was never able to attend Chris' funeral in Texas, and never had the chance to say goodbye to him.

Linda Hanley, friend of Jeanie Clarke: "I met Jeanie about thirty years ago at the Royal Albert Hall. I was talking to Mark Rocco and Jeanie joined in, and from then on we became best friends. I often stayed with her and Chris Adams, even in America, and it was great to be with Jeanie at the reunion where Chris was honoured."

Towards the end of his life, Chris Adams ended up in a desperate situation and I am more than aware of the tragedy he caused to countless others. The pain he brought to those around him is something that cannot be denied.

But I choose to remember the kind-hearted soul, who had a world of potential and brought so much love to an insecure young girl from Southend-on-Sea. I will always miss him, and he was such a supportive ear when I was going through my problems with Steve.

On the subject of Steve, I endeavoured to write the truth about our relationship when I embarked upon this project. When I first met him, he was such a humble, quiet guy, but his journey to superstardom was astronomical, and he changed as a result.

From the early days of our marriage to the end of it, Steve's commitment as a husband and father became as disparate as the 'Stone Cold' character was from 'Stunning' Steve.

However, Steve was only one half of the marriage, and I know our relationship unravelled once we realised how incompatible we were as people. I tried to find escapism from my home misery with substance abuse, while Steve pursued fame at all costs, including the dissolution of his family.

Unfortunately, Steve Austin has now become to his children what he is to everyone else; just some guy you only see on television. It saddens me when the girls try to reach out to him, and he fails to follow up on their expectations to return their calls. I could not tell you the last time he called them on their birthdays or at Christmas to wish them well, and his estrangement has left a scar that will never heal.

Steve has since told them that he will not support them unless they pursue a career that meets his approval. It's pretty hypocritical hearing that from a college drop-out and football failure whose parents allowed him to pursue a dream in pro wrestling.

Despite huge wealth, Steve has only spoken to his daughters on a handful of occasions since our divorce. As a father, he seemed to throw in the towel once he failed to beat me for sole custody. After realising he couldn't win it outright, he has not been willing to compromise.

Steve and I both know the pain caused by having to grow up without our dads in our lives. It is pretty cruel he chose to inflict the same hurt on our daughters, Stephanie and Cassidy. But it is his loss. He is the one who is missing out on the blessing of being around our wonderful children.

Throughout many of my darkest days, it was the undying love of the girls that gave me a reason to want to stay alive, and it was their intervention that led to me becoming clean. But even when I was struggling to cope with my drug addictions, they know that I never threw in the towel as a mother. I could never abandon them, despite the ongoing turmoil in my life.

Stephanie Williams, daughter of Jeanie Clarke: "Growing up in the shadows of my father's career and my mother's addiction was extremely challenging as a kid.

Cassidy (left) and Stephanie (right), 2016.

My father was out of reach, and the only interaction I had with him was every Monday night on RAW, whilst the relationship with my mother was interrupted by her addiction, and forced me to grow up. The events my sister and I endured aren't things I'd like to share, however I would like to express that I couldn't be more proud of the person, and the mother, that she is today.

I just want to say to her that I have been waiting for this woman to rise above her demons and now that you aren't lost I finally get to see the smile and hear your laughter that makes you such a joy to be around. Honestly I hope that if this book hasn't touched others it at least touches you. You have come such a long way and please know your strengths haven't gone unnoticed. Here's to a new chapter of your life.

I love you."

We have now put our past behind us, and we are looking forward to our future. The challenges we faced have strengthened our bond as a family. But my only regret is that the girls are still missing a major part of their family; their father.

Stephanie and Cassidy became the true victims in my split from Steve, which has since affected their relationship with their older sister, Jade.

Jade has not spoken to the girls for years since she cut me out of her life. Being able to tell my side of the story in this book has allowed me to bring a sense of closure to my relationship with her, giving me an outlet for the words that I never had the chance to say face-to-face.

If she ever wants to talk, I want her to know I am open to reconciliation, but I have come to accept that our relationship may never be repaired.

I am just relieved to know that Jade is safe and happily married. I hope the love of her children gives her the same joy that she brought to my life when she was a child. I am glad she has created a loving home for her family.

A stable environment was something that I never had in my early years. Due to an unsettled childhood and tumultuous life, I was never truly able to create the sense of home I always wanted.

As I write this, I am in the process of looking for a new house, and the thought of a new beginning is giving me a tremendous thrill. However, I have learned that a home is not necessarily something you create, or buy. It's something you feel. And I believe I have found it.

In a lifetime of searching, I am finally home.

It was this sense of fulfilment that made me want to share my story.

I am a person who lived the highest of highs and struggled with the lowest of lows. I will never forget sinking to the point that I held Steve's gun in my hand, aimed it at my head, and was ready to pull the trigger. I did my utmost to destroy my body, by poisoning it each day.

But even though I lost all faith in myself, I never lost my belief in Christ.

And it seemed that God never lost his belief in me.

When I look back on my life, I now believe that there was an intervention beyond my control; a greater plan which prevented my untimely death.

Bobby Fulton, former WCCW wrestler: "These days I'm a committed Christian and I speak and share the gospel. I'm also a pastor at my church and am very heavily involved in all aspects of my church in Ohio.

Hearing about the problems in her life that she has overcome I'd like to give a prayer to Jeanie.

There have been so many in our business that lost their lives to addictions. But through Jesus Christ those of us who are still here can find strength through his name, and do anything in the name of Christ. If we acknowledge Christ in all that we do then we will direct our path. I am thankful that Jeanie has seen the light and has accepted Christ, and I pray that she continues to fight the good fight, keeps the faith and holds onto that through until eternal life.

Amen."

There was a journey set out for me. It was not an easy one to live, but my story provides testament that a person can survive beyond breaking point, and find the resilience to turn their life around. Even at the last minute, when all hope seems lost.

Marc Mero, former WCW wrestler-turned-motivational speaker: "I made some horrible choices in my life as a pro wrestler. 1 Corinthians 15:33 Bad company corrupts good character. What God was saying many years ago is we become who we surround ourselves with. I choose my company; I choose to live a life opposite of what Christ would want.

So when I got to a place in my life because of sin, I remember saying "How did I get here?"

It's called consequences. I lost so much in such a short period of time; the death of friends and family. Through my faith in Jesus my life has been forever changed. He has a plan and purpose for all our lives. I now travel the world speaking at schools, churches and corporations.

As I look at Jeanie's life I can see she has also found what is truly important. There is no greater joy than serving the King!"

Through this book, I have realised my life purpose; to share my experiences with others, and spread the conviction that there is always a way out from certain tragedy.

Life is full of challenges. It is our ability to take on these challenges that defines our lives.

And that's the bottom line.

Jeanie Clarke, 2016.

ABOUT THE AUTHORS

Jeanie Clarke is a former entrepreneur, model, and professional wrestling valet from Southend-on-Sea, England. She is most famous for her appearances with Joint Promotions on ITV's *World of Sport*, the United States Wrestling Association, and World Championship Wrestling, where she performed under the name Lady Blossom. In 1991, Clarke decided to retire from wrestling to concentrate on her family life, and married Steve Austin two years later. She famously came up with his 'Stone Cold' persona, developing an edgy character which drove the professional wrestling industry to unforeseen heights. Jeanie remained close to the industry during the boom period of the 'Attitude Era' of the World Wrestling Federation, before returning to the United Kingdom in 2001. Despite achieving success in business and entertainment, her greatest accomplishments were to raise her children and to survive a seventeen-year addiction to drugs. Today, Jeanie focuses on making public appearances to share her incredible life story.

Bradley Craig is a Chartered Architect and professional wrestling historian, based in the United Kingdom. Born in Aberdeen, he founded The Professional Wrestling Hall of Fame for Scotland in 2015, and is active in the research and ongoing cultural preservation of the sport. He has contributed written articles to a number of international magazines on the subjects of architecture and professional wrestling, and is a member of various institutions which honour the rich history of both industries.

Bradley Craig

Neil Cameron was born and lives in Suffolk. After a career in the travel industry, he turned his hand to looking after the legacy of Elvis Presley for his many U.K. fans. When not behind his desk he enjoys travelling, reading, visiting as many restaurants as he can, listening to obscure music, watching bad movies and has never met a cup of tea, a slice of cake or a pint of good beer he didn't like.

Neil Cameron

Made in the USA
Columbia, SC
05 July 2024

38134586R00128